style in motion

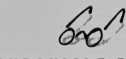

CHRONICLE BOOKS

PIAGGIO&C spa

Project Coordinator
Davide Mazzanti

Texts
Davide Mazzanti
(The History of the Vespa)

Ornella Sessa
Architect, Professor of Industrial Design,
Florence University
(The Fifteen Models)

Translation
Donald Bathgate
(The History of the Vespa)

Dialogue International srl
(The Fifteen Models)

Revision and editing (English text)
Dorothy Barrett

Contributors
Athos Bigongiali
Author

Bill Buford
Author and European correspondent
for *The New Yorker*

Tommaso Fanfani
Professor of Economic History,
Pisa University, and President of the
Piaggio Foundation

Lara-Vinca Masini
Contemporary art historian

Giorgio Notari
Technical advisor to the Piaggio Museum, vice
president of the Vintage Vespa Registry

The late Roberto Segoni †
Professor of Industrial Design,
President of Laurea Course in Industrial Design,
Florence University

Graphics and art direction
Carlo Savona

Page layout
Enrico Albisetti
(The History of the Vespa)

Carlo Savona
assisted by Paola Sardone
(The Fifteen Models)

Original photography
Studio Lanza, Giovanni Petronio
assisted by Lorenzo Borri,
Walter Mericchi and Izdeyar Setna

Iconographic research
Cristina Reggioli

First published in the United States in 2004 by
Chronicle Books LLC.

First published in Italy by Giunti Editore under
the title *Vespa, un'avventura italiana nel mondo*
© 2003 by Giunti Editore S.p.A., Firenze-Milano.

Library of Congress Cataloging-in-Publication
Data available.

ISBN 0-8118-4248-7
UPC 7-651451-0526-2

Manufactured in Italy

Cover design by Azi Rad

Distributed in Canada by Raincoast Books
9050 Shaughnessy Street
Vancouver, BC V6P 6E5

10 9 8 7 6 5 4 3 2 1

Chronicle Books LLC
85 Second Street
San Francisco, California 94105

www.chroniclebooks.com

The authors wish to thank the Archivio Storico
Piaggio "Antonella Bechi Piaggio" for allowing
us to use free of charge the iconographic
material of historical documentation necessary
to fully complete this work.

The Publisher thanks PIAGGIO & C. S.p.A.,
registered office located at Viale Rinaldo
Piaggio 25, Pontedera (Province of Pisa), for
having granted us license to reproduce the
drawings, photographs, images and trademarks
found in this book, which are the exclusive
property of Piaggio. This material cannot be
utilized, duplicated, modified, processed,
transmitted or distributed, even partially,
without the specific written authorization of
Piaggio & C. S.p.A. Any non-authorized
use will be persecuted according to law.
The marks VESPA®, PIAGGIO®,CELLA
ESAGONALE NUOVO LOGO® and P
PIAGGIO in SCUDO E FIGURA® are
registered trademarks owned exclusively by
Piaggio & C. S.p.A. Any non-authorized use is
in violation of trademark registration rights
and other applicable laws.

Thanks to the Piaggio Foundation and to
the management and staff of the "Antonella
Bechi Piaggio" Historical Archive and
the Piaggio Museum "Giovanni Alberto
Agnelli," Pontedera—President Tommaso
Fanfani, Maria Chiara Favilla, Chiara
Mani, Elisabetta Marchetti, Elisa Mazzini,
as well as Stefano Bartoli and Edo Bernini—
for the unflagging support, willingness
and ability they contributed to this project.

Thanks to Paolo Pezzini, Mario Santucci,
Gaia Stefanelli, Graziella Teta and Roberto
Maria Zerbi of Piaggio & Co. for their
cooperation.

Thanks to Gilberto Filippetti for the use
of illustrative material and his valuable
contribution to the Vespa and Piaggio
advertising campaigns he himself created for
the Leader Advertising Agency of Florence.

We thank Tam Fagiuoli for his authorization
to reproduce the photographs taken by him.

Thanks to the Leader Agency of Florence
for the advertising campaigns commissioned
by Piaggio through the years.

Thanks to Marco Lanza and especially
Stefano Marcelli for the passages drawn
from *Quelli della Vespa*, Pontedera 1996.

Thanks to Marco Riccardi of *Motociclismo*
magazine.

Special thanks to Carlo Doveri for the
willingness and patience he showed in
reviewing the fact files framed in the text.

Thanks to Silvia Bizio for the Steven
Spielberg interview.

†The thoughts of the authors turn to the
memory of Professor Roberto Segoni and
his untimely passing.

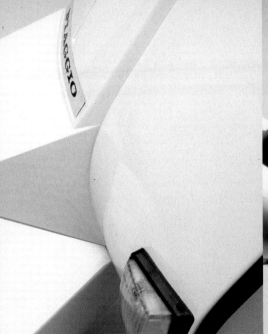

Roberto Segoni

VESPA: IT DOESN'T GET MORE INDUSTRIAL THAN THIS...

It is often said Italian design reached its heyday during the Fifties and Sixties— a truism amply borne out by design history. It is also true that those "Twenty Golden Years" were heralded in the years immediately after World War II by the Vespa, an exemplar of creative and inventive ability, the hallmark of so many other design products that were to win fame the world over by embodying the style for which Italy—where many of the world's best designers come from— is universally renowned.

These designers, it should be emphasized, have vastly different individual experience and cultural backgrounds, from the hands-on culture of the workshop on the one hand to the Faculty of Architecture on the other, not to mention the technical colleges and engineering universities, the academies and art schools.

While most of Italy's best-known designers have come through the Faculties of Architecture (the only discipline in which social sciences combine with technology-oriented subjects to produce a design culture needed if planning is to be expressed with any depth), there are several cases of equally famous personalities from the most diversified backgrounds: from the typically studio-based planner to the managerial entrepreneur able to harness, coordinate and combine the skills of others.

Ettore Bugatti had studied in the shop of his father, Carlo, an eclectic, artistic craftsman renowned for the originality of his furniture; Enzo Ferrari started as a race-car driver and went on to become a highly gifted manager of talented designers and drivers. Marcello Nizzoli was a graphic artist and painter when Adriano Olivetti summoned him to design the Lexicon 80 typewriter, which he modeled directly in plasticene.

Battista Farina, nicknamed "Pinin" ("Littl'un" in the Turin dialect) worked in his brother Giovanni's body shop as a child and grew up drawing his automobiles alongside experienced workers as they formed bodywork blow by blow or modelers as they "shaped the plaster" of the mockups.

Dante Giacosa, on the other hand, was an engineer who could design a car down to every single component, from the mechanics to the bodywork, while, as a designer, guiding the evolution of the shape, as he did for his all-time masterpiece, the Fiat 500.

Marquis Emilio Pucci, one of the founding fathers of Italian fashion, a black-sheep among Florentine nobility, was born with a creative verve and sensitivity that enabled him to design the cut of his collections.

There are, naturally, many Italian-designed products just as well known as those that come from the pen of a famous designer but whose

An innovative technique in working wood by steam bending was perfected by an Austrian carpenter, Michael Thonet, in the 1830s. More than a million copies of the famous "Model 14" of 1859 had already been produced by the 1920s. Right: one of Thonet's models of 1885.

role of the designer should be (seeking to identify the examples best suited to shed light on such a vast issue), it was perhaps forgotten that almost ten years earlier, at Pontedera, Corradino D'Ascanio, an ingenious aeronautical engineer, had already provided a highly tangible example of top-quality design in the conception and realization of the Vespa.

It would probably have been enough to take the Vespa as an example and see, even then, how perfectly it fit the requirements of such a historic event that had brought some of the most respected elder statesmen of design around the same table—those same authoritative figures who were later to lay the basis for defining the profile of the industrial designer in the then-nascent Italian industrial-design panorama.

It is true that equally famous foreign products already existed, too. Thonet furniture, the mythical Ford Model T, the Singer sewing machine, the Winchester rifle and the 1911 model Colt pistol especially come to mind, but these harked back to the nineteenth century or to the early years of the twentieth century and thus could not be properly considered as "modern" as those created in the years immediately following the end of World War II, in the mid-twentieth century.

What is certain is that these products—born between the middle of the nineteenth century

paternity is uncertain or even multiple—products designed by people completely unknown only because they work alongside more famous personalities. Suffice it to mention Beretta pistols, or the refined elegance of Gucci or Ferragamo shoes—indeed, all designer-label products in which the name of the actual designer must never appear, whether it be a collective design team or a single person.

At the 1954 Milan Triennale exhibition, just as debate was beginning on the definition of "industrial design" and what the profile and

and the beginning of the twentieth century—and the Vespa were all spawned from the same lowest common denominator: at first, each interpreted and then became the paragon of cutting-edge syle in its time. The function and appearance of each product defined its time and was aimed to last over time. Any later attempts at redesigning—save those of extremely minor significance—ran the risk of irremediably ruining its original character and hence its very identity.

This truth becomes even more significant when one considers that there are very few examples of industrial products that have managed to stay in production for a long time, even allowing for slight updates and few important changes up to the present day.

Not even the Fiat 500—which appeared ten years after the birth of another main player in the move to Italian mass motorization, the Vespa—could escape the inevitable aesthetic aging that labeled it a car of the Fifties, despite its remaining an unsurpassed example of a little/big town car. This perception gave it the (highly unusual in the automobile industry) distinction of becoming a vintage car before it became a merely "old" car during its long and honorable career.

Conversely, the Vespa underwent no aging process in either looks or function because, from the very first model in 1946, its shape was so new and different that it had very little in common with the style of either two-wheeled or four-wheel vehicles of the time. This uniqueness prevented it from looking dated like the motorcycles of those years, or the Fiat 500 or the Mini Minor, now do.

True, it was quietly redesigned more than once to keep it in line with developing changes in the market and technological evolution and production processes, keeping an eye on the parallel styling taking place at Lambretta, its only direct competitor. As opposed to the Lambretta, however, the Vespa was subjected to only very light, almost imperceptible retouching, with care being taken not to overstep the "legibility limit," which could have lost it that assertive, unmistakable shape so fundamental in such a strongly characterized product—knowledge fundamental to the designers who worked on the Vespa over the years and managed to not transform it into something else…

It can therefore be said that the Vespa is one of the select few industrial products that has kept its shape more or less unchanged from birth to the present day with only minor styling alterations.

It has kept the same performance level and expressive content as it began with, with no sign of the inertia common to most products

The Colt 1911 is undoubtedly the most famous automatic pistol ever made. With more than 5 million copies made it can rightly be called a "definitive" article—still today it is absolutely identical to the very first piece made.

The Lexicon 80, presented by Olivetti in 1948. Adriano Olivetti summoned artists and architects, representatives of a non-factory culture, to work together with the planning and study department he set up in 1929.

that causes them to be identified with the outmoded styles in which they were created.

The Vespa and the more recent Porsche 911 both belong to this select category hitherto occupied only by the likes of the Winchester rifle and the incredible 1911 model Colt, the latter being a real record breaker in design history: after more than one hundred years it is identical to the very first model produced, unchangeable down to the smallest detail, because its design was essentially perfect.

Whatever design process is followed, a well-designed product can be thought up by anyone, either alone or in a group, as long as the designer, the entrepreneur or—why not—both together have the capacity to think up and excute an idea so innovative that it will make its mark on history. This is the story of the Vespa. Enrico Piaggio's intuition and the genius of Corradino D'Ascanio gave birth to it, just as Samuel Colt and gunsmith John Moses Browning gave birth to the best automatic pistol in history, the 1911 model, until the arrival of the Italian Beretta 98F.

The Vespa was always a highly innovative product, in the context not only of the period in which it was conceived but also that of the future, which in the post-war years, was not as easy to foresee. The traffic problems and the difficulties of urban mobility today are different from that era both in terms of quality and quantity. In the post-war years, the most urgent problem was procuring a simple and economical means of transport, affordable to everyone who had to get to work and couldn't manage the luxury of a car.

Even people who viewed mopeds as dangerous and complex would find the new vehicle simpler and easier to ride. It also had the great advantage of being easily accessible to women (for whom motorcycles were out of bounds, mainly for cultural reasons) because of a certain psychological serenity—one instinctively felt from the minute one started to ride it.

Its typological unorthodoxy made it incomparable to every other two-wheel vehicle then known; it conveyed a completely new image of utilitarian vehicle, friendly and reassuring. In Corradino D'Ascanio's words, "We had to set out on a path completely new and antitraditionalist par excellence."

You drove it sitting down, it was easy to set your feet on the ground, you were protected from the rain and cold, it even had a spare wheel, like a car, its engineering simplicity made it practically maintenance-free, and it was reliable enough that drivers could embark on relatively long trips, secure in the knowledge that they would encounter no problems.

The design of the Vespa expressed all this from the very beginning. Its rounded contours,

characterized by continuity in surface and shape, made it slim and lithe. It had on the one hand the reassuring familiarity of many common household articles, and on the other the natural harmony found in nature, especially among insects (it was no coincidence that on seeing the first prototype, Enrico Piaggio exclaimed, "*Sembra una vespa!*" ["It looks just like a wasp!"] or certain creatures of the sea. The shape of the Vespa (like that of the Porsche 911) is the fascinating synthesis of natural form and the idealized motion exemplified in the tapering of its back end to a teardrop shape, like that of an insect's abdomen, or the tip of a fish's tail.

The Vespa was also conceived as a "made to measure" vehicle of exactly the proper size to satisfy the real needs of a very broad spectrum of users—an organically designed vehicle both in the layout of its parts and in the comfort it offered its user. Everything was measured: the engine power, the weight and dimensions in proportion—naturally—to the performance and the use to which it was to be put.

Power, maneuverability and ease of riding were in perfect harmony with what the public wanted: more power would have required, logically, a different size of vehicle, which in turn would have jeopardized security and practicality of use, as everyone who rides a

scooter or a motorcycle knows (and the same principle applies to cars and every other kind of vehicle).

The design's ingenuity is all the more evident when one considers how the Vespa, so measured and familiar looking, is, all the while, so anticonventional: a monocoque (integrated) body instead of the old tubular frame, thus solving the problem of bodywork design; the engine driving the back wheel directly; an offset front wheel easy to dismantle and easy to change; a spare wheel; a rear driving position instead of one seating the rider astride like a motorcycle; the controls on the handlebar; and the front shield, an integral

The Fiat 500, launched in 1957, despite its obvious identity as a vintage item, stands out as one of the most successful city cars.

Emilio Pucci, pictured in Florence in 1959, putting the finishing touches to the original sketches for one of his characteristic printed fabrics.

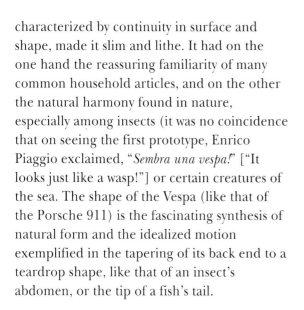

The Arco lamp of 1962, designed by Achille and Piergiorgio Castiglioni, differed from almost every other furnishing accessory that allowed for an infinite number of variations on the same theme, by being unable to be redesigned without its stylistic and functional content being irremediably compromised.

part of the body shell, to protect the rider.

The very essence of absolutely innovative design ideas is brilliantly applied and implemented on one product.

All this took place more than half a century ago, thanks to an ingenious and versatile aeronautical engineer who had gotten the world's first helicopter to fly in 1930 and received patents for innovations in aeronautics. Corradino D'Ascanio conceived and brought to reality the world's most famous scooter, almost offhand, on Enrico Piaggio's order when the

Pontedera company, destroyed by the war, had to be reconverted and it became clear that an answer to the problem of individualized transport would be a surefire market success.

The originality of the design lies, therefore, in the highly singular situation created by the circumstances of that moment in history, the farsightedness of an entrepreneur and the extraordinary ability and versatility of a designer who, as one would say today, managed to optimize in exemplary fashion the basic requirements of a project and transform them into a product able to express in terms of responsiveness a perfect synthesis of looks, innovativeness, technological content, production-process rationalization and performance coefficient.

So, the Vespa is one of the most successful examples of the vast world of industrial design, unchanged in the original qualities and potentialities that made it—then as now—one the most important icons of our times.

"The creation of a modern means of transport, with the popularity of a bicycle, the performance of a motor-bike, the elegance and comfort of an automobile, is now reality."

Corradino D'Ascanio

PIAGGIO

*W*here the tale is told of a shipbuilding
company that became a railway
engineering company that then became an
airplane company, banking on hopes of post-
war revival and on an odd-looking vehicle
designed by the man who invented the helicopter.

1884–1946

Toward the first Vespa

BEHIND THE VESPA...

Behind the Vespa there's an airplane, a train, a big steamboat and a sailing ship. The company still producing Vespas today, more than fifty years on, had already had some sixty years of manufacturing experience when it registered the patent for the world's best-known motor scooter on April 23, 1946.

Down at the far end of this time tunnel in 1884 stands Rinaldo Piaggio, who was only in his early twenties when he signed the Articles of Association of Società Rinaldo Piaggio. Splitting from his father, Enrico, on 14 September 1887, he transformed Società Rinaldo Piaggio into Piaggio & Co., a limited partnership whose head office was at Sestri Ponente with himself as director and managing partner.

The new company grew swiftly alongside the large shipping companies and the prestigious shipyards of the surrounding Liguria region, where brigantines, cruisers and passenger ships were launched. After crafting the interiors for Navigazione Generale Italiana's ships and for the beautiful *Venezuela*, owned by La Veloce and launched in 1898, it was entrusted with the transatlantic steamships of Norddeutscher Lloyd and the *Lorelei*, the Imperial German navy's flagship with accommodation for the kaiser. By the turn of the century more than sixty ships were sailing the seas bearing witness to the quality of the company's work and the ability of its cabinet makers. Elegant, luxury fittings, frequently in Art Nouveau style, were built into passenger ships while large-scale contracts called for more mundane products for navy cruisers and battleships like the *Giulio Cesare* and the *Andrea Doria*, as well as steamships bear-

Inlayers at work in the factory at Sestri Ponente. Rinaldo Piaggio, left, wanted Pietro Costa as his partner. Costa was a sculptor and was entrusted with the technical and artistic management of the decorative and inlay work for ships' furnishings.

A particular taste in decor, inspired by the Art Nouveau trend that was then the rage, is seen in the furnishings for the *Sicilia* steamship (1900).

ing the hopes of thousands of immigrants to the African colonies or the shores of the New World. The period after World War I saw some weakening in the maritime trade but the company had already been diversifying for some years into constructing and repairing railway rolling stock.

Cabinet-building and steel: rolling stock

The development of the railway system was already under way—on completion of the Frejus tunnel in 1905, Italian railways were nationalized and little time was lost in pushing this measure through in the South of the country and Sardinia also—and orders started pouring in from this dynamic, innovative industry, making con-tinued expansion seem likely. Here, Piaggio played a bold card by setting up a new company with a new fac-tory, once again by the sea, in an area defined by the coast road, the railway and the beach at Finale Ligure. It had three hundred workers in 270,000 square feet of buildings at start-up (1908) but little time had passed before both figures doubled.

Metalworking was radically new for the company but it was to be the underlying theme for the complete trans-formation the company went through. In this sense, the idea of taking on board Attilio Odero, chairman of the shipyards of the same name, was a happy one: he was to become a valuable partner. A great believer in linking iron smelting to metalworking and mechanical engineering, he, like Rinaldo Piaggio, became an Italian

"Panorama and aeronautical workshop" states the caption on this Finale Ligure postcard proclaim-ing the company's newest product diversification after railway rolling stock. The workshops looked out onto a square next to the beach where a crane acted as a mooring point for seaplanes.

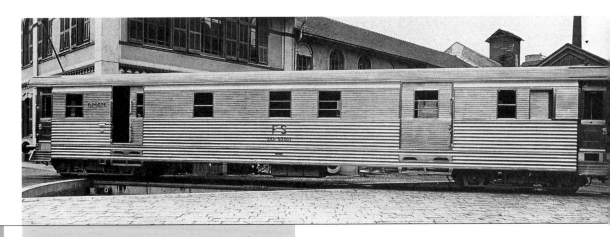

Piaggio's production of railway carriages and locomotives over more than three decades was wide-ranging, including products in stainless steel, such as this carriage, photographed outside the Sestri Ponente factory, and tramcars for the city of Milan.

In 1937, in the middle of the Fascist era, the Edward G. Budd Corporation of Philadelphia, which twenty years later would supply the molds for the Vespa, licensed advanced welding machinery to the company in Pontedera. This machinery improved the working of stainless steel, enabling innovative, ultra-light railway locomotives and carriages, similar to American transcontinental trains, to be built: a surprising initiative that was doomed to failure because of the World War looming on the horizon.

senator which gave him excellent contacts among the men who counted in heavy industry.

Railway carriages of all kinds were manufactured, from postal wagons to the carriages of the royal train of the princes of Piedmont, showing the fine taste and ability of Piaggio's cabinetmakers and decorators. Streetcars, too, were made along with all other kinds of rail transport conveyances—the possibilities for development were so enormous that in the Twenties rail-transport work emerged as the driving force of a company that had played the card of product diversification to the full. It was a decision that enabled Piaggio to get through, almost unscathed, the inevitable crisis Italian industry faced in the post-war years and the social unrest of the "two Red years" (1919–20) up to the crash of 1929, which had serious repercussions on the Italian economy of the early Thirties.

Getting off the ground

Around 1915 Italian industrial giants like Fiat, Breda and Ansaldo were struck by a sudden desire to take to the air. Just over ten years had passed since the Wright brothers' historic flight but the requirements of war pushed aviation development to the fore. In particular, seaplanes, the embodiment of technological development at the time, seemed somehow familiar to people who had always been in shipbuilding. Initially, the jobs were all indirect but very soon Rinaldo Piaggio, who was by then in his early fifties, decided to take over the Officine Aeronautiche Francesco Oneto company,

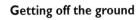

Piaggio, at last, at Pontedera. The year is 1926 and technicians and workers are standing around a test bench for a Piaggio airplane engine manufactured under license from Gnôme et Rhône.

The prestigious FBA (Franco-British Aviation) flying boats were the first aircraft manufactured under license to come out of Piaggio's factory, in 1915.

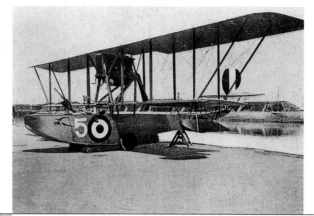

which was on the verge of bankruptcy despite a full order book of work for the war effort. With a determination characteristic of the new generation about to enter the scene, he proceeded to completely renew the technical management. He hired Giovanni Pegna, the foremost aeronautical engineer of his time, and then confidently set about moving labor from one factory of the group to another.

The new setup of Piaggio & Co., with a share capital of ten million lire ($6,000) divided between Attilio Odero and Rinaldo Piaggio, was defined in 1920. At the same time, the company's purpose was redefined as "the construction and repair of mobile material pertaining to trains, tramways or any vehicles which run on rails; naval shipbuilding; aeronautical construction; mechanical

Outside the Finale Ligure workshop a Dornier Wall built under license. On April 7, 1926 an aircraft identical to the one shown inaugurated the Società Anonima Navigazione Aerea routes that Rinaldo Piaggio had desired. Up to fifteen seaplanes, three of which were four-engined, plied between Genoa, Naples, Palermo, Tripoli and Barcelona in 1933.

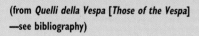

"It all started in 1924 when Piaggio took over a small factory in Pontedera and started manufacturing airplane engines."

(from *Quelli della Vespa* [*Those of the Vespa*] —see bibliography)

The outline of the P XVI, one of the prototypes manufactured at Finale, took shape around 1936.

At Pontedera, professional training was given to specialized workers and technicians who worked daily in the manufacture of the large radial engines.

engineering in general; fitting-out of ships; general woodworking; tannin extracts and wood-derived coloring material; forestry cultivation and exploitation; production of coal, its derivatives and extracts and general wood trading." It was the aeronautical sector, however, that would soon take off.

From the new headquarters that had been purchased in 1924 in Pontedera, and which some twenty years later were to see the birth of today's scooter, came the first 400 horsepower Jupiter engines manufactured under French license. Costruzioni Meccaniche Nazionali, which was already producing aeronautical and automobile engines, became the heart of engine production of the Ligurian-Tuscan group after its purchase by Rinaldo Piaggio and Attilio Odero. It was here that the

mighty radial engines were manufactured. They were destined to set more than twenty records just before the outbreak of World War II: from the P VII for upside-down flight and the P XI RC which still holds the world record for high-altitude, piston-engine flight to the P XII RC with its double radial eighteen cylinders generating a total of 1,750 horsepower, the most powerful piston engine manufactured in Italy.

Between the wars—under the protectionist umbrella the Fascist regime gave large-scale industry—the prototypes came out one after the other, from the single-seat fighter aircraft to civilian transport airliners fitted with the Piaggio-designed, variable-pitch airscrew that very soon spread to all Italian aircraft production.

And this is where one of the protagonists closest to the

Enrico Piaggio, freshly graduated from college at twenty-three, found himself at the head of the newly-born engine factory. A person of undoubted importance, highly ambitious and very determined, not easy to get along with and an unswerving supporter of technological renewal, he set the pace, increasing the workforce from 136 to 6,950 in just six years.

The same engines as those
born in Pontedera are
shown in the hold of
a P 108 transport plane
made from a converted
four-engine bomber which
took to the skies in 1938.

heart of our story comes on the scene, an absolutely brilliant aeronautical engineer. Besides the in-flight variable-pitch airscrew whose use Piaggio put under contract from 12 March 1932, the never-ending list of inventions that sprang from the mind of Corradino D'Ascanio included an "electric oven to bake bread and pastry products" (1919), a "late-firing shooting device for aircraft and its application to time-fired mortars and shrapnel shot from aircraft" (1926) an "electro-pneumatic machine for the cataloguing and swift consultation of documents" (1952) as well as a pocket cigarette case with a time-lock built in for exclusive personal use—all these besides, naturally, the Vespa in 1946.

But at this stage (1932) technology was progressing and one of the innovations called for was the building of an ambitious wind tunnel complete with tow tanks in the Finale Ligure factory. Its settings, initially gauged wrongly, were corrected by D'Ascanio, who in the process turned it into an aeronautical test bench famous throughout Europe.

When their father died in 1938, the brothers, Enrico and Armando Piaggio, took over control of the company together with long-standing partner Attilio Odero, in accordance with the patrilineal tradition of barring female members of the family from holding any power whatever their importance as stockholders. In the same year a four-engine bomber was produced, the cutting edge of Italian aviation—the P 108—that had features similar to, if not more advanced than, those of the American Flying Fortress. Dozens of these planes were manufactured for both military and civilian use. It was in one

Facing page: tension and expectancy line the face of Enrico Piaggio, in dark suit with Corradino D'Ascanio on his right, during the record-making 10.6-mile high-altitude flight of Colonel Pezzi in May 1937. His Caproni 16 aircraft was powered by a Piaggio air-cooled P XI RC engine that could produce over 700 hp.

Agreement on dividing the proceeds from the variable-pitch airscrew was reached in March 1932. With the experimentation period over, the patents belonged to the company and the inventor would receive royalties of 10 percent of both Italian and export sales, and 40 percent on licensing agreements.

The P 108 had the remote controls for the machine guns in their turrets somewhat earlier than the famous Flying Fortress. During the war years, Piaggio made the P 108 a symbol of technological excellence and commitment to the war effort.

PIAGGIO

of them that Bruno Mussolini, the Italian dictator's second son, lost his life on August 7, 1941, when his plane crashed during an exercise in the skies over Pisa.

The large Pontedera factory became the nucleus of the whole group, with more than 750,000 square feet of premises and 7,000 employees. But in late 1943 the factory's landing strip was destroyed by German mines; in January 1944, the factory itself was repeatedly devastated by Allied bombing; and later, with its typical methodical determination, the Wehrmacht blew up hundreds of Pontedera's pylons during its retreat.

From four-engine flight to frying pans

For obvious reasons, the company's factories were primary military objectives, and all of them, except Sestri Ponente, were heavily damaged—Pontedera worst of all. The workshops were almost totally destroyed and what machinery hadn't been requisitioned and shipped off to Germany had to be moved to Biella. At the end of the War the wide open spaces inside the factory alongside the railway line were taken up by the American army, and the workshops were, for the most part, inaccessible. The workforce of the group dropped from 12,000 in 1943 to less than 2,000, the white-collar workers from over 2,000 to just 300. But in '45 the Pontedera works could count only 60 blue-collar and 30 white-collar workers.

These are not the only figures that highlight the drama of post-war life: inflation rose 2,700 percent from 1938 to 1946 and doubled by the following year, although the purchasing power of wages had only risen

proportionately by 50 percent. A family whose only breadwinner was a blue-collar factory worker had to spend more than 90 percent of its income on basic foodstuffs. Industrial production plummeted to 29 percent of 1938 levels in '45 and by the end of '46 it had only risen to 60 percent. The productivity boom fostered by the War gave way to fearsome devastation of Italy's industrial fabric and infrastructure.

And yet a way out had to be found. And the main concern—at Piaggio as elsewhere—was to find a product around which the life of the factory could be progressively rebuilt. Something easy to sell, in other words: something for a country still on its knees and strewn with rubble. Italy's best aeronautical engineers had been evacuated to Biella, where they remained through-

out the last years of the war. There, they worked on the problem of how best to use men and machinery to produce aluminum pots and pans. However, events, as it turned out, were already leading elsewhere.

Piaggio, up to then, had been identified with large-scale war contracts or in any case government ones, but above all transportation vehicles of every kind, shape and size. It was no mere coincidence, then, that brought Enrico Piaggio face to face with an odd-looking two-wheeled object in the collection of Count Trossi, the Biella textile entrepreneur in whose mansion the company management was billeted. An idea was taking shape: to provide an individual means of transport that would make millions of people mobile, a Ford Model T for a Europe on its knees recovering from the war.

The 1944 bombing raids spared the technical and administrative department where Corradino D'Ascanio and others had their offices, as well as the management building between the railway and Viale Rinaldo Piaggio. The foundry, warehouse and shipping area in the complex opposite were heavily damaged and the centrally placed main workshops were almost completely destroyed.

It is hereby certified that the plant of Messrs. Piaggio & Co. of Pontedera situated in Viale Rinaldo Piaggio was partly demolished during the enemy air raids over Pontedera on the 6th, 18th, 21st and 22nd January, as well as on 14th February 1944—year XXIII of the Fascist Era.

For office use
The City Governor

1st March 1944 – XXIII

THE SHAPE OF INNOVATION

The 1921 ABC Skootamota seemed at home on the cricket field. Designed by Granville Bradshaw, an English engineer, it was powered by a four-stroke, single-cylinder 125 cc engine that gave it a top speed of 25 mph.

Little more than a kid's scooter, the motor-scooter was a two-wheeled vehicle to help one get away fast or, more exactly, to scoot away.

The Italian post-war scooter, which was to make its mark in so many different places, radically changed a concept which, at the beginning of the century, had led to the 1904 Auto-Fauteil and perhaps even earlier to the bicycle with a built-in engine and open frame made in 1894 by Hildebrand & Wolfmüller in Germany. But it wasn't until the Twenties that the motor-scooter came along in the form of the British Skootamota or, better still, the Unibus, which was dumpy but very much the shape of things to come, a true "two-wheeled car," skipping along at 25 miles per hour.

These were, however, more like expensive playthings

Le Touquet, *"le jardin de la Manche,"* in the early Twenties very probably saw many of these scooter forerunners on parade. Left, an interesting variation on the Auto-Fauteil with a padded wicker seat, final chain-driven transmission and front end suspension to boot.

Here, Eleanore Whitney, the star of a number of forgettable movies such as *College Holiday*, *Turn off the Moon* and *Blonde Trouble*, gets a driving lesson. Hollywood, before the Depression, seemed a good place for this little two-wheeled toy.

for adults, restricted to the happy few who meandered over golf-courses or along the streets of the upper-class areas of London.

Something more than a toy

On the other side of the Atlantic the time was ripe for the Cushman Motor Company of Lincoln, Nebraska to take center stage. Their company's roots dated back to the beginning of the century in the manufacture of internal combustion engines for agriculture.

In 1938, Everett Cushman and his cousin Clinton decided to gamble on producing a small number of scooters in sheet-pressed metal designed by a certain Robert Ammon in order to boost the sales of their sturdy, two-stroke engines. This rudimentary, awkward-looking vehicle, nicknamed "the Milking Stool," was the forerunner of a happy series rehashed time and again. In the Fifties, these shared the Allstate brand with Vespa in the North American market.

Several thousand units were sold up until 1965 when the line was shut down, and the Cushmans kept to the square shape and traditional configuration—a vertical engine and end-chain to the back wheel—although they updated some models with the novel variomatic transmission instead of the two-speed gear change.

This was the first time a scooter had been made as an efficient means of transport for use in town and short out-of-town trips. Despite this, it never really took off in America, probably due to the extreme popularity of the automobile and the attractively low prices of the cheapest models.

The MP6 in the words of Corradino D'Ascanio

In the cellars of Count Trossi, a motorcycling enthusiast, the Piaggio managers in exile at Biella had perhaps seen a Cushman that had been brought over by air and a Velta, the Italian scooter produced in Turin in 1938, designed by the engineer Vittorio Belmondo. From these two somewhat rudimentary objects, Renzo Spolti, himself an engineer, developed Piaggio's MP5 project that saw the light in the form of a pre-series comprising a hundred units or so.

The hybrid, powered by the same 98 cc engine with a top speed of 21 miles per hour, was a decided

It's Rita Hayworth, no less, on this Motor Glide, the American scooter which in the mid-Thirties had automatic transmission, a covered engine, front wheel brakes and easy accessibility for the rider.

Manufactured between 1920 and '22 by Gloucestershire Aircraft of Cheltenham, England, the excellent Unibus was as expensive as a car.

A Cushman 52 with its sidecar for transporting materials, in service on the ground in London's airport in May '47. It had no gears but it boasted an automatic centrifugal clutch and could just reach 40 mph. Its slender pencil springs on the back suspension were abandoned in the summer of that same year.

Very similar to other designs of the day, Piaggio's first scooter prototype did have some interesting details such as the large, front load-bearing wheelguard substituting for the usual forks and the automatic gear-change on the cardan shaft version.

improvement on both of the original machines that had spawned it, although it looked very like them. But it wasn't good enough for the managing director. The ugly duckling—"Paperino," as it was immediately nicknamed in the workshop—looked awkward, uncomfortable and slow. In a word: ugly.

Enrico Piaggio summoned his best man to Biella so that he could solve this problem as he had others.

On December 2, 1945, thanks to Corradino D'Ascanio's genius and a small miracle achieved by the technicians and workers at his side, the machine was produced, with its unmistakable form and amazing technical innovations.

One indicative example is the gear change operated by rotating the handgrip, so that the movement followed naturally from the activation of the clutch lever. This was way ahead of the 1938 Fiat prototype, which had an automobile-type stick shift, and the early Innocenti Lambrettas of 1947 were still hampered by the classic right-foot, heel-and-toe gear change.

Four years and some one hundred and thirty thousand Vespas later, a radio broadcast was to celebrate this glorious dawning. It's worthwhile highlighting the musical background, the odd-sounding new words translated from the English (in the original Italian version) and the stiff ingenuity of the ad, but also the simplicity and directness of the designer himself.

"(Motorist-type musical interlude) Announcer: And now, ladies and gentlemen, your attention please.

Even after some time had passed, the workers who gave another name to Renzo Spolti and Vittorio Casini's odd-looking creature were able to recall those days when the product was fresh on the market.

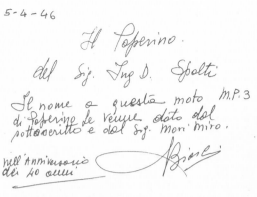

5-4-46

Il Paperino.
del Sig. Ing D. Spolti
Il nome a questa moto M.P.3
di Paperino le venne dato dal
sottoscritto e dal Sig. Moni miro.

nell'Anniversario
dei 40 anni

Corradino D'Ascanio's demand for carte blanche, and his blunt refusal to develop someone else's ideas, upset Enrico Piaggio somewhat: "You're always so obstinate. So do what you want but get on with it!" A few months later the MP6 was already a reality showing the historic Piaggio "aeronautical" logo.

What's this on my right? … It's the buzz of a Vespa!! … (a Vespa sounding its horn as it races by) … and on the left the reply from a Lambretta! (identical sound effects of a Lambretta)

Announcer: We're in the world of motor-scooters. Vespa, Lambretta, Iso, M V and so on: there are about 150 thousand motor-scooter enthusiasts in Italy and you can be sure there'll be a lot of them listening in. But what's a motor-scooter? Quite literally a scooter with an engine. Where did the idea for Mr. Quick-and-Nifty Motor-scooter come from in Italy? Let's hear from the engineer, Mr. D'Ascanio who designed the Vespa in 1945.

D'Ascanio: With no knowledge of motorbikes (indeed my business had been aviation) I thought about making a vehicle that I could use without having to be a motorcyclist. I had never liked the tangle of exposed parts common motorbikes have, always in bits on the roadside when a tire had to be changed. Previous attempts never seemed to fit what I was looking for: they always turned out like miniature motorcycles with all their drawbacks, or else little more than deluxe toys, not fit for practical use.

Announcer: Quite right. So?

D'Ascanio: Well, first of all I aimed at putting the engine-gear bloc far away from the driver and making the transmission as simple as possible, as well as making the wheels easy to take off, like on a car. Then the bodywork was designed to be as simple and economic as possible and to hide and protect the engine unit. I didn't want to have to take my hands off the handlebars (I was afraid of falling over) so I incorporated all the

The recovery work continued: until 1944, the aeronautical section was located where the building's housing management are situated today.

The Vespa was many people's new heart's desire, so it was a good promotional idea to stage a new challenge between Fausto Bartalli and Gino Coppi, two great cycling champions whose rivalry had divided the country into opposing factions.

controls on the handgrip. These were the ideas we started with. We put them together with the general layout and some constructive criticism from Mr. Piaggio, not to mention everybody's enthusiastic cooperation, from engineers to craftsmen, and the new vehicle came out at the end of 1945.

(orchestral emphasis with a bass to treble glissando)

Announcer: This, offered by Piaggio, is the first example of rapid conversion of a large-scale industrial company from war-effort production to peacetime manufacture. And bear in mind that here, at Pontedera, the production lines had been completely destroyed by bombing and plundering leaving not a single machine standing. On the basis of just one scooter prototype, Piaggio, with great courage and intuition, decided to go

ahead with the production of ten thousand Vespas without a single order to back them up."

The figure was wildly exaggerated—multiplied by four at least—but the importance of the part played by the entrepreneur is not to be underestimated. In Corradino D'Ascanio's own words "with authentic farsightedness, especially considering the times we were living in at the end of 1945 when everybody was speculating and nobody was building, he ordered the finalization of the Vespa and its mass production."

However, getting back to the design, in these few remarks, repeated elsewhere with more detail, there lies the very essence of the operation, especially in the part where he admits to being inspired by "aeronautical

Corradino D'Ascanio wrote to Enrico Piaggio on August 2, 1946: "In looks, the Nibbio borrows perhaps from both the Vespa and the Motor Glide but it's just different enough to avoid being prosecuted for plagiarism of shape. As far as the structure is concerned, the Nibbio is completely different from ours. The emergence of models that look like ours is proof that we're on the right track, and it'll be a long time before the Nibbio becomes a real threat. We will always be ahead in terms of increased production and also in improvements we'll be introducing which will take our machine very close to perfection."

Below: Corradino D'Ascanio and his brainchild have a cartoon encounter.

Below right: faced with recurring overheating that came to light in testing, Biella came up with the unhappy idea of an "air conveyance plate." D'Ascanio, however decided on the simple but brilliant idea of a fan fixed to the flywheel and solved the problem.

The clearly aeronautical origin of the front wheel support is to this day considered indispensable. The front suspension, by contrast, underwent progressive evolution throughout the years.

concepts familiar to me, such as the single-tube support for the front wheel which, after three years experience, can be said to substitute perfectly well the fork traditional to bicycles" or where he expresses satisfaction at having gone "far ahead of the most up-to-date ideas in automobile design, because the Vespa's sheet bodywork is both a frame and, because of the special way it is worked, is sturdier than the old, tubular system"— a dig at Innocenti, mother of all Lambrettas. "This answer too came from my aeronautical experience where the lightness of a part must not jeopardize its strength," he added, and in which, one feels like adding, maximizing functionality and aerodynamic streamlining is the starting point for formal harmony and beauty.

> **"P**iaggio, thanks to its experience in the field, has unreservedly decided to adopt the sheet steel option and construct a rail chassis incorporating the footrest, a generous leg shield, the steering column, and a rear box to house all the mechanical parts and support the seat … the gearbox is worked from the handlebar by means of a practical and ingenious mechanism: the left handgrip rotates and it works the gear-change transmission. The clutch lever is fixed to the handgrip. To change gear, you pull the clutch lever, then you turn the handgrip to the position that engages the required gear, then you release the clutch lever."

(from *Motociclismo* magazine, 10 April 1946)

Corradino D'Ascanio's many patents include the inclinometer, an instrument indispensable for controlling trim in flight which dates back to 30 June 1916 when he served with the Turin-based aeronautical company Giulio Pomilio.

D'Ascanio and Pietro Trojani in front of the DAT 2. A stiff blade pitch adjustment mechanism was the cause of the prototype breaking up and the injury to Trojani in October 1926.

"For me, aviation was a never-ending fever. Since childhood, flying was my greatest dream, the one I cherished most. I would stand and watch swallows with envy." A powerful calling and an unswerving ambition, a genius for mechanics and physics, an elegant way of sketching the solution rapidly—on the drawing board or the palm of his hand—for someone who had difficulty keeping up with him: this was Corradino D'Ascanio.

The father of the Vespa was the second lieutenant engineer able to fix any kind of problem of trim the pilots of the Italian army's aviation battalion complained of; the inventor of a single-seater tourism aircraft powered by a Harley Davidson motorbike engine, an authentic runabout with wings (an American dream of the Twenties); and the father of magnificent airplanes, who, in order to win back the altitude record, had no hesitation in putting pure oxygen into the cylinders of the big radial engines that had come off his drawing board. Above all, D'Ascanio was the man who introduced the load-bearing wing—in short the helicopter. In many ways this was a failure, though, and perhaps the Vespa can be blamed in part for that.

On April 7, 1925, he applied to patent a "helicopter with two coaxial rotors and an automatic slow-descent device." He didn't know then that the path embarked on so decisively—with the backing of a telegram sent by "His Excellency Benito Mussolini" to Baron Pietro Trojani, his partner and financial backer—was to be so long and difficult.

The first prototype fell to pieces in just a few minutes, although it had seemed to be taking off. The second suffered a similar fate. Success was reached at the third attempt, after a general run-through inside a hangar with the nation's Aviation Engineer Force Commission.

8 minutes and 34 seconds later

"One minute … two. Time stood still. It was like being at the dentist." D'Ascanio himself recounts that day. "Eight minutes! I couldn't stand it any more and signaled the pilot to come back down or I'd have gone completely crazy. He didn't get it and signaled back with his hand asking what had happened. Nothing had happened: I'd just won the fight. My children could be proud of me …"

INCLINOMETRO UNIVERSALE D'ASCANIO

Between 8 and 13 October 1930 the third prototype completed its trials successfully setting new world records for duration (8 minutes 34 seconds), length in a straight line (3,539 feet) and altitude (60 feet off the ground).

The DAT 3 was flown by Major Marinello Nelli who, at D'Ascanio's prompting, put his hand on the blade adjustment mechanism.

The DAT 3, the first human-operated helicopter (and the first properly equipped with a variable blade pitch adjustment mechanism) set records for duration, altitude and length of flight on the Ciampino airstrip. But the partners didn't handle the opportunities that came from this resounding success very well and the partnership dissolved two years later, leaving the financial backer in deep trouble. Who else could be blamed for the terrible error of judgment that led to an unreasonable economic proposal in response to a letter that Senator Giovanni Agnelli, owner of Fiat, had sent them the day after the historical flight?

In 1932, young Enrico Piaggio—who'd been manager of the Pontedera factory for four years—managed to get D'Ascanio on board as well as secure

Turin, 10 November, 1930 – year IX of the Fascist Era

Dear Sir,
I was at Ciampino to view your helicopter but I regret, despite many attempts to reach you by telephone, I was unable to speak with you. I wished to extend to you my congratulations for the happy outcome and the ingenuity with which you solved such an interesting problem.
Not having been able to accomplish this in person, I wish now to do so in writing and am pleased to take this opportunity of extending to you my congratulations and very best wishes, and remain,

Yours sincerely
Giovanni Agnelli

"The helicopter consists of a very long fuselage," wrote D'Ascanio in a technical report from around 1940, "surmounted towards the front by a short shaft on which is keyed the large, 43-foot-diameter triple rotor."

On the Pontedera landing strip pictured in front of the PD3 engine. Standing at the designer's right are Enrico Piaggio and the factory's general manager, Francesco Lanzara. Carlo Doveri, who succeeded D'Ascanio as Piaggio's technical manager in 1961, is shown in profile.

ownership of the patents of the in-flight variable-pitch airscrew for 10 percent of the price of each airscrew. The designer asked for 10 percent on the profits of the sale of the helicopter too because, he wrote, "my family suffered so fearfully from the long sacrifices they had to make" and here we can believe in the perfectly good faith of a man who had never been good at business dealing. D'Ascanio went to Pontedera in 1934 but the production and sale of helicopters never took place.

The Piaggio-D'Ascanio 3 (PD 3) had a surprisingly up-to-date shape and, on paper at least, boasted the performance statistics of a vehicle already up and running. But the prototype didn't make its maiden flight until 1942 and immediately afterwards it was sidelined into a warehouse because production, for the war-effort took precedence. In the meantime, on the other side of the Atlantic, the first successful long-distance helicopter flight, from Connecticut to Ohio, had been made by a U.S. Army Sikorsky, dealing a heavy blow to the Italians.

Then there was the disaster of war on the home front: bombings, moving the production lines and the war front passing through.

"Going up to Biella," D'Ascanio recalled, "I kept wondering what it was he [Enrico Piaggio] wanted from me. I knew he was reduced to making pots and pans and I had no illusions—there was nothing doing in airplanes or helicopters. He welcomed me warmly and said, 'I want something that'll put Italy on two wheels but I don't want another motorbike.'"

In the PD 4, D'Ascanio's idea of a helicopter reached its high-point. During the final stages there was a slight landing accident caused by the imperfect longitudinal inclination control system which was still being developed.

300,000 Vespas versus one single helicopter

Talk of helicopters was revived in Piaggio after the Fourth Congress of the American Helicopter Society (Philadelphia, 1948), which was chaired by D'Ascanio and Igor Sikorsky, among others. A new version of the PD 3 came out in 1949 that was destroyed in an accident two years later. The third prototype that came off the Pontedera line, the PD 4, was "a three-seat machine with double-blade, counter-rotating, synchronized, tandem rotors." Compared to its predecessors, it was ingenious and wholly innovative.

D'Ascanio was as nervous as a schoolboy when the machine took off from the Pontedera airfield on August 5, 1952. It easily went through its paces for half an hour, but then, without warning, it plummeted, struck the landing strip, spun around and fell to pieces. Enrico Piaggio ended the dream with a short, extremely sharp letter in which he said, "I was disappointed, but not surprised, to hear of the very serious accident which took place today …" He signed off with "Technical staff hitherto involved in this project will from now on be engaged in more productive tasks."

Indeed, by then almost three hundred thousand Vespas had been produced. And while this assured D'Ascanio the greatest financial comfort—he was already the company's highest paid executive by 1947 and received royalties for every Vespa and for every Ape (Bee), or Vespacar, as it was called abroad, that came off the production line—it turned out to be his downfall.

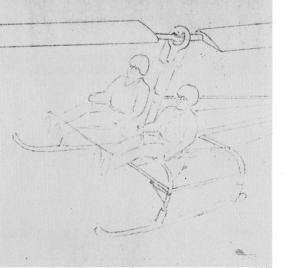

The PD 4 project shut down after a bad accident that destroyed the prototype, and D'Ascanio seemed to abandon his dream.

But many years later, after he'd retired, he used his garage as a workshop to build this small two-seater helicopter for agriculture and training.

The first of many patents protecting the Vespa's uniqueness summarizes its characterizing features. Among other details, it lists the possibility of dismantling the front wheel-guard, which, from the third production series on (1947), was abandoned.

It was natural for the managing director to preside over the birth in person: he alone could celebrate the name-giving ritual and thus give it life. Crucial to the way an object is perceived, to the definition of its identity—and thus the culmination of the effort of many—the name had to signify many things: agility, brilliance, familiarity, forthrightness, attractiveness, reliability, spontaneity and a certain amount of natural elegance without any formalism.

But history willed somehow that the thing itself, with its pinched waistline and rounded sides, led Enrico Piaggio to the laconic consideration "It looks like a wasp [*vespa*]." And that was it.

This mere whiff of company mythology was an indicator of the clear, assertive ways the man had of doing things. "The name 'Vespa' for the Piaggio motorscooter" reads the reply sent to the *Secolo XIX* newspaper when they asked the managing director for an interview in August 1962 "was given by Dr. Enrico Piaggio because he found that the shape of this vehicle (narrow waist and large hindquarters) brought to mind the hymenoptera of the same name. No other name was ever considered."

April 23, 1946, the patent

At noon on that day an application was filed in the city of Florence's patent office for an industrial manufacture patent for a "model of a practical nature" of a "motorcycle with rationally placed parts and elements

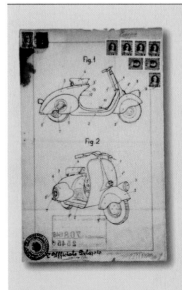
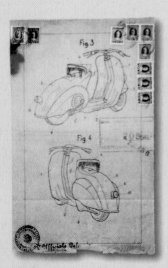

In this new phase,
the new Piaggio logo
came into being.
It was a classic heraldic
shield whose extreme
sobriety was confirmed
in the Bodoni type of
the large white initial
on the blue background.

with a frame combining with mudguards and engine-cowling covering all working parts."

Here, it is worthwhile going into some more detail.

"The model," the application goes on, "concerns a particular form of motorcycle endowed with a suitable shape and in which the elements comprising the frame, and which have the function of footrest, mudguards, and engine cowling as well as the special, arched frontal protection, have been given a rational layout; the whole shaped and combined so as to cover and protect all mechanical parts as well as make the position of the motorcyclist practical and comfortable."

A little further on, it refers to an enclosed drawing of the part in question as follows: "It should be pointed out that covering No. 6 has been shaped so that the fanned air for cooling the engine—once it leaves the fan itself—must follow a curve that brings it against the engine." This was D'Ascanio's answer to the problem of cylinder overheating and seizing: it had been perfected on a test bench with the engine running and talcum powder fed into the fan as it was spinning. A cloud of powder filled the air and started everyone coughing, but the cylinder head had been duly whitened by the airflow.

Attention was detailed, perhaps too much, for what the vehicle offered both technically and aesthetically, so much so that at the end of the description the words "while, as can be seen from the drawings and in any case is made clear by the description, the whole constitutes a rational, comfortable motorcycle offering protection from mud and dust without jeopardizing requirements of appearance and elegance" are under-

The new Vespa logo fits this hymenoptera to a T—it's the signature at the foot of a personal letter: a rounded italic, almost confidential but with a flick of the pen that without leaving the paper zips back to the beginning of the word to underline it. Moreover, the capital letter bent like a bow about to let fly its arrow is bowed to the front: it conveys a feeling of strength, held in check, and just waiting to fly.

The first pamphlet to promote the new vehicle made a point of showing a woman driving. Shown completely at ease driving the new two-wheeler, she was portrayed in a highly unusual light for the times as a privileged customer, leaving the past behind her.

At the dawning of postwar recovery: manual finishing of the castings and two photographs of the working and assembly of the vehicle. In the last photograph in particular when the machinery had been adjusted, there was a proper production line.

lined. In the handwriting of the technical head of the patent office there is a nervous note in the margin stating "a practical article, not ornamental," omitting any reference to appearance or elegance.

The office involved issued confirmation of patent acceptance on November 9, 1946.

Its introduction into society

The little Pontedera-born scooter's potential and ambition was already part of its genetic code.

The project was set up along "Fordist" lines for automobile production, which, in a company like Piaggio and with its history, meant there was nothing short-sighted or left to chance. Everything was aimed at turning out large numbers. The only question left was how the market would respond and the answer, in the early stages at least, was uncertain.

The presentation to the press was held in the exclusive setting of the Rome Golf Club and organized by Umberto Barnato, trusted ally of Enrico Piaggio and later one of the organizers of that joyous juggernaut, the Vespa Club, which appeared soon afterwards.

The American newsreel company Movietone had to be there because so was General Ellery W. Stone, head of the Allied Commission, standing side by side with the civilian and religious authorities.

Journalists from Italy and overseas were mystified by the odd-looking pastel-green thing in front of them, with its small-diameter wheels, the handlebar speed change mechanism and the seeming simplicity of the

rounded shape which was its most striking aspect. The managing director and top staff of a prestigious ex-aeronautical firm were apparently risking everything for this: a scooter, little more than a toy.

In road tests, the Vespa seemed to win skeptics over with its maneuverability and ease in start-up, the fluid, smooth performance of its engine discreetly filtered by the sophisticated, flute-shaped muffler of the first series, the astonishing power in first and second gear and going up hills, and comfort greatly superior to that of a motorcycle despite the lack of back suspension.

Despite all this, the fifty or so units made up in the pre-production series almost didn't sell. In one way or another, however, and not without difficulty, the first forty-eight Vespas were sold, the last being the most

With a novel product still unknown to the market, the logical choice was to channel through a well-known brand. It was equally logical that the biggest name on the market—Moto Guzzi owned by Count Parodi and which, thanks to the ingenuity of its engineer designer, Givlio Carcano, was then riding the crest of fortune's wave— failed to see that the potential bias against the scooter was deep-seated. Best to turn your back on the two-wheel world.

> "The first 48 Vespas got away but the 49th and the 50th just sat there—as Mr. Bartalucci, an engineer, tells it—so one fine day Dr. Piva, the foundry manager and I said to each other 'let's go to Dr. Piaggio, poor man, we'll take these last two off his hands. They'll probably never be made again...' But then the orders started to pour in."

(from A. Mondini, "*Un'elica e due ruote*" [One airscrew and two wheels]—see bibliography)

difficult to find buyers for but then day after day things picked up until it seemed they'd never stop.

Payment in installments, reliability and prestige

The company had never needed to deal with the free market before, because it had always lived on government orders and bids. For the whole of 1946, the ways and means still hadn't become clear and the year-end accounts reflected this state of uncertainty. Things, however, were beginning to move.

The opportunity arose to share the style and quality limelight enjoyed by the large Lancia sedan automobiles. Early contacts were difficult for the newly created SARPI (Società Agenzia Rappresentanze Prodotti

Start-up was difficult. Nothing seemed to indicate the coming success, which would exceed all expectations. Thanks to the more powerful model that was launched only two years after the Vespa 98, the Italian scooter became famous abroad also.

Vespa es la motoneta más conocida del mundo

In an atmosphere of rebirth, but one also heavy with dramatic political conflict day by day, the Vespa became a familiar sight in city streets and on country roads.

As valuable as jewels was the image of the brand new model projected by the new promotional pamphlet which, significantly, was printed in more than one language.

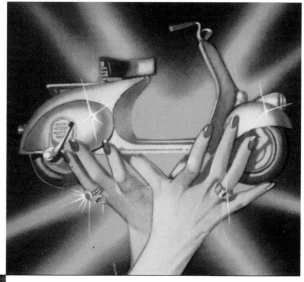

It is a vehicle which, unlike the traditional motorcycle proper, is suitable for all social classes and for both sexes. Its structure does not require excessive physical effort to get on, and is very easy to keep balanced in slow-moving traffic ... the front apron protects the legs from dust and rain ... it is the ideal vehicle for short town trips for businessmen, professionsals, doctors, etc. who may park it in a public parking place and present themselves for their appointments looking as perfect as though they had just gotten out of a car.

(from *Motociclismo* magazine, 10 April 1946)

Industriali), the small Florentine company Enrico Piaggio had set up to sell the product. The salesmen found themselves negotiating with car showrooms that had the Lancia Appia and the Ardea, flagships of Italian automobile production, proudly on show. They tried to get the Vespa 98s exhibited alongside them, perhaps because of the aristocratic associations of the old English scooters.

The idea of payment in installments was adopted, something out of the ordinary, that enabled a lot of people to buy a Vespa while assuring the company a valuable advance on capital in the time frame for delivery, at this point between ten and twelve months from order.

A technical assistance network was set up offering training courses for authorized mechanics. There was still a lot to do, first and foremost in production. There was no lack of labor in these lean years when the national economy was struggling to get off the ground, as top-management in companies seemed to understand, particularly with the dying down of the revolutionary "north winds" born of the Resistance. Already the managing director was pushing for the development of a new model that would sell in big numbers.

The first years of heady growth and deep social conflict were just ahead, the years of great satisfaction in sales, and not only on the home market: the years when an icon of our times was forged.

1945-46

MP6
VESPA98

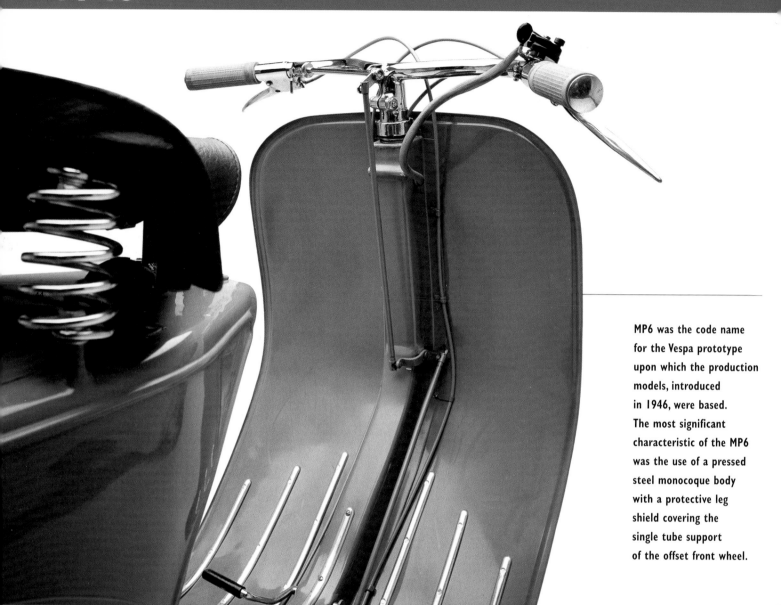

MP6 was the code name for the Vespa prototype upon which the production models, introduced in 1946, were based. The most significant characteristic of the MP6 was the use of a pressed steel monocoque body with a protective leg shield covering the single tube support of the offset front wheel.

The technical and styling cues used by Corradino D'Ascanio in the Vespa were inspired by the design of larger vehicles such as locomotives, seaplanes and automobiles and were developed further with his knowledge of aerodynamics.

The clearly bicycle-type
handlebars carried
all the vehicle's controls,
gear lever included.

MP6

Corradino D'Ascanio was given the task of designing a new type of two-wheeled vehicle that was extremely simple, cheap, absolutely utilitarian and unisex.

He realized that the project could only be successfully implemented through a rational interpretation of the typical problems of vehicle usage. This entailed identifying the needs and demands of potential users together with the possible technical/performance characteristics that the vehicle was required to have. As a result, he was able to determine a set of requisites around which the vehicle's shape and function could be defined. The choices which determined the configuration of the Vespa prototype pivoted on a number of conditions:

Excellent accessibility—the vehicle must be easy to mount. The design solution to this took a cue from the woman's bicycle, and involved freeing up the space between the saddle and the handlebars. On traditional motorcycles, this area is normally occupied by parts of the chassis, the tank and the engine.

Comfort—the riding position was more akin to the driving position in a car rather than having the rider straddled across a chassis. This was ideal both for female and male riders. Furthermore, this position allowed the rider to place his or her feet on the ground easily, which gave a greater sense of safety than did posture on conventional motorcycles.

The vehicle had to be highly maneuverable—this required the vehicle to be ridden without removing one's hands from the handlebars, which led to the decision to install all controls on the bars, including the gear lever (patented 1946).

Cleanliness and safety—D'Ascanio designed the characteristic front leg shield to provide the rider with a certain degree of protection from the weather and collisions. As for the engine, it had to be covered and isolated from the rest of the vehicle, located far from the rider but at the same time easily accessible for maintenance. He therefore decided to put the engine at the rear, making it a single unit with the rear wheel. The need to cover the engine was resolved by using a wing-shaped cowling. The upper edge of this slotted into a rubber-sealed groove on the main body of the vehicle and it was secured in place

The Piaggio logo was placed at the center of the leg shield. However, a new logo was already being designed at the time of the prototype which, together with the moniker "Vespa," was to be used in the first series.

Innovation is a Piaggio tradition. The company's ability to find new and creative solutions to technological problems or sociological needs had already been proved long before the Vespa. From the very start, in 1884, the company's success was founded on a policy of constant research into the transport needs of a continually expanding market. Thanks to this research, the company grew to became the world's leading manufacturer of light transport vehicles, both in terms of production volume and engineering innovation.

The side cowls were different in shape and size. The left-hand one was smaller and incorporates the hatch to the tool compartment. The right-hand cowl covered the engine and sported two air vent slits. The design of this component was to be modified for the production model.

MP6

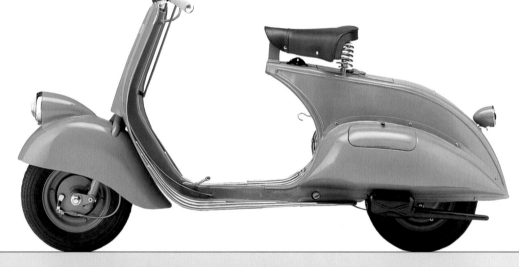

Detail of the flute-shaped silencer and the beak profile of the end of the body shell, with visible weld points.

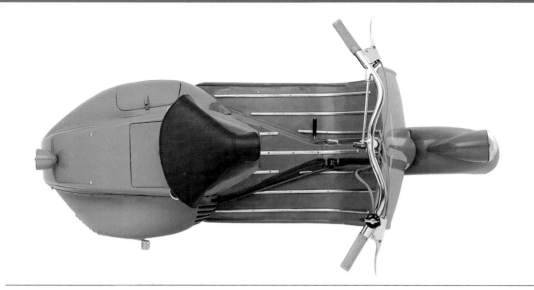

This top view shows the
footplate with the lowered
central rail, later improved
in the production version.

The shape of the vehicle
was characterized by
the "thick wing" profile
of the rear end, first
seen in automobiles
in the early Forties.

*by two studs. The chainless transmission, with the
gearbox in line with the engine and included in the
wheel-engine unit, was a result of these choices.*

*For a number of fundamental engineering solutions,
D'Ascanio took his inspiration from some constructional concepts that were rather unusual for a motorcycle. An example of this is the single-tube wheel
support, with the offset-mounted front wheel of obvious
aeronautical origin, which replaced the traditional
cycle-type fork brilliantly and which enabled the wheel
to be replaced quickly.*

*As for the vehicle's construction, a monocoque body,
which performs the functions of both chassis and
bodywork,was chosen. This, originally an automotive*

*concept (it had been used in the 1923 Lancia
Lambda), involved making parts of the body shell
in pressed steel panels which are then assembled and
electrically spot welded. This solution offered greater
strength than the classic layout in which the bodywork
was mounted on a load-bearing tubular chassis,
as well as providing a better power/weight ratio.*

*Stylistically, the Vespa was inspired by the shapes
of contemporary aerodynamic research; examples
of this styling can be seen in a number of seaplanes
(the 1932 Savoia-Marchetti, for example), locomotives
such as Sir Nigel Gresley's 1935 Mallard and the
Volkswagen Beetle designed by Ferdinand Porsche
between 1935 and 1938.*

1945

The implementation of constructional concepts such as the single-tube front fork with offset wheel, of clear aeronautical origin, or the automotive type pressed steel monocoque body, which was electrically spot welded, were proof even then of how techniques hitherto used only in more advanced industries could be perfectly suited to the manufacture of motorcycles.

MP6

The engine-wheel unit cowling was inspired by the thick wing profile in use in motor-car styling in the early Forties.

This was the result of a quest to integrate the greatest possible number of components, including the mudguard, into the bodywork: the mudguards were enclosed by the main body, allowing for a more harmonious design, defined by modeling the body as a whole and not as the sum of its individual parts.

The perfectly executed design of the rear section gave the vehicle a sleeker, lighter appearance.

This was, in turn, accentuated by the curvature of the bodywork which ran back under the saddle, continued to mold the profile of the footplate and then rose up again to form the front shield.

The conically shaped rear light with a red glass lens was mounted in a chrome-plated frame.

Through a small grille molding and the steering column cover, the shield flowed from the front wheel to the handlebars, which are still very bicycle-like in appearance.

The front wheel was covered by a large mudguard with a removable section to facilitate wheel replacement and on which the headlight was mounted.

D'Ascanio had this new vehicle ready with a speed that today would be unimaginable: only three months between the design process and the construction of the first models.

The Vespa prototype was completed in September 1945, and by April 1946 the first production models had started rolling out of the recently rebuilt Pontedera plant.

Detail of the air vent grille on the right-hand cowl, used before the adoption of forced air cooling with a fan. To the side, the tool compartment hatch.

The right cowling had the classic cooling-air outflow slits.

Front mudguard with removable section for wheel replacement and incorporated headlight. Their shapes were to change in later models.

VESPA98

The Vespa was originally powered by a 98 cc, single-cylinder two-stroke engine. The unit was air-cooled by a fan mounted on the flywheel-magneto (made by Piaggio) which blew air through a ducted casing fitted around the head-cylinder unit. The flywheel-magneto constituted the ignition system and incorporated the coils: two low voltage coils supplying power to the lights and the horn fitted under the saddle and one high voltage coil

The advertisements of its day emphasized the great versatility of this new vehicle. Ideal for work and free time, great for city traffic, the Vespa was much appreciated by women.

The Vespa, so exclusive and perfect that it stood out markedly from anything ever made before, was an extraordinary phenomenon from a unique moment in the history of Italian industry.

Detail of the gear controls on the handlebars, which operated through a system of rigid external rods.

51

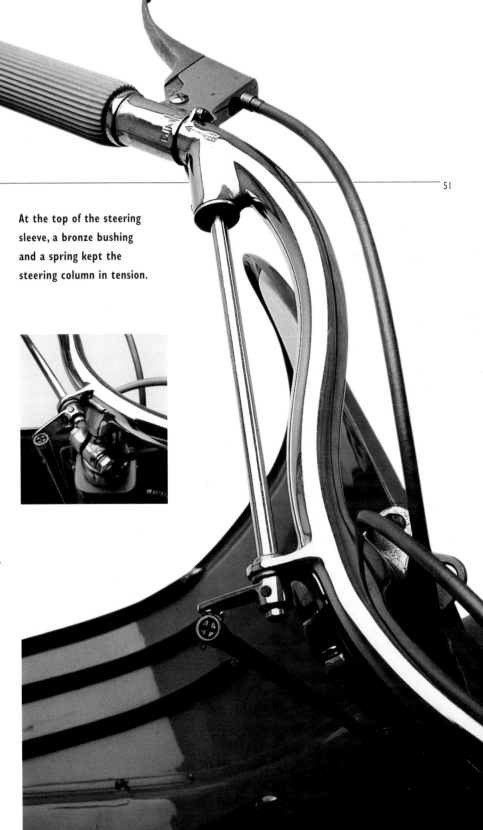

powering the spark plug. The carburetor (a 16/17 mm diameter Dellorto T2, later replaced with the TA 17 model), was fitted inside the bodywork. The three-speed gearbox was operated by a twist grip on the left handlebar via a rod linkage system. Bore and stroke were 50 mm x 50 mm (98 cc) and the maximum power of 3.2 hp was delivered at 4500 rpm: this gave the Vespa a top speed of about 36 mph and allowed it to tackle gradients of up to 20 percent in first gear, 12 percent in second and 5 percent in third.

At the top of the steering sleeve, a bronze bushing and a spring kept the steering column in tension.

The suspension consisted of a floating lever with a coil spring at the front and a swing arm layout at the rear with rubber dampers. The wheels had two-piece pressed steel rims and were fitted with 3.5-inch-by-8-inch tires.

Dimensions were: width across front leg shield, 18 inches; total width, 28 inches; wheelbase, 46.8 inches; total length, 66.2 inches; dry weight, 132 pounds.

The first series Vespa had no stand: it leaned over sideways and rested on one of two semi-circular light alloy skids fitted to the footplate. The aluminum tank had a snap release filler cap and held 1.4 gallons of two-stroke pre-mix fuel, giving a range of 150 miles (the Vespa managed more than 100 mpg of pre-mix fuel containing 5 percent oil). The pull-out fuel tap had no reserve position.

The rear light was originally conical, then later cylindrical.

At the bottom of the page, details of the three-position light switches made by Feme and of the gear control twist grip.

The Vespa 98 was made from 1946 and '47 in four different series. The improvements over the MP6 prototype were already evident in the first series. Note, for example, the shape of the headlight and front mudguard, the introduction of a horn and the resized side cowls—the left-hand one was cut to make room for the exhaust while the right-hand one had a central hole, exposing the cooling air duct.

VESPA98

The 98 remained in production throughout 1947, during which period four versions of it were made, which differed in certain details.

The main technical characteristics of the Vespa were as follows: pressed steel monocoque body with central rail lowered to footplate level; wide protective leg shield at the front; engine-gearbox-transmission unit mounted to the rear and on the right-hand side and floating together with the rear wheel suspension; easily removable small diameter wheels offset-mounted on automotive type struts; arrangement for carrying a spare wheel which, together with the luggage rack, was an optional extra.

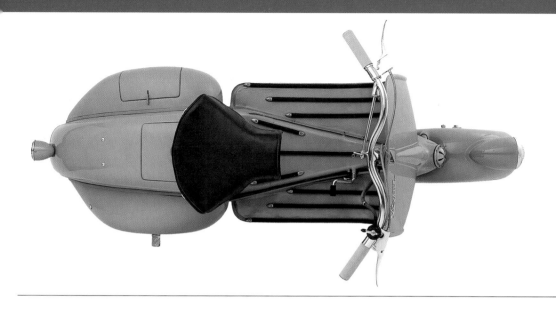

This view from above highlights the new footplate design, shorter and detached from the rear section of the body. The central rail was triangular and the brake pedal was moved to the right.

The kick-starter lever in the first two series was short and straight. It was only modified to make starting easier in the third series. The front suspension with a "pushed" front wheel and a coil spring fitted to the hub echoed the solution used on the MP6.

The 3.5-inch-by-8-inch wheels, like automobile wheels, were secured by nuts and could be switched.

VESPA98

The central compartment had a hatch for access to the carburetor. Above, the pull-out fuel tap with no reserve position. Note the shape of the body shell, designed to make opening the cowls easier and below, the gear control rods.

At the front, the horn introduced in the first series and the conical rear light which was to become cylindrical from the third series on (1947).

The front headlight with chrome-plated surround ring made by Feme. The lens was 85 mm in diameter and the reflector dish had two holes for the bulbs.

The original location and shape of the kick starter made it rather difficult to use, so in 1947 it was replaced with a longer and more curved pedal lever.

In production terms, the whole constructional concept brilliantly solved a number of problems which still today are encountered in the con-struction of modern motorcycles: an excessive number of components making up the whole; inadequately rationalized methods to connect different components together; and materials usage, which had to be optimized to save weight and, as a result, to improve the power/weight ratio. The monocoque chassis, made by spot welding a small number of pressed steel elements offers great rigidity, as well as being less expensive and simpler to manufacture, both in terms of ease of assembly and painting, and the latter is reduced to a single-step process.

Although the public, used to much more conventional-looking vehicles, initially failed to understand the Vespa, it soon instinctively began to trust it as opposed to the motorbike, which was perceived as being more for skilled and agile users.

The sales distribution of the Vespa was conducted according to a strategy devised by Enrico Piaggio, who put the Vespa in Lancia dealerships to associate the vehicle with the motorcar. Payment by installments—price at the time was 68,000 lire (about $40)—also made it easier to buy.

What made the Vespa immortal and defined its image was the concept of the monocoque body construction. It fulfilled a structural role while at the same time defining the character of the vehicle itself and is one of the most extraordinary examples of perfectly integrated form, function and expressiveness in an industrial product.

*I*n which we see Vespas turning up beyond the Alps and over the sea— in recreational areas, at track races and racing round the block—all in an "engine-powered freedom" while Italy, the country, was going through growing pains.

1946–1956

A car on two wheels

Vespa and bear-trainers: in the Spring of 1949 it was not such a rare encounter in the Italian countryside as we might think today.

"More than forty-thousand Vespa scooters are on the roads of Italy and of many foreign countries. The 'small car on two wheels' in the space of three short years has harvested an unprecedented success" says the company magazine's first edition.

"The Vespa is ours: we built it step by step."

"Whoever applauds a Vespa is applauding us and Pontedera too without realizing it."

(from *Quelli della Vespa*)

The start-up in 1946 was a cold one, yet just the following year Vespa production was going full speed ahead. Exactly one year after the first fifty units came out, monthly production topped five hundred, even though the engine shop was still incomplete, there were electricity black-outs and daily miracles were needed to get raw materials. And the numbers kept growing, so that as early as the second summer of peace an exclusive model from Pontedera was on the roads of Germany, Switzerland, Austria and Finland: the 125 *r*, where the "r" stood for "rigid" to distinguish it from D'Ascanio's new brainchild, which was already past the drawing-board stage.

An armchair built for two

There'd been a strange announcement broadcast recently, just before the radio news, heralding something important in the offing which, however, didn't seem to be getting anywhere: "It's 8:35 p.m., it's Lambretta time." This wasn't the small Gianca workshop, manufacturer of the Nibbio scooter. It was competition of another caliber altogether, an industrial colossus just outside Milan and it was just what was needed to start the ball rolling.

Enrico Piaggio had been pushing the new generation of Vespas for some time and, true to form, his ideas were clear: pre-empt the field with a new, more stable, powerful and comfortable model with better brakes than the first, which would leave the others standing.

Corradino D'Ascanio was already busy with tests, and

production start-up was swift. The 125 *e* (for "elastic" because of its back suspension) came out in January 1948, a watershed year for Italy.

Looking almost identical to its predecessor despite all the engineering innovations, the scooter joined the fray with a shrewd marketing strategy:

"This continuity in overall design, in which, quite rightly, the manufacturer takes pride," wrote *Motociclismo* magazine in the Vespa 125 *e*'s detailed presentation, "besides helping to strengthen customer trust, has also served to anchor the proper sales value of the product." The magazine, despite an editorial policy leaning towards a certain traditionalism, felt obliged to praise the significant increase in power, the effectiveness of the new muffler and the new finned cylinder head, the efficiency of the new electric commutator and above all the innovative back suspension that made it a "real car on two wheels" succeeding where others had failed.

In the meantime, the winds of change were blowing hard. Against a backdrop of galloping inflation (the price of a 98 cc rocketed from 90,000 to 168,000 lire —about $54 to about $100—in just one year), two million unemployed and the no-holds-barred campaign for the elections of 18 April 1948, Vespa produced just the right answer for the ever more pressing need among normal people to be mobile and get away.

It was a mania that made people chase this little-big dream, scrimping and saving to get hold of this newfound freedom of movement. It was an invitation to men of every social standing and to women who, if not

downright hostile to the concept, had never had anything to do with two-wheeled transport before.

The price of the first 125 *s* was equal to eight times the monthly salary of a medium-level white-collar worker and little less than the annual earnings of a bluecollar worker and although this price was still beyond the reach of everyman, the whole idea became feasible when purchasing in installments was introduced.

Still leaning askew against the pavements in front of village shops, the builder's yard, or the ladies' hairdresser, or all lined up on their stands, in front of public offices in the capital, displayed in La Rinascente department store window or surrounded by looks and comments on Sundays outside the cafés, Pontedera scooters had become part of daily life in Italy.

In June 1954, Entreposto Comercial de Moçambique in Lisbon wrote an unsolicited letter to the company management saying it would be willing to stop selling Vespa's direct competitor and confirmed *"l'expérience que nous avons eue avec la Lambretta nous sera sans doute trés valuable et utile pour l'introduction de la Vespa dans un marché si limité* [the experience we have gained with Lambretta will be of undoubted value and use in introducing the Vespa in such a limited market]." Indeed, the Italian machine raised a great deal of interest among the cotton producers for use by their surveillance staff on the island's large plantations.

lo scooter piú venduto nel mondo

Vespa

In Egypt, advertisements played by setting the marks of thousands of years of history against the modernity of the scooter, a natural complement to the modern-day, Westernized woman.

On a Vespa purring along a country road—the dark shape of the father driving, the mother riding side-saddle with the child in her lap facing backwards and looking straight into the camera's lens—there's a whole world fast approaching the Fifties.

Ways to develop a winning product

You can win market share by going downwards too, and the tit-for-tat between Piaggio and Innocenti became almost open warfare in 1953, when the Vespa no-frills model came out in response to the super-economical Lambretta E.

There was no chrome or nickel, every single thing was painted over, the headlamp was on the handlebar and the engine cowling was reduced to a minimum with no hinges, the engine the same as before, while the deluxe version started with the 125 cc with cross flow ports. This time, however, it didn't sell.

The engineers at Pontedera had learned their lesson from the model for the overseas market. It seems paradoxical but, as we shall see, the richest country in the world—"the most difficult market in the world" as the company magazine put it—was opened up only after big cuts had been made in production costs.

While the bottom-of-the-range 125 U never got off the ground, another Vespa was sweeping the boards. Developed from the model Piaggio had prepared and raced successfully, it had a 150 cc engine which, in the GS version, could top 60 miles per hour.

When the Vespa 125 U (as in "utilitarian"), of which the most typical feature is here shown in close up, came out, sales were disappointing. Later on, however, this became one of the most sought after collectors' items.

The earliest Vespa calendar, published in 1951, was drawn by Franco Mosca as was the 1954 edition which gave life to a series of postcards that became well-known in other European countries too. It was all about women, showing pin-ups dressed in Dutch and Hawaiian traditional garb, as well as one model, American perhaps, in casual camping dress with a book and cigarettes in full view.

"So the Vespa 150 Gran Sport," as a specialist magazine wrote in 1954, "is for the scooter enthusiast what the Ferrari, the Aurelia Gran Turismo or the Alfa Romeo Super Sprint is for the car devotee."

Things were already a lot different just ten years from the end of the war and the American model was making great inroads, almost getting as far as the acutely politically-conscious blue-collar workers.

Among the icons of a collective imagination striving to keep pace with the sweeping changes taking place in the country's habits and economic reality, the Vespa stood out as being able to do almost anything. It appeared in the countrified conflict between Peppone, the communist mayor and Don Camillo the priest in the film versions of the Guareschi novels, ridden by Brigitte Bardot and Joe DiMaggio, lionized on the set of *Roman Holiday*, blessed by Pope Pius XII and recommended for missions in Africa to Pope John XXIII.

Production rose steadily breaking through the 500,000 ceiling in November 1953. The event was celebrated by the archbishop of Pisa in the presence of the company leaders, the management from foreign production facilities and journalists from all over the world. That day, employees got a 5,000 lire ($3) bonus: fair recognition of everyone's commitment and, inevitably, a diplomatic move in the game of hardball being played between the company and the workers.

The celebration of company success at the time was entrusted to the high clergy: the same, almost identical scene was repeated three years later for the millionth Vespa.

Among the earliest drawings developed for the Ape, there was a military model; besides the stretcher-bearing version there was also one planned for transporting men and ammunition as a logistical back-up for motorized units which, naturally, would travel by Vespa.

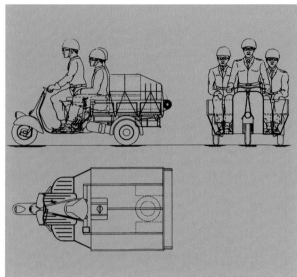

The extraordinary versatility of this motor-powered tricycle made it of great usefulness in the countryside as well as in towns. Its proverbial climbing ability was proven by all sorts of exploits, in particular its triumphant climb up Rome's Spanish Steps.

Ape [Bee] is to Vespa as ox is to horse

The birth of the first one-two-five was put off a couple of months in 1947 because a surprising tricycle with an engine was taking shape on Corradino D'Ascanio's drawing board and would proceed through to model definition and road trials.

It was an odd-looking, hybrid creature but its practicality, sturdiness, maneuverability, low price and extremely good total weight to load-bearing capacity ratio would make it a winner.

The first Ape series repeated the scooter structure and added a loading platform on the back and little more. There were, of course, some new features, such as a differential and an end transmission with dual-

chain final drive (one chain on each side), a lever-operated manual starter and back-pedal brake, torsion bars and back-wheel shock absorbers under the wooden casing.

From day one, its secret was its peerless capacity for metamorphosis, an in-born ability to change look that assured its success in small-scale transport of goods (and people) in every corner of the world.

From Gallarate to Manila, from Caracas to Berlin, from the Marina Grande quays of Capri to the triumphal Gateway of India in Mumbai; to move *gateaux* or garbage, *perros calientes*, tailored clothing or fire-escape ladders, tomatoes, manioc or eggplants, hamsters or the president of the German Federal Republic, Theodor Heuss, during a visit to Siracusa. There

was room for everything and everyone, with a bit changed here and there perhaps but nothing more.

This was the result of a new facet of the Vespa project: the launch of a new means of commercial transport that immediately became the emblem of craftsmen's industriousness, of a new dignity in working the land, of the small-scale entrepreneurship flowering in towns and in the countryside, of modernity in public services and of a new kind of relationship between customers and companies and long-established trade names.

Placed face to face, there's no comparison between the numbers of Piaggio's two "insects," and that's the way it should be. In the early years, the number of Ape coming off the line at Pontedera was some 10 percent of Vespas but its contribution to the company's

In the streets of Milan, Turin, Bologna, Rome, Naples and Palermo for Easter 1961, this was the procession organized by Nestlé.

Not only were there Ape rickshaws by the thousands in the streets of Pakistan, but in the Far East and in the United States too, they were used for transporting the most conventional types of goods.

Decidedly rare in Italy,
the rickshaw version
was developed in 1956
from the Ape C which by
then had been on sale for
a couple of years.

new-found prosperity was regularly seen in the year-end accounts.

The shape of the world's most popular three-wheeler was to prove surprisingly impermanent and it underwent radical changes throughout the years.

The engine was shunted to the back axle, an electric starter and metallic loading platform were incorporated while the driver's cabin was given greater protection and comfort. A steering wheel replaced the handlebars, a double headlight was installed, and the increased power and load-bearing capacity were to push it ever more toward an "automobile" format culminating in the final mutation, forty years later, into the Ape "Poker" with its additional wheel.

Pentarò, as in "five wheels." In 1961, the Ape was developed into the tractor of an articulated van with a load capacity of 1,500 pounds. The trailer was more than 2.5 yards long and the early design enabled the trailer to be unhitched allowing the tractor part to circulate freely. Serious registration problems, fear of doubled road tax, legal restrictions which appeared to limit the vehicle's length to a total of four yards made life difficult for this project, as novel as it was unlucky. Notwithstanding, buyers included major Italian department stores such as La Rinascente and Upim, and high-profile industries such as Michelin, Maserati, Alitalia, Olivetti.

Designed mainly for town use to carry the widest range of goods, here it is being used to ferry a jazz-band in Rome (1962), the Pentarò was also used as an agricultural vehicle.

Brief: a general means of goods transport for small entrepreneurs and companies of all sizes with an unbeatable price/quality ratio. From "who buys it doesn't spend but earns" to the Sixties Portuguese ads, and "Ape *è capace*" ["Ape can"] (1980): the means keeps up with the times but the message is the same.

MAI SOTTOVALUTARE APE

HI L'ACQUISTA...*non li spende – li guadagna*

THE APE YEARS

1947: The Ape 125 had no cabin. The driver sat atop the engine cowling. End transmission was chain driven. The wooden cargo container could hold 440 pounds.

1953: Engine size rose to 150 cc. The newly designed frame had also a version with a metallic dumper platform.

1956: The Ape C had a real cab that could hold two people and it could now carry up to 770 pounds.

1964: The Ape D had a cab with doors. The wheelbase was increased by about 3 inches, engine size now reached 170 cc and the headlight was placed in the middle of the shield.

1966: The frame was now H-shaped and the vehicle had an axle shaft and hydraulic shock absorbers, and the engine was assembled on a sled-like structure.

1968: The MPV, the first Ape with a steering wheel, double headlights on the front shield and a cargo capacity of 1,300 pounds.

1969: Non-registered three wheels, the Ape 50 could carry 440 pounds. The next year a version with a 125 cc engine was added.

1971: The Ape Car with a new body, an improved and more comfortable cabin and more than ever, a steering wheel.

1982: On a Giorgetto Giugiaro design, the Ape TM with handlebar or wheel steering could carry 1,500 pounds. Its suspension was new and it was powered by a 220 cc engine placed on the frame.

1984: The world's smallest direct injection diesel: a "clean" engine with a five-speed gearbox. Two years later the Ape Car diesel was the champion in load-bearing carrying 2,000 pounds.

1990: The Ape Poker "four-wheel engine-powered cycle"; an additional wheel in two versions: one for holders of a car driver's license and the other for sixteen-year-old junior-license holders.

1994: The unusual, colorful Ape Cross for the young customer who prefers this smaller version to two wheels.

1999: The Cargo and Auto versions of the Ape 501 began manufacture in the Baramati factory in India in June of this year.

2000: The catalytic Ape TM Catalyzed went on sale in Europe.

2002: The latest version of the Ape 50, in line with the new Euro 2 regulations, went on sale in November.

ROMAN NEW ORLEANS J.B.

THE CITY, THE FACTORY, THE MEN

The Rinaldo Piaggio summer camp was the subject of a special edition of *Domus* architectural magazine as early as 1940. "...In order to honor his memory in a way appropriate to the sentiments that made him devote his life to patriotism, family love, work and the paternal affection he had for his workers, the company has decided to create a summer camp for the children of his employees."

It was inevitable that an industry of this size would become a major player in an area of farming and handcraft traditions. A company employing more than three thousand local people can prove a difficult partner for a provincial town, but it can also be harnessed as a vital force for development, able to give a significant contribution to the infrastructure and services both internal and of the community as a whole.

The Piaggio Village, with its sports center, church, leisure center, library, hotel, and the crèche named after Elena Piaggio Odero, not to mention the summer mountain-resort center in Santo Stefano d'Aveto in Liguria, still bear witness to serious commitment in this direction. It was apparently inspired by an ideal that was having difficulty taking root in these post-war

years. Indeed, some newspapers spotlighted its inadequacy: only 140 dwellings for 3,800 employees in 1954 (but rising), plus overpowering internal regimentation and job assigning riddled with favoritism.

In June 1955, the Florentine daily newspaper *La Nazione* described Pontedera as a "happy Tuscan town," where everything seemed to center round the assembly line's magical overhead conveyance system and where everything was done in a spirit of universal goodwill, between reminiscing about the gold medals awarded for work and the company village sewing classes for young girls. By way of reply, the workers of this "happy Tuscan town" sent the journalist who wrote the article a sack filled with their paycheck receipts together with a nasty missive from the FIOM trade union.

Aumentano i prezzi - Crescono i profitti
Diminuisce il reddito reale dei lavoratori

Years of growth and harsh social conflict

Times were hard. Tensions between employers and workers threatened to boil over into open conflict. This was the Italy of the Marshall Plan, and Piaggio got credit for thousands of dollars to buy the gigantic American press-molds needed to manufacture the Vespa. This was the Italy of intense foreign and Vatican interference, with partisan ammunition still buried in the vineyard, the Italy of the Portella della Ginestra massacre (in which farm-workers peacefully celebrating May Day were machine-gunned by hired assassins resulting in eleven deaths), the attempt on the life of Communist party leader Palmiro Togliatti—and it was moving towards the Tambroni right-wing government. In short, Italy was a country teetering on the edge of outright civil strife with little or no regard for mediation.

Life in the workplace was hard. Trade unions were frowned on, surveillance by the company police was relentless, involving searches, fines and shadowing people beyond the factory grounds. Health care for workers doing the most hazardous jobs, from the foundry to the paint-shop, was far in the future. Leaving the workplace, if only to go to the washroom—where trade-union news and leaflets were passed on clandestinely, resulting in the removal of doors and locks—was allowed only to those in possession of a "pass disc" handed out by the foreman.

The company responded to strikes and no-pass picket lines by trucking the non-strikers from home to the factory under police escort. Shop stewards were divided

Work, trade-union activism, technological innovation and social conflict; what was left of old-time paternalism was carried over for a number of years as the traditional "Worker's Epiphany" dedicated to the little nursery school pupils in the Piaggio Village.

"**P**iaggio holds the key to this town" wrote Lietta Tornabuoni in *Lavoro* newspaper: "It decides who will marry whom because families always strive to marry off their daughters to Piaggio workers, and it decides people's lives." Despite the social tensions, the big factory along the railway could offer economic security and hope of a better life for thousands upon thousands of people.

A beehive, no longer a wasp's nest as the inaugural edition of the Piaggio house magazine called the "resounding workshops of Pontedera." There, where "the commitment of every single worker to production perfection is honed and strengthened by spontaneous desire and enlightened passion." Despite all this, tensions existed both inside and outside the big factory and its gates.

In front of London's Houses of Parliament, the scooter is celebrated once more despite a deep-rooted motorcycle tradition. Widely used in towns and in the South of the country giving it good promotion, the Vespa was commissioned also by the Oxford police and by the staff of the Royal Woolwich Arsenal.

between the Communist-inspired CGIL and the Christian Democrat CISL, the latter accused of being soft on the bosses but bereft of firm beliefs to counterpoint the dogmatic stance still taken by the Communists. The air was heavy with conflict. Trade-union flyers revealed names of managers and their earnings; calculations were made claiming what profit each Vespa was bringing the company; requests were made for adequate recognition of tasks; production facilities abroad were hotly contested as was the rumor pending agreement with Fiat by which Piaggio would be barred from the Italian automobile market. The fighting spirit of going one step further was already present, the spirit of getting involved in company strategic decision-making that was to characterize trade unionism for a number of years to come.

The entrepreneur lionized by *The Financial Times* and *Reader's Digest* for his undeniable courage and prodigious farsightedness—"the man who put Italy on two wheels" thus is seen in a completely different light, especially in the years in which being able to draw from an enormous workforce made available by unemployment gave him wide-ranging power. The whole country had a long road ahead in terms of full worker dignity, health protection in the workplace, economic parity between men and women and greater social justice but Piaggio too started in this direction.

The "beehives" on the other side of the Alps

Claude McCormack's Italian vacation in 1948 was no coincidence. The manager of Douglas of Bristol, a motorcycle and engineering company established in 1907, which had over one thousand employees and was on the brink of bankruptcy, had come Vespa hunting.

The first imported models, exhibited at the Earl's Court Motorcycle Show in '49 following the signing of the Douglas-Piaggio agreement, were given an enthusiastic welcome and hundreds of orders landed on the Pontedera production manager's desk. The idea of duplicating the entire production cycle in the English factory had already been talked about but in reality quite a number of parts would continue to come from

CHOOSE

AND GET THE BEST

the parent company. Two years later the first modified 125 came off the line; the headlight had migrated to the center of the shield as required by English standards. It was the only model manufactured then or later. Highly prized, its price, almost double that of a motor-cycle of comparable performance, kept it in the mid-to-high-level niche market. A precious little Continental toy for high society but spurned by purists in England, the birthplace of the motorcycle, the Italian scooter lost no time in making itself known to its public and to its major competitors, such as BSA.

In 1952 Vespas were sold from 350 sales points in Great Britain and half the customers were women. "Its name is famous" the company noted, "all over the British Empire." The Vespa-loving Mods hadn't yet

appeared on the scene, however, and oddly enough they didn't until nine years and 126,000 units later when the production line had already closed down. From 1960 onwards, Douglas preferred to act as exclusive importer only.

Jacob Oswald Hoffmann came across the Vespa at the Frankfurt Exhibition in 1949 and he made contact immediately to secure a license to manufacture.

He went home to Lintorf, concluded the agreement, and started building a new section alongside the work-shops of Hoffman Werke, the manufacturing hub of this small town just north of Düsseldorf.

Ten months later, the first model rolled off the line copied in miniature from the Italian original.

The British manufacturer, initially, played around with the logo in a combination including his company's name, an idea that was soon abandoned.

Production centers in other European cities sprang up in the early Fifties from the need to get round prohibitive customs duties on the finished product. The first Vespa produced outside Italy on 14 March 1950 was German by birth, from the Hoffman factory.

Professor Nachtfalter, 1951, directed by Rolf Meyer, was the first film to stage the Pontedera-made scooter in the scene where a handsome music teacher uses every means to get away from the advances of his girl pupils.

Tourism, runs, rallies, bathing beauties and the Vespa Club von Deutschland newsletter; but also a form to fill in to contact Vespa GmbH, the successor to Messerschmitt. Vespa GmbH introduced a special 150 GS fitted with rear indicators in '55.

The culprit: the shining Königin as Hoffman supplied it, already complete with front wheel-guard, pillion saddle, a lot of chrome work and the unmistakable search-light on the wheel in addition to the handlebar-mounted headlight.

At the next Frankfurt show, the orders deposited at Hoffman's stand covered production for a whole year.

A Gallup poll conducted in a Germany shattered by war and now on the road to quick recovery showed that the lucky owners of a Vespa were made up of "industrialists, shopkeepers and craftsmen, 34 percent: white-collar workers, 24 percent: freelance workers, 23 percent: blue-collar workers, 6 percent." Here too, as in Great Britain, the Vespa was a high-end product or almost.

A fall in sales after an exhilarating 1953 during which 400 units per week were sold, induced Hoffman to develop the deluxe Königin model. The substantial investment incurred was not rewarded by sales, however, and the modifications made to the 125 without the parent company's consent gave Enrico Piaggio, who had been waiting for an excuse to terminate the contract, the impetus he needed.

Three months later, in Spring 1955, the 150 cc in the Touren and GS versions produced by the newly established Messerschmitt-Vespa were on the roads.

A mere two years were to pass before the next crisis loomed. Vespa GmbH established in participation with Piaggio was set up in Augsburg. Besides the 150, already known to the public, the price list boasted the improved 125 of 1958: new engine, new frame and great expectations in sales. Five years later the market was in complete free-fall and it was decided to close the factory and import directly from Italy.

The fourth country to adopt *"el pequeño coche de dos ruedas,"* after Great Britain, Germany and France was

Con *Vespa* ...
Ahorrará tiempo en
sus desplazamientos

para llegar antes...

Disfrutará más en
sus vacaciones
*
Rendirá más en
su trabajo

Se cansará menos
en sus gestiones

...¡hay que a *Vespa*rse!

Spain, and its development there was different from everywhere else.

It was given a warm welcome and the February 4, 1953, issue of *El Mundo Deportivo* foresaw a bright future for *"esto tipo de vehículos, cuya calidad mecánica y cuyas dotes de turismo y de rendimiento hoy están por encima de toda discusión"*—the vehicle whose mechanicals and performance are above reproach.

Moto Vespa S.A. inaugurated its 215,000-square-foot production facility in Madrid on December 2, 1952.

The price of the 125 was 16,500 pesetas (more than $1,100), high but not prohibitive for a country by no means wealthy, which, because it had barely been touched by the war, was eager for change and modernization, especially in transport. The article with the most suitable size for this change was the scooter, not the car. After an encouraging start, sales rose well and 50,000 units of the 125 were sold in the first four years. As early as 1954, the sales and service network stretched from the Balearic Islands to Galizia and from Andalusia to the Basque Country.

In the long-term, market stability was surprising.

Hard on the heels of the 125 there came the 150 cc models, then the highly successful, Spanish-born "Vespino" and all the others up till the PX years and the present-day products.

Vespa first made its appearance in France in October '47 at the Paris Motor Show but regular importation did not start until two years later. And yet again an

Spain offered a favorable market, low-cost labor and a lot in common with Italy *"¡Hay que a Veparse!"* ... and the Vespa was here to stay.

Vespa enthusiasts swarm in front of a bullfighting arena and at Caillejas, a suburb of Madrid, Enrico Piaggio looks on as the first Vespa body comes off the line at Moto Vespa which is still going strong half a century later.

agreement was drawn up with a local licensee in an effort to get round the costly customs duties.

Ateliers de Construction de Motocycles et Accessoires, ACMA for short, was the Parisian company that committed itself to taking over an all but disused factory at Fourchambault in the middle of France, attracted by the low cost of labor there. Many resources were poured into the venture to modernize structure, update machinery and build housing for labor.

Luckily, from March 1951, production kept rising so much so that four years later output was only a third less than in Italy. Vespa had catalyzed the French market and almost a million two-wheeled vehicles were on the road, of which more than 80 percent were under 200 cc.

The contest between the big brands, with their market position already strong in mopeds, turned into total war. Lambretta, from which the French models drew inspiration, was already firmly entrenched but Fourchambault was working at full speed.

The 1956 Suez crisis and the consequent rise in fuel prices (up till then prices in France had been the lowest in Europe after Italy) and then a double rise in taxes marked the beginning of the end.

The facility closed down in '62 but France still had a card up its sleeve for Vespa in the shape of a 50 cc machine complete with pedals.

The scooter goes to war

The military version was developed in France in 1956 for the war in Algeria. With a 150 cc engine, modified gear ratio and strengthened frame showing some very obvious technical adaptations, it was in fact a project Pontedera had been toying with for some years.

After trying to make inroads with the carabinieri and the police force since 1949—"It's pitiful to see carabinieri struggling along on old bicycles, and it causes mistrust in the public to see many delinquents making their getaway using excellent means of transport, often cocking their snoot at the law," wrote the Carabinieri High Command in Rome—the idea gradually took hold in Piaggio of a special Vespa for the armed forces.

In 1951 it appeared to be coming into being but then Piaggio found itself having to talk to another organization. Oreste Bonomi, Piaggio's man in Rome, offered to "show the Atlantic Front High Command a program

The experience of the French too made Pontedera think about making armaments of various kinds: "75 mm recoilless cannons, bazookas, machineguns and submachine guns, and 60 and 81 mm mortars." All furnished with the necessary ammunition, needless to say. By comparison with the jeep that had almost become the symbol of the Second World War, the scooter had unbeatable ratio "between sale price and extent of use," coming first "over tracks, in forests and through undergrowth." Compared to the motorcycle too, generally in use by the armed forces, the scooter was supposed to be superior in the field.

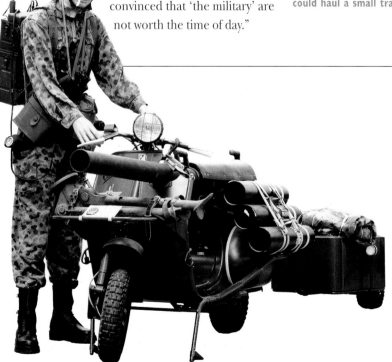

I would call 'Vespa Forze Armate' [for the Armed Forces]," then went on to describe it in detail.

What this scooter could offer seemed far superior compared to a 500 cc motorcycle. It had no transmission chain, its electrical parts were minimal but were nonetheless highly efficient, it could take two spare wheels, and had great maneuverability and lightness. Regarding performance it was noted that "in time trials the minimum imposed on a Vespa is only 3 miles per hour less than for a 500 cc motorcycle."

For use by troops escorting vehicle convoys, the Vespa squadron was to be flanked by an Ape contingent with a technical back-up function. On September 18, 1952, Fred J. Desautel of the Mutual Security Agency gave a glowing report after his visit to the Pontedera factory.

A year later, the Center for Study and Experience of the Italian Army showed similar enthusiasm after witnessing technical trials of all kinds. But nothing happened.

"The competition in Milan [with Innocenti] has got nothing to do with this" wrote Enrico Piaggio to Oreste Bonomi. As far as the army went, "I confirm we are not interested in canvassing for State orders since we know that its organs pay low prices and late." And after 27 months of the negotiations "you carried out with NATO, I am ever more convinced that 'the military' are not worth the time of day."

For the Vespa M (as in "military"), the pivot for a submachine gun could be placed on the fork on the handlebar and a radio was located under the saddle. A stronger shield for protection "against long-distance fire" was also planned.

In use, and operational in the French army, the version pictured at left could haul a small trailer.

LEISURE TIME IN EASY MONTHLY INSTALLMENTS

No more than five years had gone by since the end of the war and the desire to leave everything behind, even everyday problems big or small, made many want to join parades for two-wheelers. Organized peacefully in many cities, May 6, 1951 was Vespa Day and twenty thousand participants took part.

It is paradoxical to talk of tourism for a country which, in the early Fifties, counted no less than four million families who had meat only once a week, and at least three million of those, out of a total of twelve million, could afford it only on festivals and holidays, or did without it altogether. It wasn't until 1954 that the per capita consumption reached the meager pre-war level of about 20 pounds per year, with all the proverbial unfairness that statistics involves. Fewer than 10 percent of dwellings nationwide had electricity together with running water and inside bathrooms. More than ninety thousand of the capital's inhabitants lived in huts, cellars and warehouses, with another ten thousand crammed into churches or refitted military barracks. And yet, despite all this, Vespas took thousands upon thousands of Italians to the seaside and the mountains, to campsites, hotels and inns, to the houses in the country where their families still lived, or on out-of-town trips.

Despite the poor state of the roads there seemed to be no "natural" limit to where scooters could go. Necessity being the mother of invention, hundreds of miles were traveled with no problem. Enthusiasm, perseverance and a pinch of self-sacrifice were all that was needed to travel and to earn enough for the installments that still had to be paid to the salesroom.

The phenomenon was astonishing for its vastness—droves of people went touring on Vespas, the young and the not-so-young, couples who sometimes brought the kids along, all momentarily bound together by a

In July 1953, *Documenti di Vita Italiana [Documents of Italian Life]* dedicated a special edition to the motor-scooter phenomenon listing the percentage clientele breakdown according to age and profession. Profession: blue-collar workers, 30 percent: white-collar workers, 30 percent: shopkeepers, 16 percent: craftsmen, 10 percent: the professions, 7 percent: students, 3 percent: and doctors and the clergy 2 percent each. Age: 5 percent young people between 18 and 20; 40 percent between 21 and 31; 35 percent between 31 and 40 and, lastly, 20 percent over 40.

The Vespa transports families to weekends in the snow or at the seaside. "Italians can work miracles" wrote the *Irish Independent* "gathering everything together and bundling it up: Sunday mornings a Vespa with husband and wife, a dog, two kids and a picnic basket sets off for the sea-side, 30 miles down the road."

A brochure shows that in France, as in Italy, riders traveled between city and countryside, work and play, with Vespa runs for women which proved highly popular from the word *go*.

common code of dress and habits, with women representing the most important novelty, rather than the young as such, who would be the protagonists in the Sixties. The female users emerged from their hitherto subordinate roles, now autonomous at last and at ease, proudly riding their scooters over the most demanding routes with ostentatious panache. It was the urge to get about, to enjoy the luxury of a time and place far from work or the city's clutches—a new dimension for many—and the pleasure of independent travel on their own vehicle. It was the new "engine-powered freedom."

Some relived the adolescent urge to push themselves to the limits. Herr Diether Ebeler and Dagmar, Countess of Bernstorff, his blond companion, went round the world in three and a quarter years hauling a two-wheeled trailer through Austria, Turkey, Pakistan, Indonesia, Japan and the United States. Renzo Faroppa drove up and down Alpine passes, more than 600 miles in twenty-three hours non-stop, determined to "break through where backward prejudices" still denied the obvious superiority of the scooter. And by his side, the die-hard Vespa enthusiast Arduino Sturaro, who could do Milan to Copenhagen in "thirty and a half hours."

The guiding light of this fast-spreading phenomenon, the prophet of this celebration of femininity on two wheels, this craze for arduous enterprises and bizarre small-town festivals was Renato Tassinari. It is to this *Corriere dello Sport* journalist, hired by Enrico Piaggio right after the war, that the credit is due for the Vespa Club phenomenon.

A courageous squadron

We actors have now become spectators and we would never have dared hope that our colors, our badge, devised and drafted here in Viareggio, would ever have crossed borders and be raised in the most far-off of lands and at the most diverse of latitudes."

The words are Renato Tassinari's, spoken at the 10th Congress of the Vespa Club d'Italia honoring the glories of an association with branches from Hong Kong to Argentina, South Africa to Iceland. "As you well know, we are a movement based exclusively on goodness, with none of the poison of political hatred, none of the rigidity of hazy or unreachable idealism; a movement that comes about, expresses itself and breeds to the beat of small engines and hearts serene and free in seeking far-off beautiful countryside and brotherly friendships." It does sound a bit rhetorical but it was effective and completely in the style of the man's personality.

Backing him up there were ten years of experience in creating and running a big organizational machine able to produce rallies and excursions, fancy-dress parades, races, treasure-hunts, concours d'élegance and dances. "To promote, further and defend the interests of Vespa users: organize, protect and regulate the activities of peripheral groups with particular attention to tourism…" was the gist of the association's bylaws.

Joining the Vespa Club d'Italia, states the notice, entitles the member to the following benefits: a membership badge, a small guidebook, a road map of

Under the summer sun of 1957, competition judges stand by a checkpoint in the Eurovespa Rally. In 1953, national clubs adhered to the Vespa Club Europa which, from 1965 onwards, accepted membership from other continents too, changing its name to Vespa Club Mondial and lastly to Fédération Internationale des Vespa Clubs (FIV).

Italy, discounts and privileges in hotels, restaurants and "recommended" shops throughout Italy, a 3 percent discount on purchasing a new Vespa; a low-priced insurance policy, half-price membership to the company magazine, special terms for rally trips abroad and excursions.

Indeed, members got up to all sorts of tricks. They escorted the prince of Monaco's automobile on his visit to Rome, delivered Epiphany gifts by gondola to the Venice municipal police, got dressed up like Martians in the streets of Paris or like the imaginary Piedmontese clown Gianduja in Turin's Valentino Park or like American Indians in Denmark, rode from Madrid to the Vatican to honor the pope, gave out Christmas gifts to needy children, slalomed between the pillars and flew across the bars on the dressage fields in Oristano, Caracas and New York—all to the greater glory of the peerless scooter whose badge they wore.

Six hundred miles for daredevils

The most emphatic expression of the group spirit and an excellent test bench—not so much in terms of the scooter's reliability but also to show just how widely it could be used—was the 600-mile Vespa Audax. It was organized along the lines of an endurance test: the top speed-limit was set at 30 miles an hour, the winners declared on the average results of two of the 120-mile runs picked at random from the five completed. The prize money was almost five million lire ($3,000)—a pile of money.

The second time it started off from Brescia on 5 July reaching "that most Italian city Trieste" (the form reflecting the perceived need to bolster the Italianness of Trieste, a town that only in 1954, nine years after the end of the war, had been given back to Italy) then turning south through Emilia then back up to Milan and across to Brescia to complete the circuit.

The year was 1952 and there were 111 Vespa Clubs in Italy from which 365 competitors emerged to take part. There was a bit of everything. The sporting newspaper *Gazzetta dello Sport* drew up a colorful gallery of thumbnail sketches: Francesco Polga, profession: baker, back in time to open up shop at 3 o'clock on Monday morning without even stopping for a break; Giuseppe Angeli from Bologna, profession: plumber, in his first competition;

This photograph was taken just outside Kasangulu, forty kilometers from Kinshasa, in the mid-Fifties. Three imported 125's are lined up beside the checkpoint during a Vespa competition.

Time for a break again in the same period but this time in Italy, with an almost identical machine in the foreground. In whichever country they were, Vespa racers were all fired by the same enthusiasm.

Nearly 1,100 miles across Italy's southernmost regions: a French rider in the Three Seas Rally recalls Salerno languishing in the sun, the meager fields of Calabrian farmers, stray dogs and drilling for oil in Sicily.

No fewer than 1,500 from eleven nations participants at the '55 San Remo Rally.

Eye-catching competitors complete with chronometer and logbook in Gijon for the XX Provincias Rally.

Adriano Cielo, at sixteen the youngest competitor; Matilde Adami, a student; Domenico De Agostino the tailor from Savigliano looking for his "little bit of glory … because man doesn't live by bread alone"; Giuseppe Palma from Milan turned up at the checkpoint clutching by the ears a hare he'd run over in the dead of night; and Aldo Ambrosetti, a war-disabled engineer employed by the Edison electrical company, who had no right arm. Rearranging the controls on his handlebars enabled him to change a wheel he'd punctured and drag his scooter, now with an empty fuel-tank, searching for the nearest petrol station. He did however cross the finishing tape "in line with the Audax average speed."

And at the end of the show, the thank-you letters signed by Enrico Piaggio in person were sent to the organizing club and the service points along the route.

The managing director followed at least the main events of the circuit closely and just as he got Tassinari's editorials for the company magazine on his desk for checking before going to press, he stepped in to change the last stage of the Three Seas Rally: "an additional stage involves, obviously, an additional competition day which in turn involves additional expense. This has therefore been discarded. As a substitute, I would ask you to examine the following hypothesis …" going on to detail the route, the distance, and urging that arrangements be made for the whole retinue's overnight stays.

The Vespa Clubs' color and drollery aside, however, their undeniable logistical efficiency points to meticulous preparation and the support of an efficient organizational machine which, with no false modesty, was described as "truly colossal and high-class" during the '55 International San Remo Rally.

On February 8 of that same year the representatives of the Belgian, French, German, Swiss, Dutch and Italian clubs were called to Milan's Hotel Gallia to set up the Vespa Club Europa. This was supposed to become "the heart of European Vespa-ing, a heart that beats to coordinate and unify a whole range of associative energies … so that the Vespa enthusiast never feels alone, abandoned and more important is never made to feel a foreigner in a foreign country." So proclaimed Tassinari, elected president by acclamation.

The issue of fatherland was dear to Vespa Club mem-

"The Vespas were festooned with the Italian tricolor and many riders waved flags through the streets of Trieste"; here the delegation from the clubs of Palermo, Siracusa and Catania parade with a message for "our brothers of Istria, whom we have never forgotten."

bers' hearts, and Italian national irredentism for territory lost after World War II still ran high.

The high point of Trieste's memorable national rally was reached when the president placed alongside the war memorial the eternal flame that had been lit at Trento two years earlier by the widow of Italian patriot and martyr Cesare Battisti. The year was 1954 and after the tragedy of war, the persecution and property seizure, the signing of a "Memorandum of Understanding" gave Trieste back to Italy.

Yet again, straining beyond the celebratory rhetoric, Vespa's history entwined itself with Italy's to faithfully reproduce the nation's emotional temperature, psychological stance and most loved symbols.

When Trieste was transferred to Italy on November 15, 1954, *Life* magazine published a photograph of the Vespa procession buzzing through the city streets.

Facing page: every year saw an increase in female participants, not only at all levels in rallies but also during the most demanding competitions—here at the Three Seas Rally—in which the judges, sometimes, still seemed bewildered.

"Vespa enthusiast friends!" began Visentin, the acting mayor of Trieste to the thousands in Piazza Unità d'Italia, "you've arrived here just a few hours before the Italian soldiers we've been waiting for more than eleven years."

NECK AND NECK: VESPA AND LAMBRETTA

Three years after Lambretta appeared on the market, the 125 C, here pictured coming off the assembly line, was the embodiment of its typical features.

A young Luigi Innocenti who succeeded the company's founder, Ferdinando, pictured in *Time* magazine (12 January '62). Company vice chairman from 1958, it was he, a few years later, who decided on expansion into the automobile market.

The opposite of, and a mirror image to, the mighty antagonist that had beaten it to the market—and would beat it in the long term—Lambretta was the brainchild of a major industrialist after seeing the American Cushmans used by the U.S. Army as far back as June 1944.

The company started in the Twenties in a warehouse-workshop in Rome and managed to get a number of sizeable orders from the Vatican.

The move to Lambrate, a suburb of Milan, didn't happen until the early Thirties just as the "Innocenti scaffolding" with its renowned multi-directional jointing system, manufactured under license from Great Britain, was making major inroads in the building trade. Production itself was well organized covering

The Motorcycle Manufacturers' Association (ANCMA) set up a meeting in October 1951 for Moto Guzzi, Macchi, Innocenti, Gilera, Iso and Rumi with "Definition of the Scooter" on the agenda. Piaggio insisted that the meeting approve the agreement reached with Lambretta, labeling illegitimate "the motorcycles camouflaged as scooters ... such as the Galletto and the Rumi." The association agreed on a definition: "An engine-powered vehicle without pedals for human propulsion characterized by an open frame in the front and rear parts joined by a continuous footrest, and by two wheels the diameter of which is no greater than 12 inches," and an accompanying diagram.

With a range of 150 miles on a gallon of fuel mixture, the 125 E's cylinder was vertical. Start-up was by means of a ripcord, obviously not a great idea, which soon became a nightmare for hapless owners before the company decided to halt production in '54, just one year after launch.

metal scaffolding and pylons, water pipes for aqueducts and irrigation, conduits for gases and liquids, drilling rigs, and metal- and glass-working machinery.

The Milan workshops exalted as "a shining example of a Fascist factory" had been devastated just a few years earlier as a result of their wartime production of cannon barrels and ammunition.

Reconstruction was now the order of the day and here, too, intelligent money was backing an individual, economical and reliable means of transport. So, having discarded the initial project worked on by the Milan engineers who had been evacuated to Rome—and who were decidedly more at home with metal scaffolding, turbines and ducts—Ferdinando Innocenti entrusted the idea to an ingenious aeronautical engineer, Pier Luigi Torre. And here again the similarities were striking.

The first version was ages in getting to the market although the radio ads had been hammering out their message for months. The commercial debut was disappointing but the second version was more fortunate.

The characteristic shape of the Milan scooter, built around a large-diameter, steel-tube frame with a side fairing, did not appear until 1950 and only then, almost as a coming-of-age testimonial, did NSU acquire the license for production in Germany.

So, 1953 was the year of the Lambretta E, supereconomical and destined to failure just like the Vespa 125 U that followed it that same year. The struggle between the two great manufacturers was fierce and, not only on this occasion, led to reciprocal pursuits up dead-ends that

Until 1957, the Lambretta had two versions—with or without a fairing. Early on, Italians seemed to prefer the basic model: "Buy a Lambretta and spend the difference on something else" was one slogan. Until, that is, fortune smiled on the 125 LD, here with a woman driver in a 1953 pamphlet.

The first legal battle was fought on the grounds of possible "cheap imitation" by Innocenti with its first model with a fairing. In France, Piaggio claimed its rival "falsified its ornamental model patent" with the same motivation. The intention of Piaggio's suit was to oblige Lambretta to produce each unit in two colors or employ other similarly well-documented alterations to the front shield, to set it apart from the Vespa. Long, drawn-out discussions eventually produced an agreement in May 1953 but then new battles loomed. In Switzerland and Germany, discord grew concerning the advertising messages and now it was Hoffman and Vespa Distribution for Piaggio against NSU-Werke and Jan S.A. for Innocenti.

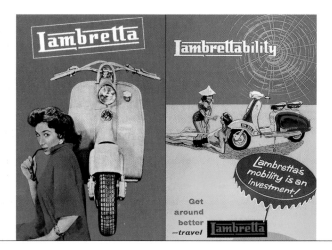

In 1954, an electric starting mechanism was incorporated in this 125 LD aimed especially at women.

Export markets were considered highly important and in Great Britain the scooter stood for originality, cheap running costs and warm Mediterranean summers.

allowed the competition a miserly 5 percent market share.

Lambrate's answer to the Pontedera 150 GS was the novel 175 TV and on and on until the Third Series in which the 200 cc model was the most powerful scooter on the market, and then the "cinquantino" ("little fifty") in 1964 up to the last series, technically excellent but sabotaged by the factory closure in April 1971.

Up till then it was all go.

In reply to the Ape, Innocenti produced the Lambro scooterized van, experimenting with automatic gear changes, electric starters and disc brakes. A new racing section was set up that developed pure speed prototypes and a scooter that could be dropped by parachute was prepared to put before NATO armed forces.

Dueling Banjos

Having chosen their weapons, the duelists got started. Roads in Italy and abroad were the dueling ground—Innocenti's dream was to supply turnkey plants abroad. This proved impossible, but licensees got underway in Argentina, Pakistan, Brazil, the Congo, Taiwan, Turkey, France, India and Colombia. Italian motor-vehicle exports doubled between 1956 and 1960, and more than half the Milan factory's production was destined for abroad, while Pontedera lagged at around 40 percent.

On the domestic market the Innocenti sales network, in an attempt to secure their position, followed the Vespa example and set up the Lambretta Clubs and published the *Notiziario Lambretta* (*Lambretta News*)

Highly original, almost heretical, this Lambretta prototype with a load-bearing monocoque body created around 1962–63 was never developed further.

reporting the extraordinary travels of scooter enthusiasts braving the rigors of the desert or Tierra del Fuego. The development of the market, the rise of competition, the increasing shift to four wheels—a sector to which Innocenti was committed by its agreement with British Motors Corporation—were to eclipse the association and the publication stopped publishing in the Sixties.

Propaganda, as radio advertising was called in those days, was full of Lambretta but Vespa was soon to make inroads spending seven million lire ($4,200) for radio announcements on the birth of the new 125 in 1964. The poster campaign of the Milan company, however, didn't come up to the level of the great Vespa campaigns that wrote Italian advertising history. Other alternatives were tried, like the one quickly brought to Piaggio's attention in '62:

gigantic billboards, obviously in the strategic "television position" in the football stadiums showing a Lambretta and an Austin Innocenti. But on the roads and racecourses the no-holds barred fight was under way.

The race round the block or along deserted suburban avenues, alongside the blocks of flats in the new projects was the same as the International Six-day Trial or the "Kilometro Lanciato" pure speed competition.

In some ways more a motorbike with its tubular frame and centrally positioned engine, the Lambretta aimed for outperformance, but comparative tests condemned the two contestants to an embarrassing draw.

All in all, though, the Vespa was more flexible, universal and feminine and continually managed higher sales than its rival that was always trying to catch up.

"Slimstyle" was how this thinner-line, single-saddle model was defined. This was the garb in which the highly envied sport version of the 175 cc came out in 1962, the first scooter in the world with disc brakes.

Just one year after the launch of the "third series" in which the Lambretta had been radically restyled, the Lambretta 150 Special was in competition with the Vespa GL on the road and on the printed page. It was neck and neck between the two competitors this time too. Performance and fuel consumption were identical and the difference in braking power was infinitesimal. But beyond better overall comfort, it was the Vespa's greater efficiency—enabling it to obtain the same racing times despite having less power at its disposal—that gave it the edge.

LIKE WASPS IN FLIGHT

Technological excellence was a given in the vehicles prepared by the Racing Department, as was ability and total determination on the part of the drivers both on trails and in speed trials on the Monza racecourse, as well as a pinch of imagination (as seen in this anti-fogging visor developed by Giuseppe Cau). This was the formula that brought victory in the Six-Day Trial as well as in every other major competition.

Few settings appear so incongruous at first sight for Vespas as the raised banking of the Montlhéry racecourse or the dirt-tracks of the International Six-Day Trial.

If legend is to be believed, the choice seems to have been lobbied by a few testing engineers, understandably eager to put the machine to the test in an open setting. However, there was also pressure from within the company to spell out in no uncertain terms the technical potential of the vehicle in order to dispel the prejudice it had always faced that the innovative small wheels were "dangerously low."

In any case, the racing season had a busy program as far back as 1948. And from the very outset this was no longer the Vespa Thousand Kilometer Rally in

which the technical service department had to deal with droves of enthusiastic amateurs, some of whose engines seized up after being filled with four-stroke fuel. The Vespas ridden by Dino Mazzoncini and the other official riders were prepared by the factory. The Pontedera Racing Department got so good over time that in the end they were turning out real racing machines, prototypes and crafted one-off pieces.

Nine out of ten in the Six-Day Trial

The high point among the many triumphs was the outstanding victory in the 1951 International Six-Day Trial; an important trophy crowning yet another win by the British team on their BSA's, Triumphs, Ariels and Royal Enfields. The Italians did not perform brilliantly, although 71 competing in Italian colors brought home no fewer than 20 gold medals, 9 of which were won by the Piaggio team. Three went to M V, the prestigious motorcycle manufacturer based in Verghera, and the leftovers went to Guazzoni, Guzzi, Innocenti, Mival, Morini, Parilla, Rossi and Rumi.

Under starter's orders there were ten Vespas—or rather eleven, the eleventh being an amateur rider named Carini who, after quarreling with the official team, appeared elegantly dressed in gabardine on the saddle of a non-functioning machine. This didn't get him a place in the history books, though.

"The simplicity of the mechanics of Piaggio's creation must surely be the reason for its great success" commented *Motociclismo* magazine's correspondent "because, despite the riders' racing expertise, they didn't look the part and their performance was nothing special." They wore a shirt showing the heraldic bearings with the capital *P*, "tiny little men like Cau and aging champions like Opessi ... who must be fifty if he's a day." Regardless, they won hands down on tarred and cobbled roads, dirt-tracks and hairpin bends, in the narrow roads of the villages they raced through and the final speed test on the Monza racecourse which, at the time, still had a porphyry surface.

The average speeds that had to be reached left little room for maneuvering: 24 miles per hour for the 125's; 29 for the 250's; and 30 for the 500's.

The Manufacturers' Trophy awarded to Piaggio cited "absolute machine perfection tried and tested

In 1950, a woman named Tina Pecol was one of the non-official riders and one of the few women to ride a "racer." Failing to repeat her success of the previous year in the Sassi-Superga race held just outside Turin, she complained to the managing director, attributing her failure to poor tuning of her machine. She also had an acquaintance send a letter voicing the same complaint. Humiliated by the Lambretta riders and feeling let down by "her" Piaggio, Pecol finished by saying that this was her first defeat and her last race. There was only one word at the foot of the letter added by hand by an exasperated Enrico Piaggio, underlined twice: "Good!"

A group photograph of all members of the racing team, mechanics and riders, in the triumphant 1951 season. Back row (l. to r.): "Lacchino" Doveri, Gianfaldoni, Castellani, Riva, Opessi, and his son, then Pellegrini, Granchi, Casini, Mazzoncini and his wife, then Biasci. Front row: Romano, Vivaldi, Nesti, Cau and Merlo.

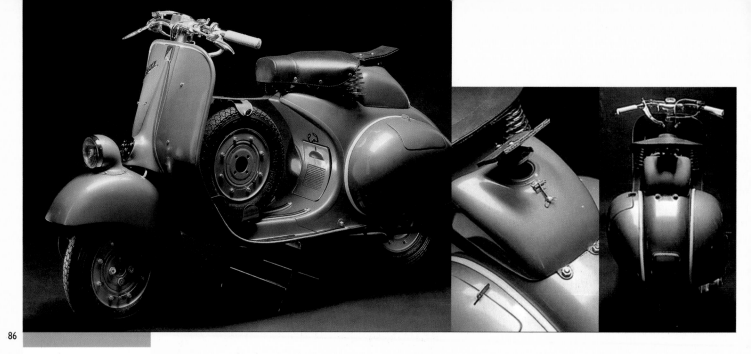

The Six-Day Trial Vespa

Turn the 1951 version of the Vespa 125 into a racing machine for mixed terrain including fast trail racing. This was the brief given to the technical department who did their job without revolutionizing the machine; indeed they improved it intelligently and changed very little.

The body was standard although slightly different. The shield was a couple inches narrower and flared at the base to improve aerodynamics, and the sides were higher off the ground.

The front mudguard was topped by a periscope headlight, more compact and less prone to damage in the case of collision than the original; a number of minor variables in configuration marked the difference between the "real" Six-Day model and the small series for the unofficial riders.

Its side-stand had a strong return spring and the front suspension was kept the same as the original but with stronger components: a thicker steering column, a sturdier oscillating linkage with the bolts uncovered, hydraulic shock-absorber and strengthened spring. The modified trim kept the scooter nearly 2 inches higher off the ground.

The compartment behind the apron very visibly housed a couple of spare wheels set lengthwise and held in place by a metal brace which also had a shelf for the log book.

One spare wheel was 10 inches and the other 8 inches in order to have available the wheel most suited to the terrain to be covered. The larger one, when placed on the front end, was better on tougher trails.

The tank also very obviously overlapped the body just behind the saddle. Its 303-gallon capacity gave 144 miles of autonomy and the inlet pipe had a rudimentary support so the rider could effectively but certainly uncomfortably drive lying down.

The knob for regulating air flow in the carburetor for the single-cylinder machine to reach top performance was on the handlebar.

Another odd feature was the hole next to the brake pedal to keep any mud or stones sticking underneath from jamming it.

Less obvious but no less fundamental was the steel engine support, the aluminum sump and cylinder head and the reinforced brakes, not to mention the wet, oil-soaked clutch, the Dellorto SS carburetor and the short play gas control. Lastly, the bolts were fixed to prevent vibration causing any problems—a measure that could be seen in the way the body had been assembled to the outermost covering of the fuel tank.

In 1952, a first, limited series was drawn from the standard racing model keeping the 8 inch diameter on both wheels. Next year a second limited run was produced with few changes, including an oval hub on the front-wheel, which marked the end of manufacture of "specials."

A lot was expected from record attempts, and not only in terms of prestige; "because speed means eliminating damaging causes of resistance, improving passive coefficients and determining the safety limits of component parts," according to the main Italian sports daily, and therefore "in a word: safety."

Among the oddities of the Monthléry prototype was the quasi-aeronautical front-end. The fuel-tank, higher at the front, was placed behind the rider, tucked in to serve as a saddle, and continued with a support area to within a couple of inches of the handlebar, keeping the "open" scooter structure required by the rules.

over six years of experience, complete protection of all vital parts" and the practicality of two spare wheels, very useful in a terrain hard on Italian tires, so different from "these great big fat tires on the British machines," adding "the effectiveness of all-round suspension, the great convenience of having the gear change on the handgrip, the powerful brakes and all the other ingenious features of this typically Italian product."

This great success was used in the presentation of the nifty 150 GS "The Sporty Vespa" as Renato Tassinari called it in his July 1954 editorial.

Tit for tat at 100 miles per hour

The race to win the speed record was just another episode in the Vespa vs. Lambretta saga. The final outcome was perhaps more controversial than the numbers on their own.

Scene 1: Montlhéry racecourse in France, an April morning in 1949.

A specially lightened Lambretta with a gigantic fuel tank and a vast front fairing wins the 125 cc-class 48 hour speed trial bringing home a trail of other, lesser records into the bargain.

That same year Enrico Piaggio gives the job of picking up the gauntlet to Vittorio Casini and Carlo Carbonero.

The vehicle designed by Pontedera's study center was at the cutting edge technically and quite something to look at. With a front fairing and large tail it folded the rider's sloped back into a single outline—aerodynamic know-how wasn't lacking in the company—but despite this it was every inch a Vespa: unmistakable, the engine can be seen outlined on the right hand side. The link to the production model was crucial in terms of publicity, and the company propaganda continually hammered this point home.

"A company's capacity to transfer an experiment to the industrial production phase, if necessary step by step, is the hallmark of its dynamism and vitality" was the comment of sports newspaper *Gazzetta dello Sport.* And so "if the Vespa, originally designed for a

speed of 40 miles per hour managed a top speed of 80 and held an average of 74.12 miles per hour for 10 hours without stopping, it means that it's making progress."

In fact from March 23 to April 7, 1950, after a first set of trial runs with a test engine, this flying wasp was passed over to Spadoni and Romano and raced round the course notching up an impressive series of results. It set the record for 500 and 1,000 kilometers, the one-hour record and then the record for two, three and then four up to ten hours running slashing more than 10 percent off the competition's time. Innocenti tried to turn the tables with a custom-built model and managed to set new records but in the meantime the scene was changing and so was the ball park.

Scene two: The Rome—Ostia motorway somewhere between kilometers 10 and 11.

Here, states the communiqué of the Italian Motorcycling Federation, "The attempt by the Piaggio company to set a 'Kilometro Lanciato' world speed record was crowned with success. The machine ridden by test rider Dino Mazzoncini ... The engine had no booster and was derived from the classic single-cylinder model that succeeded in its enterprise last year at Montlhéry ... The extraordinarily powerful single-cylinder Vespa has undoubtedly achieved a

major success ... This record is one of the most sensational set since the end of the war." It was all here—perhaps even over the top.

The rocket ridden by this "surprisingly versatile, courageous and modest rider" (as *Motociclismo* fittingly described the smiling Mazzoncini) had very little in common with the Montlhéry Vespa and even less with the placid little machines that plied their way up and down the roads of the world.

Built around a single rail aluminum frame, gathered within a magnificent fairing wafer-thin in front that opened sideways to let the rider get on and literally lie down to ride, it was something from another world.

Here again though the alien look of this speed machine compared to that of the common or garden Vespa was hushed up.

Anyway, it was a splendid result: 103.26 miles per hour on average in two runs over a measured distance.

But Lambrate wasn't resting on its laurels and a brief two months later a missile with the Lambretta badge rocketed along at 114 miles per hour near Terracina and did the double ton on the Munich-Ingolstadt autobahn. A magnificent performance but the engine was boost fed so it couldn't really be called a fair fight.

It was, however, a great chapter in the history of motorcycling brought to an untimely end by the tragic death of a racing rider, Renato Magi, flying along on an extremely unlikely scooter prepared by M V.

The one-kilometer pure speed race prototype was ridden lying down with the knees bent up and the chest leaning on the central lever that opened the "doors." In deceleration, the rider raised his chest pulling the lever and the doors opened like a fan, acting as an aerodynamic brake.

Its distant lineage to the scooter could be seen in the shape of the steering column and the front suspension and the rear with its oscillating arm and the offset wheel, or the laterally mounted engine, but the distance from the standard product was astronomical.

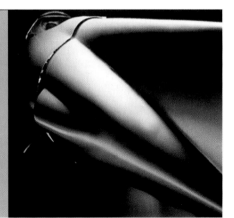

The announcement of an agreement between Piaggio and Sears, Roebuck & Co. was dated 14 November 1951. The ANSA news agency stated there would be a first lot of one thousand units as a trial run for a market as vast as it was untested for this type of vehicle.

There came the day when Elvis Presley himself wanted one in his collection with the purple Lincoln and the red Messerschmitt, the yellow Isetta and the red Cadillac, the black limousine and lastly his silver gray Harley Davidson; a white Vespa, standing there alongside them all. But we're still at the beginning and the road was long and uphill.

The possibility of an agreement emerged with Indian Motorcycle Company of Springfield, Massachusetts, "the largest American firm of its kind," wrote Piaggio to Cesare Merzagora, Italy's minister of foreign trade, in July 1948 when he applied for an authorization to buy up raw steel in the United States. But the deal fell through soon after.

During a trip to the United States in March 1949, the managing director paid a visit to Sikorsky and Bell Aircraft for the helicopter business, then on to Ford, General Motors and Chrysler in Detroit for the Vespa. He also called on Budd Co. in Philadelphia, supplier of the giant molds bought with funding from the Marshall Plan.

For Byron C. Foy, Piaggio's man in the United States, the scooter's future was bright but the practice of giving big rebates to the retailer and the low starting price for buying a car made things difficult. So while quality was never questioned, the price "was $100 more than for a lower quality machine"; the new compact motorbikes too that came out under the Indian–Harley Davidson brand were cheaper by a long chalk.

The "American" Vespa was delivered right to the customer's door. Sears, Roebuck & Co was even then a colossus in distribution owning a department store network and a powerful mail order organization. Richard Sears, a watch and jewelry representative, prepared the first general catalogue containing a wide selection of merchandise in 1896. The first sales point opened in Chicago in 1925 and on the eve of World War II more than six hundred had sprouted all over the country. The sales turnover in 1947 (thus shortly before the agreement with Piaggio) was in excess of $1 billion.

Chanel's success in the United States was supreme: many American designers copied the maison's European style and the scooter often appeared in fashion magazines.

Vespa reached a fair level of penetration in Texas, California, Pennsylvania and New York which together took up 50 percent of the imports but the great expectations of the beginnings were not completely borne out.

Back in his hotel room Enrico Piaggio wrote his instructions longhand replying to Francesco Lanzara, his most trusted employee and factory manager from 1946 to '59. The stand at the Milan Fair, the new Moscone outboard motor, the second issue of the magazine, some bits missing here and there and the Vespa, reluctantly touched on, "interests a number of American groups but there are some problems to be overcome."

Sears: we've got ideas

Two years later, Martin Selfridge, of Sears, Roebuck & Co., "the largest commercial concern in America with monthly sales of some $250 million," got off the train at Pisa, came to Pontedera and then left for his never-to-be-forgotten Italian vacation: "Three thousand kilometers; town and country, in the dust and in the rain"; on a Vespa, of course. An ideal way of doing a test run to confirm their decision to import a scooter, now famous the world over, into the United States. He was grudging with compliments and pointed out every defect: the sparkplugs had to be cleaned every 500 miles and the engine de-carbed every 1,200 miles. But if not, it kept going just the same.

As far back as the Spring of 1951, Selfridge had been given a long list of things his technical manager considered "unnecessary" which if eliminated would have made the retail price more acceptable. These included the horn, the anti-theft device, the rubber strips on the

"Go with style ... go on a Sears Scooter" followed by "three versatile beauties" of which two at least were Vespas.

"Piaggio and Innocenti are seeking the success that eluded Cushman for twenty years: to convince the Americans that the scooter is an efficient and fairly dignified means of transport," wrote *Business Week*

in its 22 September '56 issue, "Piaggio alone has invested $250,000 in one year: a large amount by European standards."

A Vespa was chosen for the cover of this fantasy novel by John Steinbeck: a suitable mount for a sovereign during the French Revolution and among Texan millionaires, as well as teenagers bitten by the reading bug.

!GO!

Places to go! . . . things to do! . . . you're part of today's vibrant crowd that's on the go. So go with style . . . go with fun and excitement . . . go on a Sears Scooter. We'll show you three versatile beauties . . . all sleek 'n sassy, surging with power and lots of get-up-and-go to match your adventurous spirit.

footrest, the baggage rack, all the chrome work, the whole electrical circuit and even the front brake that "could be made optional."

When Enrico Piaggio heard about this he OK'd getting rid of a lot of bits and pieces from the prototype being prepared at Pontedera but he dug in his heels on the brakes and the electrics: the sizeable price cut of over two thousand lire (about $1) in the license price did not justify leaving the vehicle "incomplete." "I have not therefore deemed it advisable to abolish such parts." Pontedera opened negotiations with its suppliers but the 3,500 lire ($2) it clawed back on the price of each unit was still too little.

Despite all this, the idea of a Vespa for America was already on the way to becoming reality and the ANSA news agency hastened to point it out. In the beginning they were sold almost at a loss in the United States, but in the following year, 1952, a second lot was ordered, this time for five thousand units—and so on.

The numbers from across the ocean were sensational. Towards the end of '55, *The New York Times* pointed out that "thirty million American families need a second car but can't afford one"; so the twenty thousand Vespas sold there in four years might only be the tip of the iceberg. Piaggio's great expectations led to the founding of Vespa Distributing Co. in New York, Denver and Florida and the setting up of Vespa Clubs American-style. Vespa's eternal rival pointed out to *The Wall Street Journal* that it aimed to spend over $200,000 in advertising and promotion for that year. But, by then, Vespa looked like increasing its lead.

1948-55

VESPA 125
125U
150GS

VESPA125

Two years of testing and experience gained from a constant dialogue with users made a number of technical and performance improvements possible.

The result was the Vespa 125, which went into production in 1948.

The most important feature of the new model, which was more practical to use and more agile than the previous version, was its larger, 125 cc engine. This engine size has been maintained throughout a whole series of technical updates and is still in use in the Vespa today.

The engine was still the same unidirectional valve unit, but with bore increased to 56.5 mm,

The success of the Vespa 125 (to the left, the sidecar version with its characteristic tubular frame) encouraged Piaggio to increase the factory's production capacity.

Contemporarily, a policy of expansion into foreign markets was under way, with new plants being opened in a number of European countries.

Costing 68,000 lire
(about $40) the Vespa
125 was the perfect
answer to Italy's need for
affordable mobility. The
version shown in the
photograph is from the
second series (1949).

VESPA125
95

giving a top speed of 40 mph. The carburetor, which could be reached through a hatch at the front, was still a Dellorto TA17, but with a redesigned air filter. The choke shutter valve for cold starting was located under the saddle.

A lot of attention went into making the vehicle quieter: the engine was now fitted with a more efficient silencer than before, and some of the transmission gear wheels were redesigned to reduce mechanical noise.

The implementation of a longer travel spring and a telescopic hydraulic damper in the rear suspension and improvements made to the front suspension, which now had a support arm (the steering column) on the right and used a compressed coil spring, ensured greater comfort.

The brake drums and shoes were strengthened to provide smoother, more powerful braking as well as require less frequent adjustments.

One of the problems noted was that the Vespa was difficult to park: therefore a bicycle-type side stand was fitted on the left. This soon proved to be inadequate, however, and was replaced in the following series (1949) by a proper central stand made from metal tubing with flattened, rolled ends in order to provide a more stable surface to stand on.

As for the controls, the light switch on the first models was the same as on the Vespa 98. Later models, however, were fitted with a fan shaped switch with a black plastic case and a chrome-

plated cover. The shape of the horn also changed and it now had an external adjuster screw in the center.

A crest shaped ornament in chrome-plated zinc was added to the top of the headlight, while the rear light was now cylindrical.

The gearbox control rods, which were previously entirely exposed, were modified in correspondence at the footplate, and now entered the chassis at

After the initial stages of production, a different light switch from the one used on the Vespa 98 was fitted.

Detail of the rear with the new parcel rack. The rear light was cylindrical with no surround ring.

The steering column was shifted over to the right-hand side of the wheel, the engine cowl was cut open at the bottom to allow for the vertical travel of the engine, and the tank now had a new tap with a reserve position. To improve comfort, the saddle was now also sprung at the front. A bag-holder hook was added and finally, there was now also a stand.

VESPA125

The front suspension had a new "pulled" wheel layout with a vertical spring aligned with the steering column. The mudguard was sleeker after the elimination of the removable side panel.

The black horn was fitted with a centrally mounted external adjuster screw.

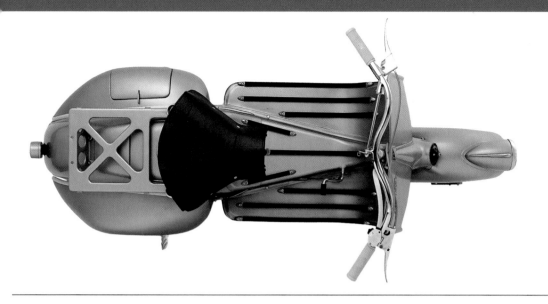

The gear control rods were modified near the brake pedal, where they now entered the chassis. This improved both the cleanliness and safety of the footplate area.

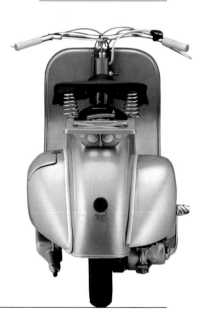

the brake pedal to exit near the engine cross member pivot.

The fuel tank was fitted with a new tap, with a hook-shaped twist lever which now also had a reserve position.

Theft protection, which in the first series consisted of two drilled plates through which a padlock was inserted to block the handlebars, was now ensured by a more convenient lock incorporated in the steering column, blocking the front wheel to the right.

No significant changes were made to the monocoque, apart from reinforcing some parts to improve stability. The lower middle part

This side view shows the rear brake cable exit point from the bodywork.

This rear view also shows the rear light, a characteristic feature of the '49 model.

As a result of experience learned with the first model, the kick starter lever was redesigned to make starting easier.

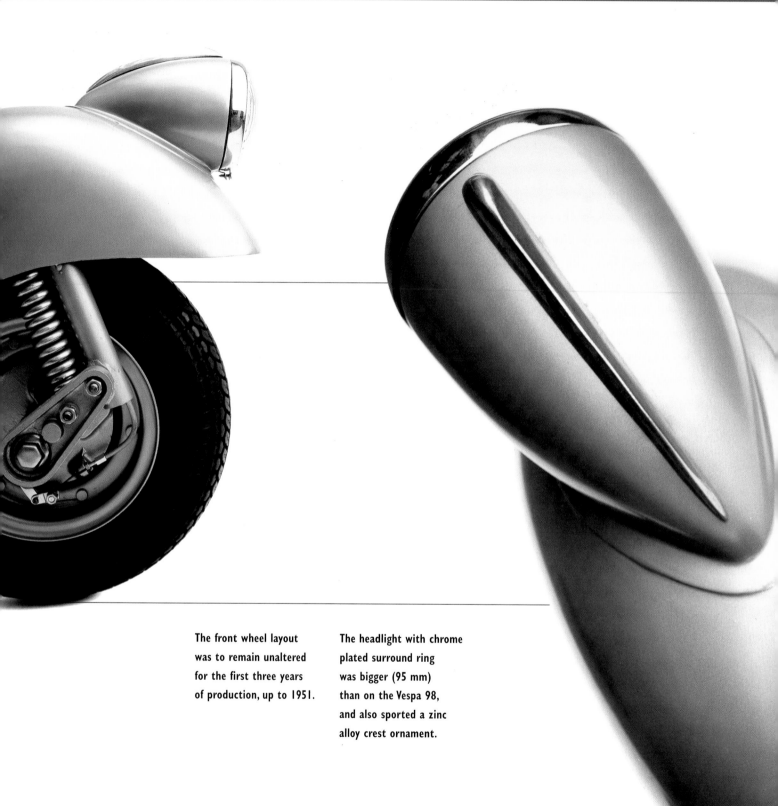

The front wheel layout was to remain unaltered for the first three years of production, up to 1951.

The headlight with chrome plated surround ring was bigger (95 mm) than on the Vespa 98, and also sported a zinc alloy crest ornament.

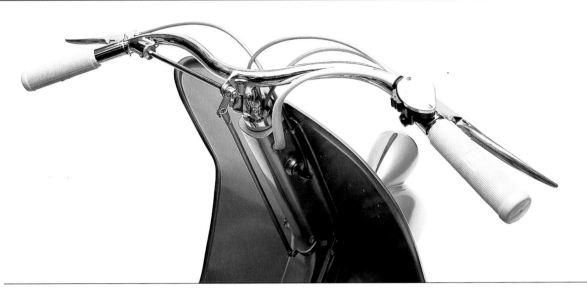

The handlebars carried
a new fan-shaped light
switch with a black plastic
case and a chrome-plated
cover. The rubber handlebar
grips now carried the
Piaggio logo.

of the engine cowling was now cut open, however, to allow for the vertical movement of the engine.

The front mudguard was made slimmer and the removable panel was eliminated, simplifying wheel replacement.

A number of other components were also modified: for example, the handlebars now looked better finished, thanks to new rubber coated hand grips embossed with the Piaggio logo.

Changes were made in maximum height (from 34 inches to 38 inches), footplate height (from 6 inches to 9 inches) and

saddle height (from 28 inches to 30 inches); the saddle was now also sprung at the front as well. Length remained the same, but weight was increased from 132 pounds to 154 pounds.

A major patented feature for 1948 was the fitting for a sidecar. This development was part of a project to make the Vespa an extremely versatile vehicle, suitable for urban mobility needs and long distance traveling.

The Vespa 125, already a worldwide success, thus also affirmed itself as a vehicle for touring and recreation.

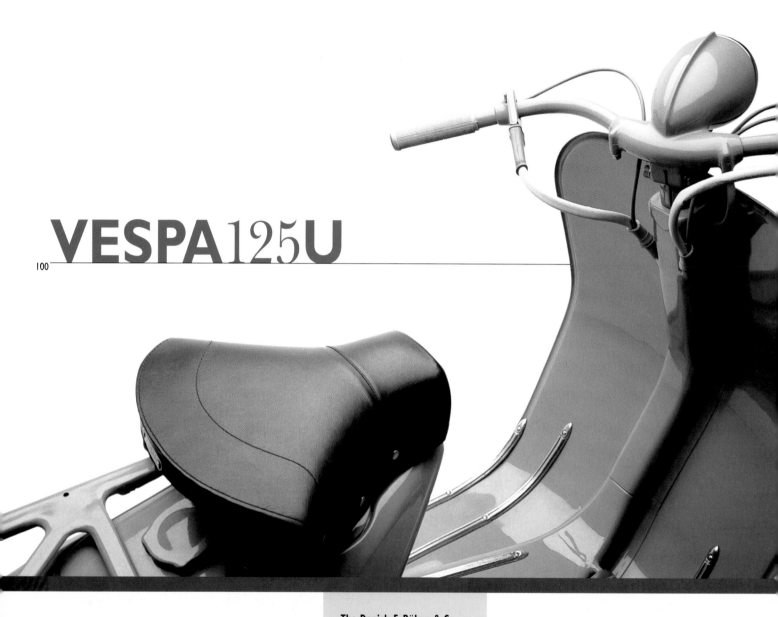

VESPA125U

VESPA – MODEL STANDARD

The Danish F. Bülow & Co. promoted the 125 U as the "standard model"— in addition to the "deluxe model," the new 125 of 1953—but only two years later it was no longer on the market.

The configuration of the Vespa Allstate (1951) for the U.S. market proved very useful in the preparation of the 125 U.

Characterized by spartan styling, the utilitarian version of the Vespa cost 20,000 lire ($12) less than the basic 125, but was destined to be a resounding flop.

The smaller front mudguard, now for the first time not carrying the headlight, was molded around the bend in the steering column.

The early Fifties saw Piaggio engaged on two fronts. On the one hand, there was the creation of an advertising image suited to the distribution of such an innovative product in a wide variety of markets.

This led to a corporate communication system organized on a number of levels—retail, assistance and end user—and actuated through different channels, including billboards, magazines, informative pamphlets, gift items, post cards, calendars and the cinema.

On the other, the structuring of a production system capable of meeting the rapidly developing needs of the market. The system was organized following criteria from the automotive industry, with a complete cycle production process synchronized with transport and assembly lines.

The increase in production was already evident by 1950, with 6000 units per month being made. This new state of affairs made a number of modifications to the Vespa possible in order to achieve levels of performance that were, at the time, considered impossible for a scooter.

1953 was an important milestone in the evolution of the Vespa, which was available in two versions: the 125 U—"Utilitaria"—of spartan design, low priced and available for purchase by installments, and the 125 cc new series model 53, with a more elegant, refined design.

The two models both used, in part, some of the features already developed in the 1950 series, and

This top view illustrates how the protective strips along the footplate are fewer in number and not covered with rubber. The saddle is smaller and dark green in color, like its support springs.

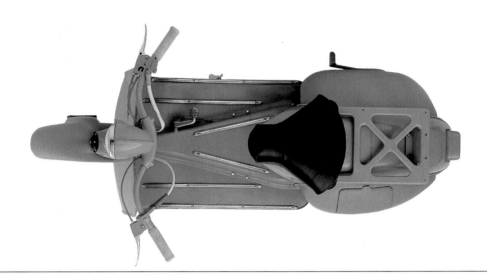

VESPA125**U**

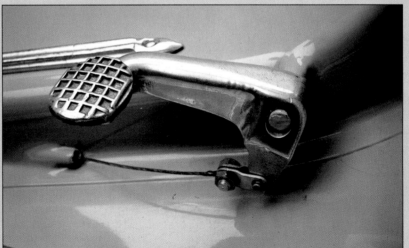

Detail of the brake pedal in rough aluminum with the gear control cable entering the chassis underneath.

The front view (left, above) shows the steering column around which the front mudguard is molded.

On this model a number of highly innovative features were tried out which were to be implemented only several years later. For the first time in Italy, the headlight was now mounted on the handlebars. This configuration had already been used on some export versions. The mechanicals were immediately accessible due to the very small engine cowl and the front mudguard was also much smaller to facilitate wheel replacement.

The gear lever with exposed half bars and flexible cables.

above all in the 1951 series. The latter introduced a new body shell with a redesigned structure in which the ribbing along the rear bodywork was eliminated, resulting in a continuous curved shape.

The silencer also changed position, and was moved from its original location at the side to a central one, ahead of the wheel and hidden by the bodywork. This also allowed modifications to be made to the shape of the lower edge of the left-hand cowl. The footplate was extended towards the engine, providing a more comfortable position for the passenger. The handlebars were mounted on an anti-vibration support— considered a major advance when introduced in

the 1951 series—and the gearbox was no longer operated by a rod linkage, but by flexible cables.

These solutions formed the foundations of the two 1953 models, which set the styling standards on which further models were to be based.

7000 Vespa 125 U's were made. They cost 110,000 lire ($72)—20,000 ($12) less than the standard 125 cc 53 model, putting into practice the company's intention of offering the public a budget Vespa (this was also an answer to the extremely low priced Lambretta E of the same year).

The engine was a baffle type unit, similar to the one used on the 1951 Vespa. Top speed was 39 mph and fuel consumption was more than

Detail of the cast aluminum headlight, similar to the component mounted on the Allstate model for the USA. The headlight was small (3.8 inches in diameter) and made as a single piece incorporating the handlebar mounting bracket. It was surrounded by a chrome plated ring—the only chrome on the vehicle.

VESPA125U

100 mpg. The model was extremely simplified and was put together with surplus warehouse parts. All chrome plated parts (except for the headlight surround) were eliminated and all parts were painted, like the bodywork, in pastel green (Piaggio code 334). There were *no finishing details and no rubber covers on the stand (which was now galvanized with the end section bent at a right angle) or on the brake pedal and kick starter. These components were now made of aluminum with a griddle pattern stamped onto the contact area. The protective strips on the footplate were now fewer in number and made of raw aluminum with no rubber covers. The saddle, now smaller, was fitted with*

The word *Vespa* was painted directly onto the front leg shield in dark green.

Opposite: the rectangular-shaped rear light is identical to the one mounted in the standard Vespa 125 from the same year.

The extremely minimized
engine cowl offered
immediate access
to the spark plug.

Due to its disappointing
commercial results, this
model was manufactured
in a limited number and
is one of the versions most
sought after by collectors.

VESPA125**U** 105

dark green conical springs at the rear and was
unsprung at the front. Two other interesting
details in this series were the engine cowling and
the front mudguard.

The mudguard was smaller and contoured
around the bend in the steering column, whereas
the engine cowl left the cylinder head exposed—
the spark plug was visible and easily accessible.

The two side covers (engine cowl and tool compartment) were made of sheet steel and were fixed
to the body with exposed screws and gray rubber
seals. The color of the seals contrasted with the
green of the bodywork to emphasize the shape of
the wing-shaped side cowls.

For the first time in Italy, the headlight was
now mounted on the handlebars.
This configuration had
already been used on some
export versions.

Although this model
launched a number of technical solutions that would
be seen again in
later versions,
it was rather
unsuccessful
and was taken out
of production
after only
a year.

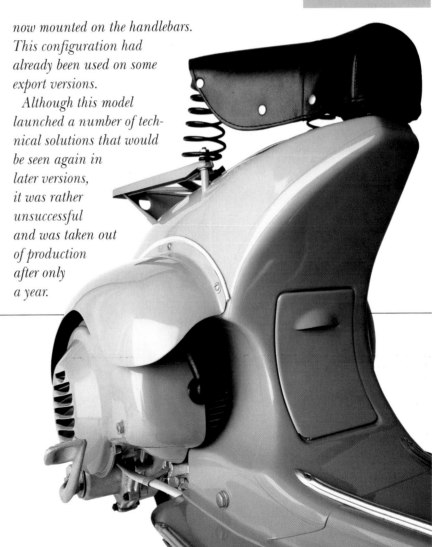

150GS

The 150 GS was a milestone in the history of the scooter. It is remembered by enthusiasts as the greatest scooter the world has ever seen and is today highly sought after by collectors of vintage Vespas.

Although this is in part due to its distinctive styling, with that typical Vespa elegance, it is more because of this model's higher performance. The 150 GS was specifically intended to appeal to "sportier" customers, for whom the model would be a status symbol perfectly in keeping with their own requisites. Speed, immediate acceleration, good handling, lively uphill capability and powerful braking in all conditions: these

From 1955 the Vespa was manufactured in Germany by Messerschmitt, a name well known for its fighter planes in World War II.

Offering outstanding performance, yet still appealing to female users, the much envied 150 GS was also successful abroad.

GRAND SPORT — en maskin utöver det vanliga!

The handlebars carried a large 4.5-inch-diameter headlight, with a chrome-plated surround. On the Piaggio shield, made of fire-enameled brass alloy, the word *Genoa* no longer appeared.

The "Vespone" immediately met with the enthusiasm of the public, which wanted a more powerful, quicker vehicle also capable of long distance motorway journeys.

characteristics were, in a nutshell, what made the GS "one hell of a scooter."

It was the result of experience that Piaggio had acquired from speed and trial racing with the Six-Day Trial Vespa (Vespa Sei Giorni).

The first GS models were delivered at the end of 1954, although most of them are dated 1955—the same model year as the basic 150. However, there were many new features distinguishing it from the basic version.

It was powered by a square (bore and stroke 57 x 57 mm) 145.6 cc engine derived from the unit developed for the Vespa Sport Sei Giorni and reached the remarkable (at the time) speed

of 60 mph. Until the Vespa 200 Rally was made in 1972, this was the fastest Vespa ever.

The higher speed demanded highly efficient brakes. Large-diameter light-alloy drums were therefore fitted with an incorporated cast iron ring and cooling fins. The rear brake pedal lever was lengthened to allow more brakeforce to be applied. The increase in brake diameter necessitated modifying and reinforcing the wheels which now, for the first time, were fitted with 3.5-inch-by-10-inch tires.

To ensure faster pace even when riding with a passenger, a four-speed gearbox was used (note that the normal 150 only got this in 1960)

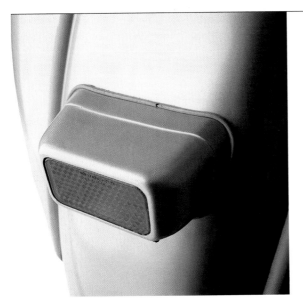

The rectangular-shaped rear light is similar to the one mounted on the Vespa 125 from 1953, but larger in size.

The design of the kick starter lever was new—it was now longer, highly polished and fitted with an anti-slip rubber grip.

These views show off the Vespa's elegance and the perfectly proportioned design of the individual parts making up the whole. The new body shell was larger and more rounded, giving the vehicle a particular aggressive and sporty appearance.

The long saddle could accommodate two people or allow a single rider to adopt a prone, racing style position.

The sporty aspect was emphasized by the use of larger wheels (3.5 inches by 10 inches).

150GS

with a reinforced clutch to cope with the higher power. The plates, springs and all other clutch components were now larger in diameter.

The machine's original and attractive appearance is the result of a harmonious balance of its individual parts: newly designed handlebars, with incorporated headlight, a sleeker leg shield, metallic paint (metallic gray, Max Meyer code 15005) and a long, dual-purpose saddle, suitable for head-down riding but also comfortable with a passenger.

Compared to the normal version, the GS had a more aerodynamic shape with a dished leg shield and raised footplate. The side cowls were taller

and very large, due to the different location of the Dellorto UB 23S3 side chamber carburetor, mounted directly above the cylinder. The front mudguard now hugged the wheel more closely, and was fitted with a highly polished aluminum ornament in place of the headlight, which was now on the handlebars.

The handlebar-headlight assembly (introduced with the Allstate in 1951 and thus on the '53 125 U, then adopted on the '54 150 cc model and now further refined) was constructed from a single-piece cast aluminum casing. The cables continued to be mounted externally, arranged symmetrically with the sheathed cables entering

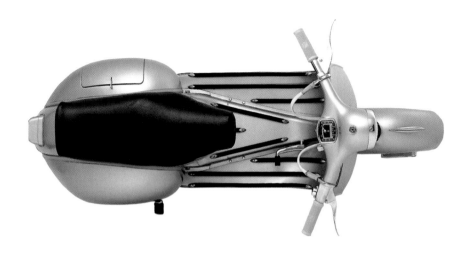

The pre-production example in this photo is fitted with a black saddle that is slightly different from the definitive production article.

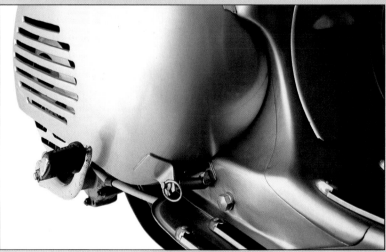

Detail of the engine side cowl fastening: as on the "Six-Days Trial Vespa" ("*Vespa Sport Sei Giorni*"), it was secured by fitting a plate welded onto the cowl over a dowel protruding from the body, then fixing it with a split pin.

The 150 GS is considered to be the "most loved, imitated and remembered" model of Vespa ever and is today highly sought after by collectors of vintage Vespas.

150GS

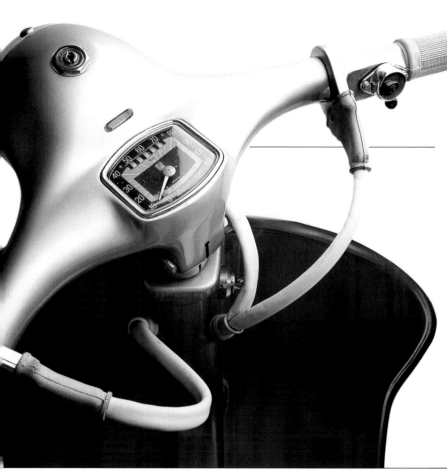

the leg shield under the steering fitting. The elegant, original handlebars incorporated a speedometer with a scale on a green background reading up to 72 mph, a key-operated switch for the ignition and the lights and a headlight indicator lamp. A switch on the right handlebar toggled between full beam and dipped beam and also incorporated the horn button. The headlight was now larger in diameter (4.6 inches) and surrounded by a Siem chrome-plated ring. The electricals had a 6 V–12 Ah battery to power the lights and horn. This was located in the left-hand compartment next to the maintenance toolkit. Recharging was via a metal rectifier next to the battery.

For the first time the Vespa was fitted with a long, double saddle with a grab strap for the passenger. Initially dark green, from 1956 the saddle was made in dark blue. (The saddle seen here is black and has no grab strap, as the Vespa photographed is a pre-production example.)

If you pushed the back of the saddle forward, it opened to give access to the tank, which held 3.5 gallons including the fuel reserve. On this model only, the filler cap was secured by a quick-release clip.

The GS continued to be manufactured, with a constant series of improvements and evolutions over the course of more than 6 years, until 1961.

Detail of the die cast handlebars with speedometer, key-operated ignition and headlight indicator lamp. The external sheathed gear control cables entered the leg-shield under the steering fitting.

The wheel-hugging mudguard was topped by the characteristic highly polished aluminum ornament, in contrast with the black horn.

ROMA MILANO
LA DOLCE VITA

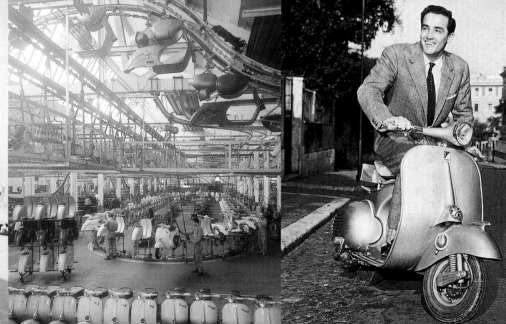

In which Vespa tops its first million just at the dawning of the "economic miracle." Seemingly never-ending progress: the fabled years of "Get Vespa'd," Hollywood, the Mods and a daring foray into the world of four wheels.

1956–1963

Italian Style...

THE MILLIONTH VESPA

Staff are assembled to celebrate the event with salesmen, the press and the company management. At this time, the "factory strength" is 3,781 workers (of which a mere 169 are women), 402 male and 99 female clerks, and 13 managers.

The big factory along the railway line was dressed up in its Sunday best. The year was 1956 and on April 28 the gates opened to a big crowd of guests flocking to see the millionth Vespa, blessed by the archbishop of Pisa, coming off the production line. There were 284 journalists and sales agents from Italy and abroad, as well as representatives of the licensees, and Vespa Club chiefs.

The managers and foremen were at the managing director's side to welcome the guests as were 160 senior employees including thirty or so due to receive company awards after lunch and right before the air show that would be followed by the visit to the Village, the customary way of rounding off factory tours.

"The biggest motorcycle company in the world," which now lay before the guests' eyes, with its avant-garde production facility spread over 68 million square feet, churning out two hundred thousand units a year, celebrated the event with painstaking meticulousness, special attention being paid to making the most out of the publicity. Italy was then in the middle of a boom period that favored other large-scale industries too, first and foremost Fiat.

Full steam ahead, with statistics to prove it

The consensus is that the Italian economy really took off in 1958; industrial employment overtook agricultural labor and yearly growth was over 6 percent. Over the next five years, industrial production more

"**H**is August Holiness congratulates praiseworthy success of mechanical industry at Piaggio factory, Pontedera and is pleased to note harmonious industriousness management and workers and sends heartfelt auspices divine assistance and blessing."

The incomparable Domenico Modugno—"Mr. Volare"—one of the best-known symbols of the new Italy at the dawning of the economic boom, won the crown of success at the 1958 San Remo Song Contest.

Center stage at the big celebration was taken by a Vespa 150: a model launched in 1954 and restyled for the occasion.

This happy event was important enough for the issue of a letter-sealing stamp colored light blue and gray, the company colors.

than doubled as did exports to the European Common Market. But this unruly growth had its bitter fruit: mass migration of over a million people from Italy's south to the industrial North and speculative building that wreaked havoc with the landscape corrupted public administration and spun a never-ending web of clientelism.

Throughout all this, the evolution in social customs continued with unrelenting vigor. This was the era of "Volare"—the refrain of the winning song in the '58 San Remo Song Contest that became famous the world over—Visconti's film *Rocco e i suoi fratelli,* and the Rome housing schemes dear to Pasolini in his film *Una vita violenta* and the TV quiz shows freshly arrived from the USA and the *Carosello* television program's advertising sketches celebrating the splendors of modernity showing a girl in trousers sporting a head scarf and sunglasses astride a Vespa.

At the dawn of the economic miracle—central Italy with its small and midsize industrial structure felt neither the harshness of emigration nor the culture clash with southern immigrants, and drew from the substantial pool of labor made available by the break-up of sharecropping—scooter manufacture was not the only area to enjoy prosperity.

Manufacturers of large appliances, such as Candy and Zanussi in Italy's northeast, are cases in point. But among the producers of the 1,750,000 "light motorcycles and mopeds" around 1954—almost double the number of four-wheeled vehicles counting private cars, trucks and buses—Piaggio, with its exports

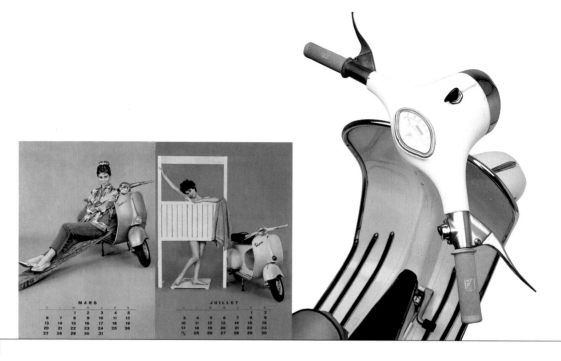

Little Joe on his Vespa is smiled on by Lady Luck: the pen of Benito Jacovitti, creator of Pippo, Pertica and Palla, Coconut Bill and Jack the Mandolin invented him in 1959 for boys' comic paper Lo Scolaro [The Schoolboy].

to sixty countries, turned out the lion's share: over the course of the decade, 60 percent of Italian scooter enthusiasts chose a Vespa.

Piaggio's main competitor, Lambretta, was also gaining ground and in '59 leapt forward reaching 70,000 new registrations. Now, Piaggio, which had flattened out at over a hundred thousand units a year in the wake of the new 125 and the rotary distribution engine, launched the splendid 160 GS and shot ahead.

Gilera e Guzzi—manufacturers of the Galletto, the only scooter they produced and one very much *sui generis*—stood for tradition and prestige among scooter manufacturers. Yet these long-established manufacturers sold only 880 units in 1958; the two-wheel market was for machines under 200 cc.

Offstage, and unnoticed to begin with, the Japanese were elbowing their way in.

The specialized press talked about it and were nonplussed at seeing 880,000 motorbikes manufactured in 1959 and 600,000 in just the first six months of 1961 with exports that for some time had been doubling year by year.

The progress of Vespa sales seemed unstoppable, but it wasn't.

However, the first crisis of the scooter industry, which coincided with the requirement in 1961 of a driving license for two-wheeled vehicles, injected new life into the strongest, as so often happens. Upon Enrico Piaggio's death in 1965, three and a half million Vespas had been manufactured in Italy.

Models sported drainpipe pants, sneakers and printed blouses made of synthetic fibers. Two years after this highly modern 1960 calendar, an all-white Vespa with a lot of chrome work and a pearl-gray saddle was launched.

The hypnotic flow along the line

Francesco Lanzara, a Piaggio's general manager, facing a Rotary Club audience in December 1957, stated, "American production specialists say every piece specially made is a special enemy—and we've had to make a lot of enemies"; 1,457 to be exact, on a Vespa 150 as the company magazine pointed out elsewhere. "It's the engineer's job to cut them down to as few as possible."

Only inflexible standardization and substantial investment can guarantee the quality of the end product, he added; once the standard is set, according to conventional wisdom, "go on repeating it with no unprogrammed changes."

"Once quality drops, rhythm falls and stalls and delays crop up, and rhythm is what productivity is all about, the indispensable tool of the producing worker, the mainstay of his earnings," Lanzara said. Consequently, "Systems of remuneration structuring are being constantly perfected … and the factory you have just visited can be safely said to have reached a level of modernity in this area, too, which is studied and sometimes admired by visitors from both home and abroad."

Concluding, the general manager noted that a company is healthy and prosperous "if the industrialist has courage, intuition, organizational skill, as well as faith in his job and in the usefulness of his efforts and of his workers.

"If he has faith in the future, it doesn't matter if, as in 1945 and '46, it looks more dark and uncertain than it eventually turns out to be."

Francesco Lanzara (1914-90) professor at Pisa University, manager of the Piaggio factory and chairman of the Confederation of Pisa Industrialists, shows a group of visitors the metal body of a scooter as it goes into the next stage of production.

The factory is organized along the same lines as large-scale automobile manufacture with modern-day, complete-cycle systems of productivity and synchronized conveyance and assembly. The cycle, starting from steel sheeting, aluminum ingots and pig iron, and steel, is carried out in five big production workshops functioning as a single synchronized unit linked by overhead conveyance systems that feed the shops and absorb their output, shunting the various completed components to the assembly line. In the sheet metal workshop, presses of up to 500 tons produce the molds of the frame, then built on automatic production lines using electronically controlled and commanded welding machines. Every two minutes a frame is conveyed overhead to the paint and assembly shops. The foundry uses the modern-day technique of pressure die-casting; the castings produced are moved by the conveyance system over the heads of the assembly workers in the engineering shop in accordance with a rhythmic distribution program. The engineering processes take place in two workshops: one makes the gearing and the other the engine. Many machines were expressly designed and built for Piaggio by companies in both Italy and abroad in accordance with the most advanced concepts in automation. All the components of the gearing and the completed engine come together, synchronized with the frame, to the main assembly lines.

Breve notizia sullo stabilimento di Pontedera
[Brief notes on the Pontedera factory] **March 26, 1956**

118

The long strike of 1962 showed the trade union eager to be involved in the company's strategic decisions.

The streets of Pontedera see Vespas head the May Day celebration parade during a season of major conflict and expansion. The future Italy of affluence and youth revolt, revolution in customs and fierce social dispute had its roots here.

Rhythm, Lanzara stressed, was "the constant, even unceasing flow of the assembly line: no jumps or jolts and no stops."

Fifteen hundred "piaggists" turned out 1650 vehicles a month in 1948. Just a few years later 4000 "unit workers" managed no less than 13,000 pieces—undeniably a lot and the sign of an excellent state of affairs according to the management or a now unbearable one according to others.

Parallel development between national reality and company life can be seen here also. Between 1953 and 1960 national industrial production all but doubled and worker productivity increased by 60 percent while salaries had moved however slightly in the opposite direction.

In less than a year after the big party celebrated in Viale Rinaldo Piaggio, the triumphal statistics of the Vespa were brandished by FIOM, the metalworkers' union, to launch another—and this time more ambitious—broadside by publishing the so-called Green Paper on "matching technical progress and increased labor output with substantial improvements for all workers."

The detailed report with the well-meaning title—in which a well-documented item-by-item cost-benefit analysis was conducted that made no bones about setting Innocenti as the wage model and the example to be followed—resulted in the struggle for "a lira for each Vespa," with the bitterest clashes of the Sixties already looming on the horizon.

"The Piaggio family" as Bob Considine wrote in a New York magazine article in 1956 "has found an answer to Italian Communism by giving birth to this highly practical single-cylinder means of transport that can do 100 miles on a single gallon of fuel."

A small car on two wheels

The new VESPA G.L. offers some further improvements that make the scooter still more confortable.

- **Four speed gearbox,** for greater acceleration and better performances

- Lighting equipment of improved photometric characteristics.

- 10th inches wheels to secure a great stability on corrugated and ice-covered roads.

- New cromed of tail light with stop - light of higher luminous intensity

MORE POWERFUL AND BRILLIANT ENGINE

Technological innovation was one of the features Vespa was highlighting most in its promotion campaign in Italy and abroad.

By comparison with the traditional configuration, the rotary distribution (below) among other things ensured excellent cooling and the most effective lubrication of the connecting rod big-end bearing.

2-stroke innovation

"The two-stroke engine didn't look as though its classic configuration could be much improved but confidence in the engine kept us looking and we were eventually successful: the new rotary-type of distribution we developed made the new Vespa 150 engine something truly revolutionary" as Vittorio Casini, the engineer in charge of the Servizio Tecnico Esperienze e Prove [Technical Experience and Testing Department], wrote in April 1959. So it did have a new configuration that resolved a number of long-standing, thorny problems.

The carburetor was assembled directly on the sump, which enabled the air-intake duct to be done away with. This reduced resistance to the gas flow.

The sump gas intake port was now placed just by one of the driving shaft counterweights and was opened and closed depending on the position the latter was in. This enabled the combustion chamber to be filled better, eliminating backflow to the carburetor and increasing engine performance. Using slightly more technical language, the distribution diagram was no longer necessarily symmetrical with respect to dead center as it is in traditional systems where the port is opened and closed by the piston, but can be determined in the design stage to get the best volumetric yield from the pump.

The gas now flowed directly onto the connecting rod big-end, the traditional weak point, giving improved cooling and lubrication to the bearing. This enabled the mixture to be thinned from 5 percent to a cheaper and intrinsically cleaner 2 percent causing less combustion chamber coking and less exhaust smoke.

This was a splendid development which, besides, became more effective as engine temperature rose, allowing proper separation of oil from gasoline. This explains why the test riders, despite driving miles and miles, couldn't find anything wrong, whereas in the very first production series the big-end bearing inexplicably wore out in the most normal town-traffic conditions. This was an apparently insoluble puzzle, as engineer Carlo Doveri recalls, which was eventually got round by carrying out a number of exacting changes.

But that wasn't all.

The rotary distribution axed fuel consumption by 10 percent and gave the engine more elasticity. The technicians found a "very flat efficiency curve": the engine elasticity factor rose by 15 percent, thus eliminating, for now at least, the need for a four-speed gearbox.

For millions of new users riding a post 1960 Vespa meant cheaper running costs and a zippier engine in acceleration or on hills.

And all this, Vittorio Casini emphasized, "was done without adding a single piece to the engine but just honing the performance of what there was to the job on hand."

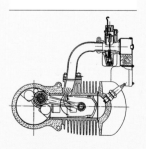

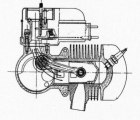

GET VESPA'D!

A highly successful and freehand version of the French original, "Vespizzatevi" ["Get Vespa'd"] became part of everyday language and in turn was translated in many foreign ad campaigns of those years.

"Ne courrez plus ... roulez Vespa ... roulez Vespa." This invitation, one would think would inject some calm into the frenzy, as the happy couple puttered away: "he" with his hat and pipe, "she" with her skirt and windswept, medium-length hair. All the while the crowd ran alongside—lots of stylized, black legs round about pounding the tarmac— in Villemont's poster of 1954.

All this was translated with a certain amount of latitude and some genius: "Don't run ... Get Vespa'd!" The message was reiterated, with a shade less graphic elegance, in an Italian poster soon after: "Get Vespa'd, if you want to get to work relaxed." And since this, observed the *Salesman's Newsletter*, "meant more time for workers to rest as well as costing them less fatigue,

there could be no doubt that bosses, if faced with this issue in an intelligent way, would be interested in purchasing significant numbers of scooters." Why not?

"Get Vespa'd for work and play." But the duo advertising the scooter, fresh as a couple of daisies, and with a vaguely Nordic, countrified look are nowhere near anything that looks like work. Firstly they take it easy— she offers her consort a lunch basket without getting off the scooter—then they set off looking for all the world like a pair on their way to a rural party complete with fireworks and accordions—on a Vespa of course.

The neologism took root in common parlance.

It is curious that almost fifty years later, the word *Vespa'd* has disappeared from the dictionaries. But still firmly rooted is the word *Vespa*, as well as *Vespino* ("little

The original ad by Bernard Villemot (1911–89), a highly original billboard artist who loved to say how much Henri Matisse, among others, influenced his work.

Vespa"), *Vespista* ("Vespa driver"), *Vespistico* (adjective: "concerning the Vespa") and also *Vespone* ("big Vespa"): "a motor scooter with cylinders and size superior to those of the Vespa" reads the entry in the *Sabatini Coletti Dictionary of Italian* or, as it appears in the long established Devoto-Oli *Italian Dictionary*: "Vespa with cylinder capacity of 200 cm."

Vespa in heaven and paradise on earth

The *style français* noted for its "good taste and elegance" can be seen in the Savignac illustration with a Vespa rampant on a yellow background or in the originality of the advertising campaigns like the one in 1958 when illustrated French magazines cheerfully celebrated the first day of spring with a full-color ad with a circulation of five million, scented with lily of the valley.

Vespa was considered deserving of the collaboration of people of stature like Erberto Carboni, a graphic artist and architect well-known in the history of Italian design, not to mention the Turin designer Sandro Scarsi famed for his innovative vivacity of ideas, and put its in-house communication and graphic department to the test on promotion and advertising, at least up to the end of the Sixties.

This was the birthplace of the campaigns, where billboard projects and newspaper ads were developed as well as the exhaustive documentation fed through agencies and service centers, obviously with all the alternatives and in all the necessary languages.

A few years after the beginning of the advertising campaigns that kept the slogan going, illustrator Sandro Scarsi made a contribution in his highly personal idiom, and in the strong colors characteristic of his work.

Raymond Savignac is one of the giants of the Vespa advertising campaigns. From 1933 he produced work for Perrier, Dunlop, Monsavon, Olivetti, Pirelli and the daily newspaper *Il Giorno* among others. He also worked for Vichy, Renault and Bic and was involved in cinema production. The Italian postal service derived the stamp and cancellation for Vespa's 50th anniversary in 1966 from his "Vespa towards the sun" poster.

Erberto Carboni (1899–1984) created some of the most renowned campaigns for food manufacturers Pavesi and Bertolli, and much of the RAI's (Italian State Broadcasting Corporation) graphic work. His was the poster "In tutto il mondo Vespa" ["Vespa the world over"].

The sales management defined this poster as "motivational" and in '61 suggested it be used in "underdeveloped areas"; at the same time, it tried bus advertising.

Right: "A paradise for two" was the new spirit of youth announced in spring 1962.

in tutto il mondo

Vespa

Throughout years and beyond, countless brochures were prepared for distribution in thousands upon thousands of copies for the sale points and every opportunity that arose. Elegant, bejeweled feminine hands—we had seen them earlier—proffered the first Vespa 98 as though it were a precious stone. In the ad that followed, the beautiful black background cover developed, in the subsequent pages, into stylized comic strips praising the small, interchangeable wheels, the monocoque body, the shielded engine and many more "auto-style," meaning modern-day, features the scooter could boast.

"Everyone knows what a Vespa is" crops up elsewhere in '58 "but not everyone knows … " that the number of units produced in ten years borders on the unbelievable. Put together it could power a wartime navy or supply enough energy to light up the whole of Italy, France and Austria combined or form a line that would stretch unbroken from Milan Cathedral to Red Square. Famous personalities from Italy and abroad lent their names to the campaign in the pages of the glossy weeklies. In France the Vespa's elegant shape was spotlighted, while in new markets statistics were used to emphasize the vehicle's unsurpassable ease of use, underlining the importance of technical data in this period: it wasn't easy to avoid making constant mention of weight, horsepower and top speeds.

Marketing cemented the Vespa's shape in the imagination of the general public, exciting its curiosity and evoking ideas of freedom and wide-open spaces. The most innovative campaigns of the Sixties playing on

the power of slogans with a whiff of transgression and seemingly void of common sense were still to come, but with the "Get Vespa'd" campaign of 1954 they didn't seem at all far off.

But as a secret weapon in the daily skirmishes with traffic problems, Vespa stimulated the irony and humor of the ad men in the United Kingdom and Northern Europe. This was a feature carried over into the whole "low wheel" message—a playful touch, a bit ingenuous and stilted in the long run perhaps but endearing nonetheless and certainly in sympathy with the young, carefree, holiday-like atmosphere increasingly conveyed in the ads and captured by the public at large. From the very beginning it represented the idea of a car with two wheels for those who couldn't afford a four-wheeled one. There was a "he" and a "she" with kids. These parents were youngish but not juvenile. "To complete their happiness, all they need is a Vespa"; and indeed off they go again, set against the a yellow background smiling for the camera.

Surprisingly modern by comparison in both graphics and message was the "A paradise for two" campaign: "every trip, whether short or long, can turn into a rendezvous with happiness." The year was 1962 and the style was already different for a different public and a different world.

"Genuine Master" Vespas

Many personalities had their photographs taken for the pure enjoyment of it while sitting, wreathed in smiles, astride the world's best-known scooter. Louis Armstrong, Dominguín, Jimmy Durante, Italian sprinter Livio Berruti, and Lord Brabazon of Tara were among them as were stars of the screen like a seraphic-looking Henry Fonda, not to mention artist Oscar Kokoschka, who climbed onto a Vespa but never painted one—that is, to the best of our knowledge.

But Salvator Dalí painted *on* a Vespa.

The story goes that Antonio and Santiago, law students at Madrid University, set off for Italy hoping to get a private audience with the Pope, no less, and then board ship at Brindisi for Athens. However, before crossing the border into France, they stopped off at Cadaqués to pay homage to the artist, and their honest little sky-blue 150 was irremediably marked by the experience. Dalí

Some interesting forerunners: it was only 1955 but there was already a duo in the air astride an invisible Vespa, drawn by Leo Longanesi.

Oscar Kokoschka in Italy to receive the Premio Roma in 1960.

Thousands of miles after its fateful encounter, the Dalí Vespa was duly restored and put on view in the Piaggio Museum.

Renato Guttuso *The Trip by Vespa* (1957), oil on canvas paper, 42 x 42 inches, New York—John D. Rockefeller III collection.

set his signature on it, painting the name of his beloved Gala with a crown above it on the right-hand side panel.

A number of sketches the intensely Italian magazine *Il Borghese* published in 1955 showed just how blasé its editor-owner was. Leo Longanesi saw the Vespa as a woman, a silhouette from the Belle Époque with just a hint of the libertine. Another illustrator pictured a melancholy looking well-dressed gentleman on a Vespa chasing a pear dangling in front of his nose that hangs from the branch of a potted tree he's carrying. Next, the Vespa name meandered like a creeper turning into an arabesque.

John D. Rockefeller III's collection houses a beautiful Renato Guttuso canvas: *The Trip by Vespa* of 1957. In it, "she" in the foreground—they're seen from the back—with her legs folded to one side; leaning against

Writer, journalist and illustrator, Leo Longanesi (1905–57) was known not only for his publishing house and his membership in the editorial board of *Il Borghese* magazine, but also for a particular kind of graphic humor with its roots in the nineteenth century.

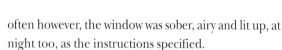

"he," a darker figure absorbed in driving, she leans against for shelter, and the white road below them carries them on and on.

The sales network …

There were four main branches—Milan, Turin, Genoa, Catania—and five sales management groups in Padua, Bologna, Florence, Naples and Rome, plus five hundred agencies, subagencies and minor branches and three thousand service stations all over Italy. Sales and after-sales service were the means of contact with the public. Showroom windows, quality of service, local promotional initiatives all had to reflect a coordinated, coherent image. Pontedera gave clear instructions.

"It is necessary that a Piaggio style exist, just as, today, an Olivetti style exists and a Necchi style is coming into existence" declared *Vespa Servizio* the sales staff newsletter. A consultancy department was set up to advise on how to dress showroom windows bringing to the streets of Italy examples of real scenarios for local agencies to reconstruct with Father Christmas's sledge pulled by a team of Vespas, or, in a corner setting, a lakeside campsite situation, complete with tent and scooter, both coming with a detailed layout scheme so anybody could reproduce the enchantment. If the more important showrooms so asked, they could prepare a "metaphysical window" with magical devices designed by Corradino D'Ascanio in person in which a Vespa perched on top on a jet of water or shot across a wire held in balance by a gyroscope hidden in the bodywork. More

often however, the window was sober, airy and lit up, at night too, as the instructions specified.

Communicating with the sales force was no small task involving, as it did, combining information on how export sales were going, the technical features of the new models, the most wide-ranging series of promotional initiatives launched by individual agents, together with the exact way to go about setting up a service workshop and its workbench, as well as a constant exhortation to get involved in promoting at local level—the fair, the carnival, local folklore shows of every kind and sports competitions: "But Vespa must always in any case be shown up in the best light … care must be taken not to link it with a second-rate team."

"The particular difficulty in assembling this delicate configuration," shown here in the shop window of the Milan 'La Rinascente,' "makes the participation of a mechanic from the factory in Pontedera essential." At the start of '59, the sales management made this latest Corradino D'Ascanio brainstorm available to the sales agents.

The enormous media impact of the events organized by Italy's Vespa Club as far back as the early Fifties was reflected in the steady increase in club membership: from 6,500 in 1950 to 15,561 in '53 and from 31,792 in 1956 to 50,810 in 1959 and to 61,327 just twelve months later.

In the wake of the redhead in the bathtub—Angie Dickinson, "America's most beautiful legs"—came actress Cristina Gaioni with her shocking-pink, pure nylon lingerie. In the mid-Sixties, the models appearing on the Piaggio calendar made way for stars of television and cinema.

... and the enchantment of the *Carosello* ads

At the end of 1959 *Vespa Servizio* published the results of an in-house poll on the advertising and promotion plan for the following year. In a nutshell it asked: "How would you have divided the budget over the various channels of information if you had been in charge?" Feedback from the people in daily contact with potential customers is a valuable resource.

From north to south through central Italy and in the islands too, everyone unanimously would have spent at least a quarter of the budget on *Carosello*: the television program at the forefront of everyone's imagination, which brought considerable influence to bear on the sales force. Next came the cinema "shorts,"

The actual items in the advertising and promotion budget for 1960 given by the company in percentage terms were: daily newspapers, 22 percent; magazines, 4.4 percent; technical journals, 3.2 percent; other publications, 2.3 percent. Vespa Club: printed materials, management, excursions, 16.7 percent. Advertising materials, 11.6 percent; cinema, 8 percent; roadside billboards, 8 percent; competitions, discounts, complimentary giveaways, 6.8 percent. Branch offices, 5.4 percent. The *Piaggio* and *Vespa Servizio* magazines 4.2 percent. Fairs and exhibitions, 3 percent; sales organization support, 2 percent. Miscellaneous, 2.4 percent.

The 1960 Rome Olympics were a special showcase for Italian-made products. More than one hundred Vespas and ten *Apes* were made available to the athletes in the Olympic villages of Rome and Naples, where the yachting events were held. The scooter is pictured with Italian middleweight Nino Benvenuti or with Harry Jerome from Canada, record holder for 100 meters (10 seconds), on the pillion.

common at the time, then the national dailies although this latter only in the more advanced north of the country. That aside, third place was taken by the Vespa Club races: the aggressive promotional machine perfected by Tassinari, considered effective in the north (8 percent among regional and national competitions) was a real ace up the south's sleeve that would have given it a fourth of the whole promotional budget.

Today, the prevalence of national over regional dailies is normal. In 1959, according to the sales force's preferences, in the north the preference was almost 2-to-1, although in the center of the country they ran neck and neck, and in the south the regionals were ahead. The advertising budget assigned a scanty 8 percent of all newspapers combined in the south, against 24 percent in the north. The islands, by contrast, got a reasonable 7 percent but for the local press only, with the national dailies there getting nothing.

At first, it seems odd to see so little advertising in women's magazines considering how Vespa had so often combined its image with women, not just in the Piaggio company calendars but also from the very first SARPI brochures, in 1946, that showed "her" very often in the driver's seat. It had been hoped "she" would have ridden off with ease, panache and skill testifying to the extreme ease of use the machine offered but the sales feedback seemed reluctant to see "her" as a potential customer.

At this point the management stepped in to say its piece on "the bone of contention: TV." The "goggle box" was more suitable for consumer goods purchased "consequent to what one's memory suggests which, if we may be excused the elementary psychological citation, draws from the subconscious."

"There are few products costing more than a few hundred lire with the sole exception of Singer and its sewing machines."

"And if we weren't afraid of being accused of back-biting we could also mention the competition who, some time ago, used *Carosello* without reaping much success from it … if we're not mistaken!"

The staging of the Martian was another classic. The little green men act as Santa's helpers in this 1954 Christmas shop-window scene inspired by American sci-fi cinema and by such a host of "sightings" that everybody felt spacebound.

CUL DE SAC

The French-made "petite voiture de grande classe" was ready to compete with the early compact cars. The novel configuration of the front suspension and the ease of accessibility to the battery by means of a sliding plate behind the false radiator grille, as well as other features, showed how original this "2 CV racée" really was.

Back in 1949, Enrico Piaggio had sent his general manager to the Paris Motor Show. Francesco Lanzara, attaching brochures and materials, reported on the event. "Obviously, we concentrated our attention on small-engine cars especially the Renault 4hp, the Citroen 2hp and the Dyna Panhard."

"Obviously," he said, because something along those lines was being talked about at Pontedera, the general feeling being that "compact cars like those manufactured in France don't exist in Italy."

Eight years later, again at the Paris Motor Show, Piaggio launched its new four-wheel Vespa, built in the Fourchambault facility for reasons of "suitability," surrounded by rumors of a tacit agreement with Fiat.

Vespa 400 on the new auto market

This was a small, new gem. Small, certainly: 9 feet long and a wheel-base of a mere 5.6 feet.

With two seats and little else there was the luggage to worry about, but you could also buy a model that seated four, as long as two were children or slim grown-ups: with the canvas hood rolled up, for its passengers it was like riding a motorbike. It was basic, functional, pretty, innovative and apparently set for great things in Europe's emerging compact car market.

It did fairly well, at least in France and Belgium (bearing in mind that France was Europe's biggest market) and in Italy, 30,000 vehicles produced by Piaggio between 1957 and '61 were sold despite the drawback of a sales network that had not been created with this kind of product in mind.

If the Italian nut seemed hard to crack because of the excessive power Fiat held, Germany was little different thanks to the overriding presence of BMW and others. Besides, German highways were dotted with Goggomobils, little vehicles with 300 cc or 400 cc, two-stroke engines of which no fewer than 300,000 units had been manufactured in a ten-year period by a scooter factory trying to make the great leap forward.

In the United States, the sales effort behind the Vespacar was considerable. There, it was seen as a

Vespa 400

1958

A two-stroke, two-cylinder 393 cc engine with rotating valve and three gears, with second and third synchronized, was extremely lively and could zip the Vespa 400 along at 54 mph.

The four-wheeled Vespa set itself out as a second car in France, at that time Europe's largest market in terms of registered vehicles and city cars. Therefore, and in accordance with company policy, particular care was taken of how it appeared to the female public from fashion magazines to its presentation on the Côte d'Azur as well as the layout in the Vespa GmbH brochures for Germany.

second vehicle. A micro-compact had to face competition from the gigantic used-car market, not to mention the prejudice it faced from the public "worried about the vehicle's size because it had never tried to figure out what a second car should be like … even though it would never be used on the freeway, never have to carry the whole family and never be used for long trips."

It was too small and too European.

"Why don't they develop a bigger version with a four-stroke engine?" wrote the agents in Massachusetts, California and Georgia, showing just how little they'd understood the idea.

None of this surprised Enrico Piaggio. "Apart from the present problems," he reminded Alessandro di

Since sales were sluggish, various promotional events were planned to work alongside commercial agreements with major automakers. Peugeot especially seemed interesting in integrating its range with the little Italian but nothing ever came of it.

From Stockholm to Monte Carlo in January '59. Of the four that left, three made it over the finish line in the under-1000 cc category—a noteworthy result even though two of the three failed to meet the time limit by just over one hour after no less than 2,035 miles.

Montezemolo of the Vespa Distributing Company, in Long Island, New York, in February 1960, "you know how I have always been rather pessimistic about the American vehicle market."

A few modifications were made in the finishing and, in 1961, production of a GT, four-speed version got started. A right-hand drive version designed for the United Kingdom market was left out.

Too late (or too early?)

"In 1953 and in 1955 too the Vespa 400 could really make a dream come true, technically not just a means of transport but a proper, well-designed car at an accessible price" commented the specialist German

magazine *Roller Mobil-Mot*, in September 1960.

"Built on five years of experience, it was designed and developed in 1952-53. In 1957 it was priced at some 4,000 DM ($2,400) with even the sales staff saying it was crazy. The Parisians used the 400 as a second car for the city but in West Germany there were only a couple hundred on the roads. Vespa could have launched its 400 in a big way in '55—at least in Italy—when the Fiat 600 failed to carry over the affection it had gained with the users of the Topolino ["Little mouse," a small, popular, pre-war compact car]. It should have been launched much earlier and maybe it would have won over most of the market which later went to the Fiat 500."

Maybe bad timing *was* the culprit.

"At the starting line, spectators and fellow competitors smiled at our daring. Halfway through the race they started to pay attention. At the finish line, they were applauding."

(The Vespa 400 at the 28th International Monte Carlo Rally.)

Shortly after it was underway, the P3 project was substantially updated with many innovations including a single gull-wing door. The photograph compares it with the Fiat 600. Below, the scale model.

The original project (1966), in the lower left-hand drawing, had sliding lateral doors.

Four wheels and a faux pas

Vehicles shorter than 9 feet, whether private cars or mini-cabs, or cars to rent by the hour but in any case falling within certain well-defined security limits. An innovative road network, outside city centers at least, with underpasses in place of crossroads. Multi-story car parks like the German Parkhaus, again based on the 9-foot standard, intended as a source of income for local municipalities, and shuttle trains for out-of-town commuters. The very low price of these micro-vehicles guaranteed by massive-scale production runs without jeopardizing security or reliability in any way.

The Corriere della Sera *newspaper of 11 September '64 broached the traffic problem with commendable anticipation publishing an article signed by Pio Manzù, a young, up-and-coming designer whose pen was to give birth to the Fiat 127 just a few years later.*

In this direction, the project thought up by Carlo Doveri, who'd already managed the Vespa 400 project, and perfected by Piaggio in 1966 seemed to have boundless potential.

Just under 9 feet by just under 4 feet–20 inches shorter than the Fiat 600 and four inches shorter than the Fiat 500—the P3 gave its two occupants more space.

A functional luggage compartment, improved suspension to make the best use of space, innovative sliding doors "a real plus point for the client" reads the note put out by the planning office and "tackling the added construction problems it will evidently cause seems a reasonable proposition."

The choice of a two-cylinder liquid-cooled engine would hopefully have solved the recurring problems of the Vespa 400 and thought was given to developing a four-stroke engine giving 20 hp against the 12 of the earlier version.

But on 8 March '66, the chairman informed the general manager Francesco Lanzara that the project would clash with the company development directives "especially because" wrote Umberto Agnelli "over and above the issues still not clarified there is to be added the certainty that Fiat's next program includes replacing the present 500."

UNDER OTHER SKIES

In the early Sixties you could rent a Vespa in Tahiti. British, Salvadorean and South Rhodesian (now Zimbabwean) police used them. It could be seen on the streets of Phnom Penh, and proudly shown off at the feet of Oscar Niemeyer's skyscrapers in Brasilia. But—as the company magazine pointed out—if Moscow, Idaho boasted just one Vespa "the real Moscow had a lot more but they were all counterfeit."

From Russia without honor

The "motoroller," which appeared on the pages of Moscow's daily newspaper *Izvestia* and was produced in the Kirov district, looked like a Vespa 150 GS. Presented to Moscow's public during the Agricultural and Industrial Fair of June '57, it was immediately reviewed in *Svet Motoru*, a Czechoslovak motorcycling magazine.

Infinite effort had gone into adapting Corradino D'Ascanio's project to local needs—meaning the precariousness of the Soviet road network. Just slightly more bulky and heavy, but powered by 5.5 horsepower instead of the GS's 8 horsepower, the Viatka had a sturdier electric circuit and a massive adjustable headlight. The tool-and spare-parts box was a substantial, fully-equipped repair kit complete with piston rings and carburetor jets; it had no spare wheel but a tire repair kit and a hand pump. It was curious that the large air-filter disappeared just as the GS flywheel had been done away with, given the lack of tarred roads in country areas. Some 50,000 units a year were planned with, obviously, no

"Batron, je veux acheder une Bespa!" We're in the far-off year 1957 when letters of this tone could still be seen in the Piaggio magazine. "Beyond Leopoldville, in the bush, where you come across money-hungry whites, missionaries in search of souls to save and melancholy blacks, I found among the most primitive tools the happiest of all mechanical animals that has come to light in recent years: the Vespa. Easy to ride over these earthquake-ruined, burned and muddy roads, their black riders 'understand' and dominate them; two very difficult things for them to do, having only just learned the use of the wheel and the alphabet in the last seventy or eighty years."

LO SCOOTER PIU' VENDUTO NEL MONDO

Una produzione giornaliera di oltre 1300 Vespa viene diffusa in 114 Paesi

LO SCOOTER PREFERITO DAGLI ITALIANI

Nel 1959 ogni 100 acquirenti di scooters, di tutte le marche e cilindrate, immatricolati in Italia, 61 hanno scelto la Vespa

acknowledgment to the Italian parent company.

At the end of the Sixties appeared the New Viatka—completely new; unluckily for it, one is tempted to add. A cross between a Lambretta and a Vespa, with some resemblance to the Italo-American Topper Harley Davidson, it was powered by a three-speed 150 cc engine with a chain end drive. It was infinitely heavier, slower and thirstier for fuel than the beautiful little Italian from the other side of the Iron Curtain.

Vespa and the racing champion

The Vespa exported regularly to about a hundred countries, and the 1962 quota of 70,000 doubled its total exports compared to '55. Vespa's fortune on international markets was somewhat seesaw in nature despite an overall constant trend in growth and a number of assembly plants had been built in various parts of the world outside Europe.

Detailed exploration had been going on for some time among metalworking and engineering companies in the Buenos Aires and Rosario regions to assess the feasibility of a factory. Frequent world race-car champion Manuel Fangio who was Piaggio's representative there had direct access to Enrico Piaggio and the relationship, though somewhat variable, was satisfactory to both. But reproducing the required network of outside suppliers wasn't quite so easy at these latitudes—working systems were often different, using outdated technology with inadequate quality standards; in short, the area had a relatively poor industrial fabric. The decision

forced upon other Italian motorcycle producers such as Gilera was for almost total self-sufficiency: "with the exception of very little, everything is to be imported or made in house." The management from this Milan-area manufacturer on loan to Argentina were peremptory on the matter. "This was the only way," in their view, "to sidestep disappointment and line halts because of local suppliers that are, save few exceptions, untrustworthy or incapable."

The case of Panauto is singular.

With a 25 percent stake held by Pontedera, factory start-up took place in 1958 in Santa Cruz, in the Brazilian state of Rio de Janeiro. Government restrictions on imports meant "nationalizing" the product requiring an "almost total" manufacture of the four-speed 150

With no acknowledgment to Piaggio or Corradino D'Ascanio, Russia's viatka looked like the offspring of a multitude of parents: "La Viatka n'est qu'une copie servile de la Vespa Française" ["The Viatka is nothing but a cheap copy of the French Vespa"], or so the French press broke the news.

A well-conserved example of the derivative Soviet scooter (G. Notari collection).

In 1956, Manuel Fangio visits Pontedera. He met Enrico Piaggio and visited the factory with managing director Francesco Lanzara and had the project explained to him in detail by D'Ascanio himself.

In every part of the world, competition between the two great Italian manufacturers was often to the fore. It was ironic that in Brazil, the Vespa became a *lambreta*, the word for "scooter."

Daniel Sauvage, after 15,500 miles round the Mediterranean with his wife Françoise on a Vespa, had no qualms about using the woman fakir Nadia Jo to promote his book *Ma Vespa, ma femme et moi* published in 1956.

which, in 1960, succeeded the Vespa 125, the first model to be produced. Despite this, a number of components, such as the carburetor and the dynamo flywheel, were still produced in Italy. In the early years, "the Vespa sold by itself" but as early as 1963 the factory manager was reporting the serious local economic situation, the substantial hard-currency indebtedness of the company and the increasing difficulty of the market. The political instability that had been dogging the country for some time was to prove the coup-de-grace for Piaggio's Brazilian adventure, at least for the moment.

So go east, young man! Bajaj Auto Ltd. of Mumbai was to be a very different story. The contract was signed in 1961 and to this day the Indian Vespa is alive and very much kicking despite the difficulties in mutual understanding. The distances between the two worlds looked insurmountable at times and the differences irresolvable—but of this more later.

Pictures from around the world

The Vespa universe is chock-a-block with heroes. In over half a century of scootering there was always someone, burning with competitive ardor, foolhardiness and the spirit of adventure, ready to throw himself into the most daring ventures.

A French soldier declared the Vespa to be the best way of getting back to France from its colony in Indochina, and news of this got back to Pontedera. In the summer of '57, a Brussels photographer, Victor Englebert, took the road south and didn't stop till he reached Cape Town. He

managed it virtually on a shoestring: 30,000 francs ($5,300) and 180 gallons of fuel for a four-month vacation.

The great motorcycling champion and amphibious scooter enthusiast nonpareil Georges "Jojo" Monneret had done the short hop from Paris to London only a few years before. On arriving in the customs shed in Calais, he set his Vespa on top of a 16-foot-by-6-foot double-hull raft, coupled his 125 engine to the propeller shaft and set off escorted by a fishing boat. The first attempt failed because he collided with a tree trunk halfway across and damaged the transmission. The second attempt, however, using a powerful three blade propeller, was successful and in five and a half hours he landed at Dover and from there carried on in orthodox trim to Trafalgar Square.

Facing page: group photograph in front of the Caodaist temple in Tây-Ninh, Vietnam.

Right to your door—"White Crane saké delivery" is written on the typical blue apron worn by shop assistants. The luggage rack holds the traditional wooden barrel used only for New Year celebrations or for weddings.

Three years later he was in Paris presenting Captain Dupuy, representing the Ministère du Sahara et des Départements et Territoires d'Outre-mer, a symbolic can of "French" petrol drawn from the Hassi Messaoud oil-well after having run his "Raid du Petrole."

Others took on a different challenge, this time in a race between various types of vehicles in the middle of rush-hour traffic in Manhattan. Victory was the scooter's, ridden by Betty Kent, a total unknown, followed by a taxi a couple of seconds later, then a limo three minutes after that. The horse and carriage rolled in much later, and last to arrive was pedestrian Kyle Rote, captain of the New York Giants.

"Clerics all over the world are going modern," read the heading in the *Piaggio* magazine for a photo essay

The incredible amphibian Vespa touches land at Dover after sailing five and a half hours: 20 miles in second gear on 4 gallons of fuel mixture but the scooter had surprisingly good sea legs keeping trim on the waves.

Two terribly hip young Americans in Bangkok in the summer of 1961, subjected to puzzled stares while posing for the *Piaggio* magazine.

Opposite: then fifty-one years old, Monneret completes his first 2,100 miles between France and Algeria during the 1959 Eurovespa Rally.

"Clean living under difficult circumstances": the motto inspiring a movement still in its infancy (1959) points to the elite spirit behind these Modernists. All this had very little in common with the gang violence that exploded in 1964–65.

of prelates on scooters "just as long as they don't say we're stirring up the old question of reformers or the much more recent issue of worker priests for goodness' sake."

But this two-wheeled troupe wasn't just navigators, heroes, lunatics and saints. A new urban aristocracy had emerged among young people in the United Kingdom. Their ranks were soon to swell, and the Italian scooter was adopted as their badge of identity.

Mods and rockers: the first wave

Be cool, neat, sharp, hip and smart: this was the order of the day for "teenagers," itself a neologism in the late Fifties. Forget the dusty deadness of British conformity with its extenuating, never-ending rituals, its class men-

tality and its narrow-minded domestic shabbiness.

Modernity! Modernists! The Mods, as *Melody Maker* called them, brought in more a style than a substance that was nonetheless vital, emancipating and sincere.

Children of the petty bourgeoisie, kids growing up in working-class families that could afford something extra, they could identify only with others in their group.

Mods stood out for their dress code and dress codes can turn into a real obsession: dark, made-to-measure suits with narrow trousers, ankle boots or low-cut shoes—black, white, red or even two-tone with laces and rubber soles—pullovers, often with stripes, sometimes 4 inches wide, with clashing colors. Later on Prince of Wales check came into fashion, then Levis, first bought from the GIs based outside London, and

"It used to be the Young Ones... then it was the Wild Ones. Now it's Mods and Rockers. A few young idiots use violence in seaside towns and the next thing you know, Beat stars are being asked to comment on these riots. Why? Why not ask teenage butchers? Or teenage grocers? Or teenage rat-catchers? Before you know it, the young rioters will be called Beat fans.

Lay off young people's music. Like long hair, it's harmless until the knockers get to work."

(from *Melody Maker*, May 30, 1964).

The magazine that tells you what's on and where to go in London.
August 17-23 1979 No.487 35p

Time Out

Striking a familiar Chord.

This picture was taken last week, not in 1965. Inside Phil Shaw dusts off his parka, talks with The Chords and checks out the Mod Revival.

from 1960 onwards a Gitane cigarette dangling from the corner of the mouth like Jean-Paul Belmondo. This was all stuff for guys. The girls were just there to look good.

Their music was recognizable too. A Mod listened only to R&B and went to the clubs in Soho. The heart of a real Mod managed to beat to the Stones but only just, and they hated the Beatles. Muddy Waters and Chuck Berry, though, figured high, until the real "Mod bands" came along: the Small Faces and then High Numbers, later to become the Who. But his heart really raced to the sound of a two-stroke single cylinder.

That's the way it was: an Italian scooter, be it Vespa or Lambretta was part of a real Mod's soul. The scooter stood for style, modernity, elegance, passion for foreign things, individuality, a canvas for creative spirits to paint on: a Vespa GS, the best of the best, could be made into a rolling exhibition of rear-view mirrors, at night a circus of lamps and lights, it could be full of chrome work and the windscreen often bore the owner's name and address.

After 1964 and the battles with the sordid, greasy rockers who had absolutely no style at all, something changed. The group turned into a pack and the scooter started to be associated with juveniles of the delinquent variety. After '66, when the range of scooters was still ballooning out, sales crashed through the floor. Apart from that, the youth scene was moving on, the times they were a-changing, and the hippies were about to appear on the horizon.

The passion of Anthony Quinn an "American" from Chihuahua in Mexico on his way to fame. His story was a fairy tale. Born into a poor family he won a scholarship and became a pupil of Frank Lloyd Wright, the man who suggested he go to acting classes to regain fluency after a minor operation to correct a speech defect.

"That Oscar that Hepburn won in 1953 for *Roman Holiday* should have gone to the Vespa, because while Gregory Peck was courting Hepburn, the rest of the world was falling in love with the other 'she'" noted *Forbes*, America's renowned financial magazine, and, here at least, authoritative observer of custom.

The incomparable grace of the 24-year-old Audrey Hepburn by the side of a splendid Gregory Peck set the world's heart beating faster, but their image is irrevocably tied to that little 125 scooter painted metallic green—as far as the black-and-white film shows color.

This William Wyler film will always undeniably be *the* Vespa film and the greatest (but not the only) contribution to cementing the image of that era.

The long catwalk for the Vespa and sidekicks

It was San Girolamo's Day when on that 1949 *Domenica d'agosto* [August Sunday] a group made up of youngsters on bicycles, a taxi and some cars, not to mention the Vespa making its debut, set off along the Cristoforo Colombo highway for the Ostia beach on the Roman coast. Director Luciano Emmer set a young Marcello Mastroianni on the scene in his first leading role as a traffic cop wearing a pith helmet with his voice dubbed by Alberto Sordi.

From then on, the Vespa was seen on and off in films of all kinds and qualities. "If our calculations are right, a Vespa has made a major appearance in no fewer than 64 films," a surprising statistic, the manufacturer probably noted in Sprin 1962.

The two of them, Marcello and the Vespa, were often to meet again on the set.

In 1959, when Anita Ekberg made her triumphal entrance hounded by journalists and photographers on their scooters, Mastroianni didn't lose his cool. Yet little time would pass before she was to be driven down the narrow streets of the Eternal City in a British sports car leaving paparazzi and all the other hangers-on in their wake.

The blonde Sylvia-Anita, the petulant Hollywood diva and unaware symbol of absolute femininity, was unattainable, even for whoever jumped after her into the Trevi Fountain whose jets were soon quietened in the never-ending sleepless nights of *La Dolce Vita*.

> "The Vespa did everything we couldn't: travel the world, race on race tracks and hobnob with actors and actresses."

(from *Those of the Vespa*)

Six years after William Wyler's film, in a very different Italy, Marcello Mastroianni lives out his untidy existence in the heart of Roman life. And then comes Sylvia from the USA, almost as though it was another planet, a blond, sumptuous Anita Ekberg (lower left) on her way to Rome.

Cinema's most famous Vespa (right). A delightful, incognito princess tries out her driving skills in the center of Rome and runs over a hawker and his cart and then into street artists' easels in Via Margutta.

Ernest Hemingway is quoted as saying of his friend Gary Cooper: "If they invented a character like him nobody would believe it: he's too good to be true."

John Wayne relaxing on a Vespa.

The young Henry Fonda, looking even more glowing and elegant than usual.

Other major films with Vespa's by Italian directors

Bolognini's *La notte brava* was based on "Ragazzi di vita" ("The Ragazzi"), written by Pier Paolo Pasolini who then cast Franco Citti as Anna Magnani's protector in *Mamma Roma* and had him run around the capital's streets on a Vespa in the opening scenes.

Then there was Luchino Visconti, in *Bellissima,* from 1951, who chose a Vespa on which the small-time swindler, played by Walter Chiari, would burn the savings of the character pivotal to the whole film, Maddalena Cecconi, played by a superb Magnani.

Then came *Belle ma povere*, the 1957 Dino Risi film, sequel to the better-known *Poveri ma belli* and prelude to *Poveri milionari*. Romolo and Salvatore, one a lifeguard

That unequaled performer personifying Italian social custom, Alberto Sordi, takes to the road with Aldo Fabrizi on the pillion (1956). Sordi, who was to chalk up an impressive list of film performances, had already appeared in Fellini's *I Vitelloni*, *Un Giorno in Pretura* directed by Steno and Monicelli's *Un eroe dei nostri tempi*. In '55, Harry Truman invited him to Kansas City after his acclaimed performance as Nando Moriconi in *Un Americano a Roma*.

in a lido on the Tiber and the other a record shop assistant, are friends but rivals in love, and they become brothers-in-law after marrying each others' sisters. Then the shades of neorealism fade into the spirit of the play and, in the last of the series, Maurizio Arena loses his memory after being run over by a showy and very wealthy Sylva Koscina. In the meantime "she," the Vespa, is on proud show from the first billboard of the trilogy on.

That was also the year Alberto Lattuada filmed *Guendalina*, a "pretty, clever little play that weaves the first torments of adolescent love into the hypocrisy of the stereotyped couple only concerned in keeping up appearances": in telling the story of the daughter from a good family and her friends in the long Viareggio summer, the scooter inevitably became one of the main characters and a means of amorous seduction, a tale that repeats itself endlessly along that very same coast to this day.

The next step forward leads us to the beach films and the musicals. Often they were mere flimsy pretexts with non-existent scripts to show off the popular singer of the day. On the other hand, it is fun to see Adriano Celentano alongside Chet Baker with Mina and Peppino di Capri, Joe Sentieri and Marilú Tolo, all together in the 1960 film *Urlatori alla sbarra*.

Through this first series of images can be seen the beginnings of a country starting to grow.

After having been the central figure in the trilogy starting with *Poveri ma belli*, Maurizio Arena was a movie director and leading man in 1960. Also in the cast of *Il principe fusto*, stigmatized as the "poor man's version of *La Dolce Vita*," was Catia Karo, shown here on the pillion.

Ben-Hur and Messala, also known as Charlton Heston and Stephen Boyd, on the set of the $14 million 1959 blockbuster, *Ben-Hur, which* won eleven Oscars. The production involved six years of work and six months of shooting in Italy and a chariot race in the Circus Maximus, a milestone in cinema history.

Dino Paul Crocetti passed into the history of show business as Dean Martin. Already a successful crooner, he made his debut in the cinema as a duo with Jerry Lewis. His first film after the breakup of the pair—*Ten Thousand Bedrooms*, a mediocre film in comparison to the next ones in which, among other things, he won an Oscar (*Rio Bravo*, 1959)—was shot in Rome.

142

A movie that started with great ambitions but met with a poor reception from the public and critics, *A Farewell to Arms* is from 1957: Rock Hudson rides a model with the headlight at the center of the handlebar.

The screen of youth

Les Tricheurs, like Laurent Terzieff, rode their Vespas up and down the streets of Paris: the rebels without a cause of Saint-Germain-des Pres can already be seen careening towards a tragic end to the music of Dizzy Gillespie and Oscar Peterson.

The ideas behind the varying worlds of youth meet and show up on the screen in different epochs and with different stories to tell with, in common, the unmistakable sign of autonomy and freedom that Vespa has represented for more than a generation. It came back at the end of the Seventies with the revival of the Mods phenomenon in *Quadrophenia* where Sting plays Ace Face, the incomparable gang leader astride his splendid GS.

The film reflects the cultural phenomenon at least a year later than when the young "modernists" came on the scene, in a London where the Chords play the Who, and Pete Townshend co-authored the script bringing to the screen scenes he had experienced first-hand some years previously.

Meanwhile, Vespa, with impeccable timing, launched a model that was to enjoy enormous success not only in the United Kingdom: the PX series has sold two million units worldwide and still going strong today. The glossy "White Duke," alias David Bowie, in 1986 too brought vintage models to the screen in reconstructing the swinging London of his beginnings under the direction of Julian Temple in *Absolute Beginners*, an enjoyable and lively film with an excellent soundtrack.

The marriage of Lucia Bosè with bullfighter Dominguín (1956)—here we see them in Rome with Villa Medici in the background—marked a period of almost total interruption of her career as an actress. From 1968 to '76 she returned again to work with Fellini, the Taviani brothers, Mauro Bolognini and Liliana Cavani.

Jessica—that is, Angie Dickinson—is a beautiful American midwife, an especially attractive widow who practices her profession in the Sicilian provinces. She travels from one village to another aboard a Vespa—and that's enough to start tongues wagging.

Beside Broderick Crawford, in 1955, Giulietta Masina starred in *Il bidone*. In the history of Fellini's films this movie, not highly appreciated in Italy but famous in France, takes its place between *La strada*, from the previous year, and *Le notti di Cabiria* from '57.

In his free time between shots of *Exodus* (1960) in Israel, Paul Newman loved to explore the countryside riding a Vespa; but he prohibited his wife, Joanne Woodward, from doing the same, on the grounds that it was unsuitable for her and too dangerous.

In 1979, Sting was the symbol of a Mod revival that had started in Britain. Franc Roddam's film *Quadrophenia* became a milestone so much so that among the in crowd, the initials "B.Q." stood for "Before *Quadrophenia*."

A pause on the set of *102 Dalmatians*, with trained puppies and a brand-new Vespa ET making its debut on the big screen.

A 180 SS able to dive under water and fly in the air equipped with radar and all the necessary armaments: *Dick Smart*

2007, directed by Franco Prosperi in 1967 with Duccio Tessari's screenplay, portrayed a likable, second-rate James Bond.

The series, and Vespa's, appearances on the big screen become countless.

Also worthy of mention are *Of Love and Shadows* with Antonio Banderas directed by Betty Kaplan in 1994, and *The Talented Mr. Ripley* by Anthony Minghella (1999).

Unexpectedly, the Vespa ET put in an appearance in one of Disney's recent productions, *102 Dalmatians*.

But earlier, in '73, just after the titles, Terry "Toad" Fields, the bumbler of the group in *American Graffiti*, risked disaster parking a brand-new 160 GS beside Mel's Drive-In. George Lucas's film brings us back to the early Sixties, on the other side of the ocean.

Regardless of time, the Vespa myth in the cinema is irrevocably linked to the image of Audrey Hepburn. The charity benefit auction named after the actress was held in '99 in Geneva. Besides jewelry and evening gowns, a Vespa ET fell under Christie's hammer almost fifty years after the William Wyler film.

145

A U D R E Y H E P B U R N
THE
FOUNDATION SWITZERLAND

"I auditioned for this job for forty-five years and I finally got it. I always felt very powerless when I would see the terrible pictures on TV. But I was offered a wonderful opportunity to do something [and it] is a marvelous therapy to the anguish I feel." Audrey Hepburn, referring to her role as UNICEF ambassadress (B. Paris, *Audrey Hepburn*, Putman & Sons 1966).

Audrey maintained she felt indebted since 1945 when she was sixteen and UN humanitarian aid in the Netherlands saved her from extreme poverty.

From 1988 onwards, she visited Ethiopia, Turkey, Sudan, El Salvador, Honduras, Bangladesh and Vietnam, taking on these tasks without sparing herself in full awareness and with deep emotional participation.

On returning from her last trip to Somalia in September 1998, just a few months before her death, she declared: "I have been to hell."

And again, on another occasion: "I'm filled with rage at ourselves. I don't believe in collective guilt, but I do believe in collective responsibility."

146

Fortune magazine published a survey held by the Illinois Institute of Technology: 80 designers worldwide selected their 100 best-designed articles.

In Italian in the original, the Cushman ad speaks to the love of things foreign presumably hidden in every American who bought this functional and yet so very high-class little vehicle.

Joe DiMaggio, the damnedest Yankee of them all, had in common with Senator J. William Fulbright making some kind of appearance in support of Vespa while visiting Rome.

While the legendary New York Yankees' "third base" gave photographers few chances, the senator who often rode it in Washington said he was sure "it had development potential in the U.S. market." The statement was made in January 1957 and its reasons were amply detailed.

Statistics seemed to bear him out with more than 10,000 units exported to the States—a big increase over the previous year's figure; in 1958, 70 in every 100 scooters imported to America came from the factory on Viale Rinaldo Piaggio, Pontedera.

The Vespa Distributing Company had been in a joint venture of a kind with the powerful sales force of Sears, Roebuck & Co. but they split up in 1960 when Vespa signed an agreement with former rival Cushman Motor Works, now part of the Outboard Marine Corp., makers of Johnson and Mercury boat engines. Other companies took on the agency for the northwest and New England.

The Italian style, vigorously advertised by the media, Hollywood, and exclusive store windows on Fifth Avenue seemed to take the shape of this little scooter.

When the Illinois Institute of Technology Center for Industrial Design awarded first prize to the Olivetti Lettera 22 from among the one hundred best industrial products nominated by a highly-qualified international jury (1958), Vespa was cited as the best two-wheeled vehicle ever designed.

Its undeniable ease of use did the rest.

A different public, youths of every age

Youth was then Vespa's natural market, and more here than elsewhere, especially college students.

As a Boston daily pointed out, widespread use of scooters would be a good way to solve the problem of something like 5,077 students homing in on Harvard's campus, five days a week, all driving their traditional American autos "weighing a ton and a half."

The scooter was seen as a possible second car for many, but it had only a niche market among the

At the dawning of the Sixties, famous brands chose Vespa for a get-together in Central Park or to say "Italy," while other, perhaps less weighty matters also took the stage. The League of Honest Coffee Lovers of the Pan-American Coffee Bureau have it parading in arms under its banner.

middle and upper classes, often women and city dwellers. The type of consumers Madison Avenue was aiming to reach, young American Vespa owners, were already pretty affluent; they'd had a good education and on average dressed better than their age-group peers. Many had been to Europe but certainly not during the war. Vespas appear in the most varied settings synonymous with joie de vivre, good taste, beauty.

A fleet of six Vespas was supposed to symbolize Italy and Europe in general in the sumptuous first anniversary celebration of the opening of *Around the World in Eighty Days* produced by Michael Todd in 1956 and starring David Niven, featuring a hot-air balloon moored in the center of Madison Square Garden. The godmother of the celebration was the twenty-five-year-old Elizabeth Taylor.

A caricature in the *Village Voice* showed an Ape van lying on the psychoanalyst's couch with the punch line "So, you say you get the feeling you're being used by people for their own benefit ..."

The Broadway Show League organized a procession through the streets of New York of almost two hundred *Vespisti* (Vespa enthusiasts), carrying famous players from sixteen baseball teams that were linked to sixteen musicals then showing in the 1959 theater season.

But this didn't happen just on the East Coast. There were other vital centers of this American low-wheel colony in Chicago, Seattle, and California, too.

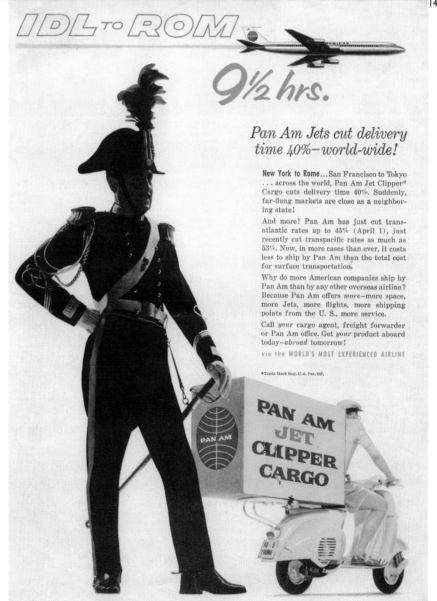

IDL TO ROM

9½ hrs.

Pan Am Jets cut delivery time 40%—world-wide!

New York to Rome...San Francisco to Tokyo ... across the world, Pan Am Jet Clipper® Cargo cuts delivery time 40%. Suddenly, far-flung markets are close as a neighboring state!

And more! Pan Am has just cut trans-atlantic rates up to 45% (April 1), just recently cut transpacific rates as much as 53%. Now, in more cases than ever, it costs less to ship by Pan Am than the total cost for surface transportation.

Why do more American companies ship by Pan Am than by any other overseas airline? Because Pan Am offers *more*—more space, more Jets, more flights, more shipping points from the U. S., more service.

Call *your* cargo agent, freight forwarder or Pan Am office. Get *your* product aboard today—*abroad* tomorrow!

via the WORLD'S MOST EXPERIENCED AIRLINE

*Trade Mark Reg. U. S. Pat. Off.

PAN AM JET CLIPPER CARGO

In the first ten years, 1953–63, just over eighty thousand Vespas were sent to the USA confirming that the market was certainly prestigious but in the end not so important. In 1953, a start was made with 2,451 units which grew to 6,901 two years later, reaching the top limit of 13,342 in 1958. The three successive years saw a fall to an all-time low of 8,310 units in 1961 rising again to the 10,889 scooters Pontedera exported to the United States in 1963.

A Broadway procession of the Show League parades along 44th Street west on 14 May 1959 with the lanterns of *The World of Suzie Wong* and *Flower Drumsong*.

Where mobility is one of the basic values, the little Vespa can hitch a ride on the bumper rail of a gigantic car as a complement to the big recreational vehicle.

Despite all this, Piaggio's exports to the USA never got beyond that promising 10,000 units a year.

By contrast, motorcycle imports into the USA were being increasingly dominated by Japanese manufacturers. In 1963 they made up almost two-thirds of sales with Honda alone getting more than 65 percent of the Japanese total.

Italian scooters fought on defiantly in defense of their 7 percent market share as similar-looking German and English products were progressively eliminated. After a rather difficult start, the market for larger motorbikes grew well, bringing prosperity to Harley Davidson as well as to the historical British brands and a few well-placed Italian ones.

The Italian Institute for Foreign Trade attributed the Japanese success to a shift in the image of the motorbike away from the black-leather, greaser stereotype and the ongoing work of technical perfection, highly effective advertising and sucess in the organization of the sales and service networks. Not that Pontedera had much to learn on that score.

1958-64

VESPA 125
160GS
180SS

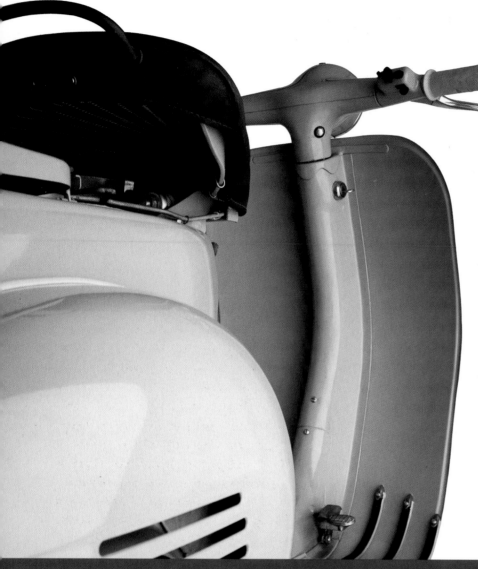

VESPA125

In 1958 Piaggio terminated the production of models in which the headlight was mudguard-mounted and launched basic models—a 125 cc and a 150 cc—with identical chassis. The only differences between them were the engine capacity and a few details on the handlebars. In fact, the most important innovation of the 1958 model was indeed the standardization of the body shell, now possible thanks to a new central welding process.

For the first time, the classic monocoque of the Vespa was made of two sheet steel half shells welded lengthwise and connected by a transverse bulkhead. The front rail, now thicker, was made

French advertisements drew attention to the introduction of the new rotating valve engine that ran on 2 percent pre-mix, shown here on the larger capacity model.

The new centrally welded body shell as it rolls down the production line: here it is shown during paint checking.

from two elements electrically spot-welded
together along wide mating surfaces.
The engine support cross member was
now incorporated in the left-hand half of
the engine casing. The right-hand one
incorporated the air-cooling circuit, which
had previously been separate.

The new design kick-starter lever, now with
a toothed selector and a crown wheel meshing
directly with the multiple gearbox gear, was
fixed on a shaft protruding from the engine case.

The new technology permitted a narrower,
lighter chassis, offering major advantages both
in terms of production, by optimizing manufacturing processes, and for the user, a less bulky
vehicle more agile in urban traffic.

The body profile generally followed the classic
Vespa shape, with evident modifications made
in the upper rear section, under the luggage
rack. Here, there was now a small hump, with
a flat top surface. This was to accommodate
the fuel tank, which was also now flat topped.

The rear cowls were decorated with parallel
rows of ribs which, as well as being a styling
feature, improved resistance to collisions.

The engine cowl, which could be removed
completely to facilitate maintenance, was fixed
to the body at two points and secured by quick
release levers. The engine cooling air intake slots
were redesigned, and were now similar in shape to
the fan cover underneath. In this configuration,

The central column and the handlebars with completely integrated controls from this innovative 125 model. Theft protection was improved with the introduction of a key-operated steering lock.

In this rear view can be seen the central weld of the half shells. The redesigned parcel rack was smaller. The rear light was still the rectangular component with a metal case.

This front view shows the smaller dimensions of the chassis—now 26 inches wide compared to 31 inches for the previous version. This made the scooter more agile in city traffic.

These side views show the different profile of the body shell under the parcel rack.

The new design required the resizing of the tool compartment (now with a hatch at the top and a molded contour below), of the engine cowl, (also with redesigned air intake slits) and of the parcel rack. The kick starter mechanism now acts directly on the secondary shaft.

VESPA 125

the Vespa 125 was lighter (180 pounds) and more rigid than the previous models. The new, more compact 4.5-hp engine gave better acceleration, making the vehicle more agile and responsive and giving a top speed of 45 mph with lower fuel consumption (75 mpg). With its 2.3-gallon fuel tank, this Vespa had a range of 250 miles.

As always, much attention was paid to the quietness of the vehicle, which now did not exceed 81 phon as a result of the new location of the Dellorto UA16S1 carburetor, over the cylinder (as on the GS). The air filter, contained in an easily removable box, was connected by a flexible rubber bellows to the chassis,

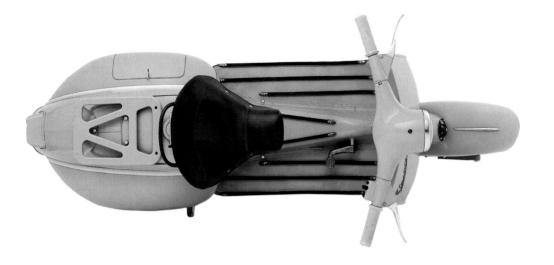

This view from above shows the new chassis profile, with a length increased (67 inches to 69.5 inches) and with a narrower central rail. The footplate strips and studs were also narrower.

The hinged saddle was dark green, like the plastic covering the passenger grab strap. The second saddle was an optional extra and was installed over the parcel rack.

Front wheel with suspension using variable rate coil springs and dual action hydraulic dampers.

The saddle was hinged and its central spring could be adjusted to the weight of the rider; at the front the bag hook can be seen. Under the saddle was the choke lever, already introduced on the 1956 model 125.

through which air was aspirated. The new location of the carburetor meant that the inspection hatch on the compartment behind the legs could be eliminated. This compartment was now defined by an unbroken curved surface between the footplate and the saddle. The only protrusion from this surface was the fuel tap.

Another refinement, both in terms of function and style, was the new handlebar with incorporated headlight and, at last, internal control cables. This component was made of two pressed steel shells which could easily be disassembled for maintenance work to the gear and accelerator cables. A 4.2-inch-diameter headlight at the center of the handlebars was connected to a new closed circuit electrical system, made exclusively for Piaggio.

The three-speed gearbox had a new easily installed selector mechanism housed in a steel case which in turn was protected from the weather, dust and collisions by a cover.

The saddle was dark green, as was the plastic covering of the passenger grab strap, and had a central spring which could be adjusted for the weight of the rider. The choke lever was located under the saddle.

Among the optional extras available was a speedometer (fitted as standard on the 150), the small rear seat, which could be easily and quickly fitted to the rear luggage rack, and a spare wheel, which was carried in an easily

Detail of the right-hand side of the handlebars. Note the assembly of the two half-shells. The upper one could be opened for maintenance of the now completely internally routed cables, which were connected to the grip via a metal case housing the front brake lever and the controls for the lights and horn. The Vespa name was applied to the leg shield in dark blue.

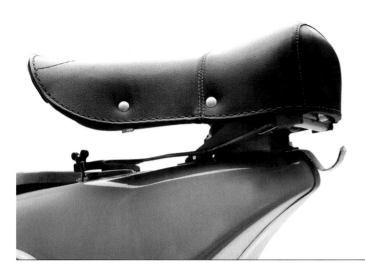

accessible location on a strong bracket on the internal side of the leg shield.

This model of Vespa was produced with two different chassis number prefixes and in three colors.

The first series, VNA1T 01001/068031, made in 1957–58, was initially gray (Max Meyer code 15046), but was later made in light beige (Max Meyer code 15099). The second series, made in 1959 with chassis number prefix VNA2T (068032/116431) was metallic light blue (Max Meyer code 15099), and mounted the new rotating valve engine, which ran on 2 percent two-stroke mixture rather than 5 percent.

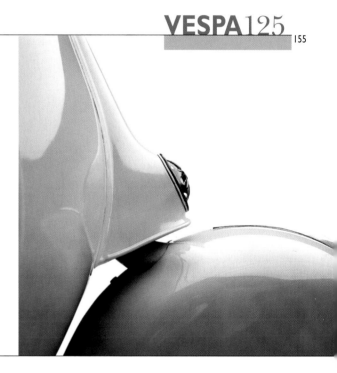

The front mudguard was made of two parts welded along the middle, like the whole body, and reiterated the curvature of the rear part of the chassis. The wheels were interchangeable and were fitted with low pressure 3.5-inch-by-8-inch tires.

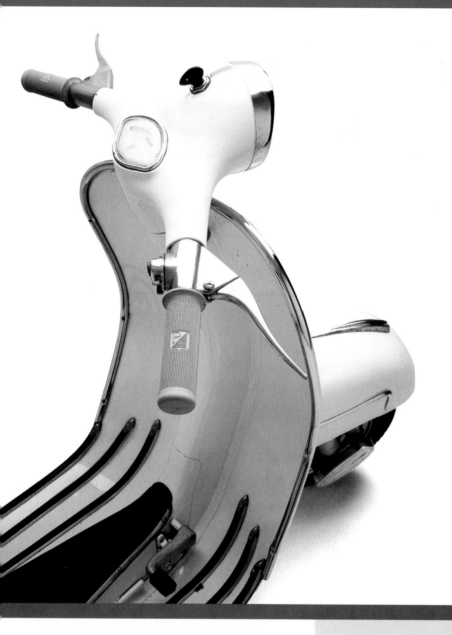

160**GS**

The 160 GS was built to rekindle the success of the 1955 GS. It was modern looking, it had class-leading performance and it responded to the functional and styling demands of an increasingly experienced, sophisticated clientele.

The technological improvements employed were in keeping with the company's policy of product renewal, which had already been implemented in the basic 125 cc and 150 cc models.

This version of the GS had a newly designed engine, which was more powerful and offered better acceleration, the suspension and saddle were now more comfortable, the bodywork was

From 1960, the German Highway Code required even this luxury sports two-wheeler to carry rear indicators. These were incorporated into chrome-plated dashes on the side cowls.

The carry-all compartment in the rear of the body was a characteristic of the first series (1962).

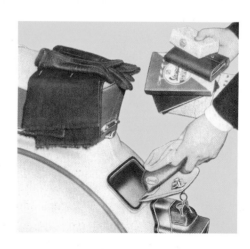

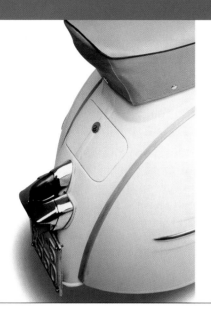

The GS was an elegantly designed, refined model in which minute attention to detail in the design and build was confirmed by clever color combinations and particularly high quality details and finish.

The rear had soft, sleek lines. The large, well finished rear light also incorporated a brake light.

less bulky and it had more comprehensive equipment, with the spare wheel (now fitted as standard) inside the bodywork. The engine cross member was incorporated in the chassis and engine size was increased to 158.53 cc (bore and stroke 58 x 60 mm), producing 8.2 hp at 6500 rpm and giving a top speed of 60 mph.

A number of important structural modifications were made, including a high strength crankshaft mounted on two crankshaft bearings (a roller bearing on the flywheel side and a ball bearing on the clutch side) and lubricated with gearbox oil. All major engine components and their supports, internal transmission components and gears were resized, the silencer was much larger with an indentation for the wheel and the carburetor was now an automotive Dellorto SI27/23 type with a shutter throttle valve and an incorporated choke.

The new body shell design, which was lighter and slimmer thanks to the central welding process, gave this, the most powerful Vespa to date, a modern, elegant appearance.

The styling was influenced by the 1961 150 cc model, which anticipated a number of the design ideas featured on the 1963 150 GL, considered the most elegant version ever designed by Piaggio.

The GS was built around the needs of the user who traveled frequently, who wanted power, rational space usage and immediately accessible mechanicals. These prerequisites led to a number

The mudguard, made from two half-shells reinforced internally along the join line, was decorated with a newly designed polished aluminum crest.

of the constructional details that distinguished this model from the basic versions.

Both cowls could be removed and were secured by a new easily operated fitting mechanism. The left-hand cowl (there was now no longer a tool compartment hatch) covered the spare wheel. The square battery and its rectifier were located at the center of the spare wheel. A sheet steel half shell painted the color of aluminum (Max Meyer code 1.268.0983) and fixed to the chassis by a central bolt covered the lower portion of the wheel. The air vent slots in the engine cowl were also redesigned. They were now all the same length inside an inclined rectangle to give a

The steering caster angle, visible in this side view, was changed to improve riding behavior and stability, especially in curves and at high speed.

The large, rounded side cowls stand out when seen either from behind or from the sides. An important new feature was the spare wheel housed in the left hand cowl. A half-cover held in place by a central bolt protected the bottom part of the wheel.

The incorporation of a locker compartment behind the leg shield in 1963 contributed to visually balancing the volumes of the front and rear.

160GS

Detail of the horn and lights control block, incorporated in a removable case.

more dynamic appearance. This new air vent design was to be kept unchanged in future models and became a hallmark motif for the Vespa.

The side cowls and the new shaped mudguard were decorated with a rounded motif stamped into the metalwork and outlined by an anticorodal aluminum border. The mudguard ornament crest was also redesigned as was the label "Vespa GS."

In the rear of the body-shell, between the saddle and the rear light, was a cubbyhole with a hatch fitted with a lock and key. This feature was used only in this series. It had already been abandoned in the '63 version, as it was decided that the rear side of the leg shield in front of the legs was the

This view from above shows the long gray saddle, in key with the body paint scheme, and the improved footplate design, now with a mat and more harmonious rubber strips.

The engine cover was fitted with an anti-corrosive aluminum strip and had equal length cooling air slits.

The elastic element of the front suspension was now a single component, consisting of a coaxially mounted hydraulic damper and coil spring.

Although this particular model offered high performance together with great elegance, it was not very enthusiastically received by the public.

The legacy of the definitive sports model—the 150 GS launched in 1954 but revised several times up until '61—was a hindrance, not an assistance.

160**GS**

ideal location for a proper, much larger hold-all compartment. This compartment was rounded in shape to fit in with the overall design of the scooter and also became a definitive feature, used on the majority of subsequent models.

The rear light with incorporated brake light (introduced on the 1958 GS to comply with the new highway code) was identical to the component fitted to the VS5 (150 GS, 1959/61) as were the handlebars and respective controls. The long, ergonomically designed saddle was light gray to fit in with the gray-white body paintwork (Max Meyer code 1.298.8714). This gave the scooter an exceptionally refined, elegant appearance, emphasized by the rubber mat on the footplate and the fluid, uniform shape of the bodywork between the footplate and the saddle, which was no longer broken by a hatch for the carburetor. The bag carrier hook was now more functional and theft protection was improved, with a new steering lock which allowed the key to be removed only once the handlebar was in the locked position.

The 160 GS was so successful as it catered to the needs of customers who wanted a competition-derived vehicle worthy of its prestigious historical precedents. Sixty thousand 160 GSes were built during its production period from 1962 to 1964.

Detail of the handlebars and controls, with the fan-shaped speedometer and highly polished half bars.

The innovations and solutions experimented on this version formed the basis for the subsequent 180 SS (Super Sport) model in 1964, which was much more successful.

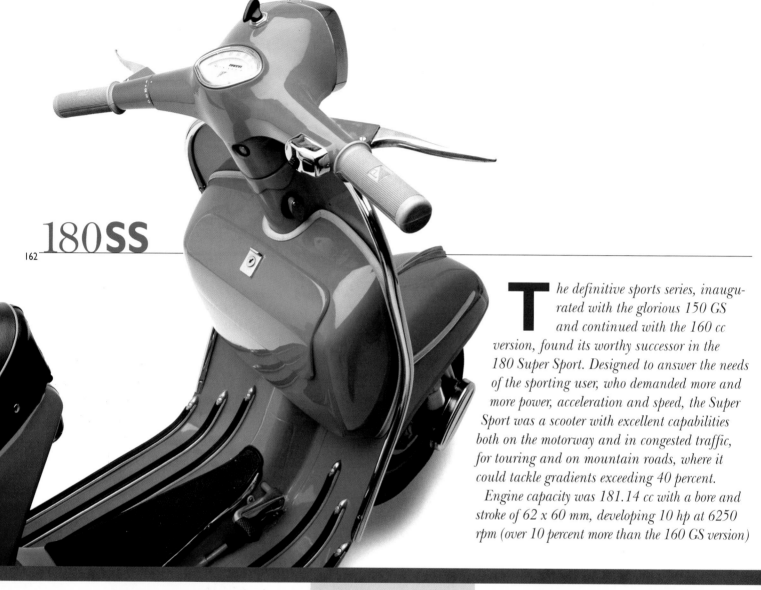

180SS

The definitive sports series, inaugurated with the glorious 150 GS and continued with the 160 cc version, found its worthy successor in the 180 Super Sport. Designed to answer the needs of the sporting user, who demanded more and more power, acceleration and speed, the Super Sport was a scooter with excellent capabilities both on the motorway and in congested traffic, for touring and on mountain roads, where it could tackle gradients exceeding 40 percent.

Engine capacity was 181.14 cc with a bore and stroke of 62 x 60 mm, developing 10 hp at 6250 rpm (over 10 percent more than the 160 GS version)

The big sports Vespa was the last model to use the crossed port engine. The model name was the main focus of billboards and in advertising slogans, and was given even more emphasis than the Vespa logo itself.

Piaggio fared very well indeed during the boom in the automobile industry in the Sixties. Numerous versions of Vespa were launched to satisfy the demands of a constantly growing market.

In addition to the "Vespa SS" badge on the front shield, another was fitted at an angle on the back bearing the script "Super Sport." This badge, which was also used in other versions, identified the model immediately.

and giving a top speed of 63 mph in a head-down position or 57 mph with a passenger. Fuel consumption was 85 mpg with 5 percent pre-mix.

The slender, dynamic shape of the scooter, which was only 27 inches wide, was the result of a fluid yet bold design of its individual elements, some of which had already been used in other models. The handlebars were from the 1963 GL, while the trapezoid headlight and the rear light were from the Vespa 150 Sprint of the same year. The handlebars were open underneath, exposing the gear and accelerator control bars. These components were protected by two sheet steel dust guards painted the same color as the bodywork, and secured with four 0.32-inch diameter round-headed aluminum bolts. These could be removed to allow the windshield support rods to be fixed by steel bolts in their place.

The steering column cover and the horn housing were incorporated in the leg shield. This solution had been developed for the 1963 GL and was confirmation of Piaggio's constant quest since the very beginning to rationalize presses and to reduce the total number of components.

The modifications made to the bodywork could be seen in the tail section, which now tapered towards the number plate support and in the compartment fitted to the rear side of the leg shield (as on the last 160 cc series models) which was now complete with a lock opened by the same key as the steering lock. The mudguard and side

This was the first model in the sports series to use the new centrally welded body shell. The now narrower front mudguard still wore the aluminum crest ornament. The horn housing is similar to the one on the 1963 Vespa 150 GL.

The new body gave the vehicle a slim, sporty appearance which was further emphasized by the dashes adorning the flanks.

This model was smaller than the GS 160, with a maximum width of 27 inches (instead of 28.5 inches) and a total length of 71 inches (72 inches for the GS).

Comfort and handling were improved by the new suspension configuration that set the vehicle lower at the rear while raising the front end and handlebars.

180**SS**

The new fan-shaped speedometer read up to 72 mph and also had a trip counter. Above, the ignition key, which was to be eliminated in the subsequent series due to changes in the electrical system.

cowls were now narrower and were decorated with a linear, dynamically shaped ornament that like a pencil stroke emphasized the outline of the scooter which was already defined by the rubber seals between the side cowls and bodywork and the stainless steel trim edge running from the footplate to the leg shield. As on the 160, the cowls could be removed. The left-hand cowl covered the spare wheel.

Among the modifications made to improve comfort were revised suspension settings to improve stability and road holding. The rear suspension was lowered whereas both the front suspension and the handlebars were hiked up.

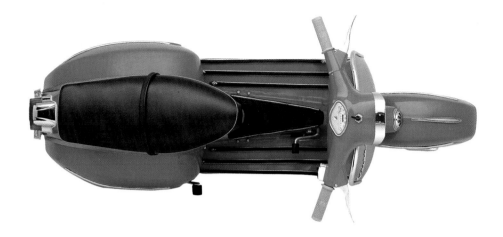

A locker compartment was fitted behind the leg shield: this was not only the perfect location for the compartment, in front of the rider's legs, but also helped form a better visual balance between the rear and front of the vehicle.

Detail of the front suspension, which reproduced the layout introduced on the 160 GS two years earlier.

In keeping with Vespa tradition, the tires (3.5 inches by 10 inches) are interchangeable.

The end of the tail was modeled to carry the number plate also. The rear light shown here is not the standard production component.

Except for the contact key, the handlebars were similar to the ones on the 1963 model 150 GL, with a trapezoid headlight and of single piece construction. The underside was open to permit maintenance of the cables and to give access to the windshield mountings.

180SS

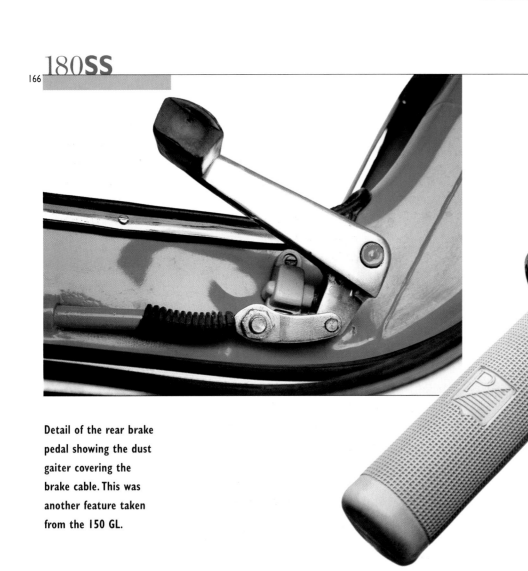

Detail of the rear brake pedal showing the dust gaiter covering the brake cable. This was another feature taken from the 150 GL.

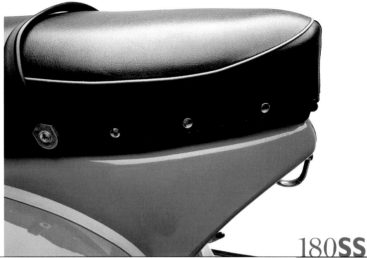

The AC ignition system now had a key operated ignition switch mounted on the handlebars. In the following series, the electrical system was modified, eliminating the ignition key, the battery and the rectifier. The zinc alloy flywheel fan, with incorporated annular magnet, now had modified vanes to increase the flow of cooling air. It was fixed to its hub by six bolts.

The Super Sport was available in a range of different colors: three shades of red, hawthorn white and peacock blue. This was the first time that a model requiring license plates was available in a different color.

The 180 SS was manufactured between 1964 and 1968. It was followed by the 180 Rally, built between 1968 and 1973 and the 200 Rally, built from 1972 to 1979. This was considered the most prestigious Vespa ever made by Piaggio. It was the first with electronic ignition and it had a top speed of 69 mph.

In 1965, like in '64, Piaggio had a very productive year in which the results of research and experimentation were applied to several models, but it was also a year sadly marked by the death of Enrico Piaggio. He was succeeded by his son-in-law, Umberto Agnelli, the first company director from outside the family. Agnelli implemented a series of changes, starting with the redefinition of the company logo and image, which were to affect all future production.

This was the first license-plated Vespa model available in a variety of colors. This Vespa offered potent performance yet was light, colorful and fun. It symbolized a generation that wanted to break its ties with the past.

W here unpredictability sets in, from the plains of Pisa to Woodstock, from Pop Art to youth revolt and a revolution in custom; the difficult times of the early Seventies with a bit less verve and a bit more of new words like austerity.

1963–1976

...and a Vespa for Peter Pan

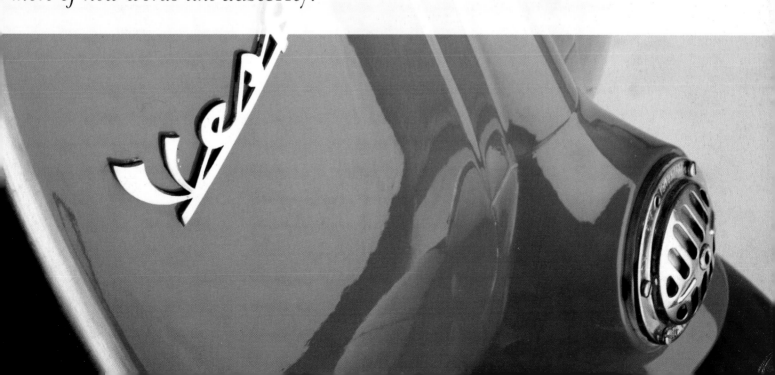

"Nineteen sixty-four saw the highest number of Vespas manufactured—more than 210,000—only bettered ten years later," General Manager Francesco Lanzara recalled on receiving the Rotary Club Paul Harris Fellow award on behalf of Enrico Piaggio. "But '65 started off worse and Piaggio died in October: these were trying months and even years but things eventually picked up."

On Thursday December 21, 1961, the *New York Times* published an article covering the four-month report of the United Nations Economic Commission for Europe. It appeared, with photographic illustrations, on the financial page.

The caption for one of the photographs was inexact: Genoa was the location of Piaggio's head office, not that of its production facilities. The caption read, "Satisfaction of market demand: the assembly line at Piaggio's factory in Genoa, Italy is working full steam ahead. The demand in Europe for machine tools shows no sign of slowing."

And the photograph was the one—used time and time again—of the final, overhead carousel of the line at Pontedera in the engine-to-body assembly plant.

Such was the importance of the Vespa phenomenon almost twenty years after its creation that this image became representative of the whole of western europe's magical period of expansion and growth.

The local scene close up

All this was taking shape, day by day, in a valley in the heart of central Italy: an unlikely place, if you think about it. "With no important urban center but very near two provincial capitals, its labor resources are scant but it can count on substantial reserves from the surrounding countryside." You needed to go no farther than the surrounding hillsides: according to a 1961 ISPES (Institute for Social and Economic Develop-

At only 60 years old, Enrico Piaggio died suddenly on October 17, 1965. His plane, which had departed from Milan that morning, landed on the little airfield by the Vespa plant. Piaggio drove himself home to his Villa in Varramista, just a couple of miles away. After lunch he was admitted to a hospital with severe abdominal pains. They feared the worst, considering that one of his kidneys had been removed when he was young. After unsuccessful surgery, it was decided to bring him home to Varramista in critical condition.

Clocking in at the Pontedera factory. In the ten years between 1950 and '60 the workforce almost doubled, rising from 3,320 to 6,321.

In the period from 1958 to 1962, there was an increase of the lower-middle classes (from 34.9 percent to 58.5 percent) in clientele and a fall in the number of white-collar workers, shopkeepers and entre- preneurs (from 37.5 percent to 14.3 percent). For work and play, Vespa was the ideal means for those who couldn't yet afford a car.

171

ment) document, sharecropping was widespread over more than half of the Pisa Plain.

The closed-off world in which the family patriarch held sway blended smoothly into the new in which it was normal for the younger generation to commute towards the new production centers downhill. More and more young people were seeing the farm as "a suit- able jumping off point to get into industry" without this necessarily endangering the farm since its existence was underpinned by the "extended family" model so preva- lent in these parts. Others immediately took the places, in the home and in the fields, of those who left the land to work down in the valley.

The big "wasps' nest" at Pontedera alone employed more than 70 percent of the total labor force in the local metal-working and mechanical sector, with the rest of the area's industry orbiting round it.

Large-scale short-distance commuting prevented uncontrolled urbanization of the main towns. In 1965, only half of the 6,000 Piaggio employees lived in Pontedera; all the others came in every day from the surrounding villages and countryside to work in the fac- tory on Viale Rinaldo Piaggio alongside the railway line.

There were a lot of young people and many had had some kind of trade schooling. Others had been to spe- cial training courses. The job of skilled worker in a large-scale industry had the attraction of seeming a safe haven against the risks of life and an inside track to the enormous market of consumer goods.

In 1957, youth unemployment reached 32 percent but this situation reversed in the years immediately

Carry on Cabby (1963) was the first of a popular British film series set around taxi driver Charlie Hawkins (an excellent Sid James), his mates and his married life. Shown here on a Vespa, one of the "lovelies" used by Peggy Hawkins who has decided to open a taxi company in competition with her husband.

Growth in consumption and establishment of the product abroad as well as in Italy did not give protection from the market backfiring.

after, to the point that droves of students abandoned professional training schools to get jobs right away, no matter how lowly.

Those were years of dynamic change and harsh social conflict. Many industrial sectors made widespread use of overtime and sham fixed-term contracts to hire unskilled labor at as low a wage level as possible: big assembly lines made do with unskilled labor. When the market went slack, they simply put workers on short-time weeks and short-time pay.

In negotiating workers' claims, the trade unions put forward requests for longer holidays and a work week of 44 hours instead of the current 48, but with no cut in pay. More free time was pretty much everyone's aim in this new, affluent Italy.

The accelerating pace of life pointed towards the car, and the less-affluent were discouraged by the cost of meeting new government regulations: the license plate, the driver's license, the increase in road tax for two-wheeled vehicles, enrollment in the PRA (State Vehicle Registration Authority). In 1960, sales fell 6 percent, in '62 they fell 14 percent and in '63 they fell 20 percent. "In such conditions," wrote the general management of Piaggio, "the government has taken measures to arrest the enormous growth in the acquisition of consumer goods... The results were seen in 1964, when sales plummeted 25 percent. The cost of labor has risen 50 percent since early 1962. The plant usually operated 44 hours per week in winter and 40 hours per week in summer; but in 1965, only 40 hours per week all year round. Something must be done."

1 Engine assembly shop
2 Press mold and frame construction shop
3 Foundry
4 Engine construction shop
5 Engine assembly shop
6 Engine testing shop
7 Galvanizing shop
8 Paint shop
9 Vespa assembly shop
10 Vespa finishing shop
11 Vespa shipping department
12 Ape and Pentarò workshop

A Managerial offices
B Technical and data processing offices
C Experimental workshop
D Manual workers' center
E Mechanic training school
F Office workers' canteen
G Raw material testing department
H Spare parts workshop and warehouse
I Test track

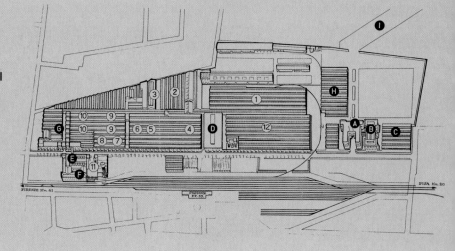

Intermission in black

The craving to have and to do and to spend made selling by installments spiral out of control: a vague "promissory note" now seemed the only currency when buying retail or dealing with wholesalers, craftsmen and small-scale industry.

After the long growth phase that followed reconstruction and the miracle years of 1958–63, a period set in that many had not foreseen, fraught with economic hardships that caused serious repercussions on the standard of living. The sharp fall in the amount of money in circulation put a stranglehold on economic growth, forcing harsh measures to restrict credit availability. The cost of money rocketed from 5 percent in '59 to 15 percent in '64.

Everyone watched in disbelief as consumer prices rose and workers' demands exploded. Capital and new, potential investment resources fled the country alarmed at rising labor costs. Consumer activity shrank substantially. The center-left which appeared in several controversial political configurations between 1962 and '68 was a let-down compared to expectations and, dragging on through three successive coalition governments headed by the Christian Democrat leader Aldo Moro until 1968, showed itself unable to carry through structural reforms, even though every day the economic situation made it clear that these were necessary. Behind the scenes, the ambiguity of the highest offices in the state facilitated a tendency towards authoritarianism that could wreak havoc with democracy and civil society.

The updating of the production lines, especially in vehicle assembly and finishing, resulted in a lesser need for the ability and experience of expert craftsmen.

The Pontedera factory at the beginning of the Sixties.

"The water seemed to have had a great time making hills of headlights and horns and mountains of saddles all over the place..." noted Umberto Agnelli after the flood. "Cases containing plastic components and light-weight materials were even found halfway along the road between Pontedera and Pisa."

In this dark interlude that was opening up unexpectedly after years of acceleration and growth, industry in general was hard hit and motorcycle manufacturers especially so. The measures adopted to combat the crisis in 1964 curtailed selling by installments and created serious difficulties for thousands of potential customers, especially in Italy's South.

Developments of a few years before in Germany and Great Britain in which motorcycle sales had fallen dramatically in the wake of a strong rise in the automobile market were seen here in a less drastic way, Italy following more closely the pattern of what had happened in France despite the difference in real terms.

The crisis was hard for everyone, but major manufacturers suffered no critical downturns and, in the final analysis, even broadened their market shares. Piaggio, despite seeing its sales fall by half between 1960 and 1965, made a great leap forward raising its share of new registrations from 33 percent to 47 percent.

These were the statistics the trade unions brandished in questioning the legitimacy of a swathe of dismissals in early 1966. The unions maintained these measures were politically motivated to get rid of a number of workers who, two years earlier, had called a strike whose aims had only partially been met but that had dragged on for more than sixty days. There was no denying that major investment in new production technology had enabled the company to axe more than 700 jobs in two years. The struggle, however, was making itself heard outside the factory walls, echoing throughout the surrounding countryside in a call for government intervention.

And then the flood

Then the 4th of November happened. The waters of the Arno brought disaster and devastation to the center of Florence and its artistic treasures. Venice looked on in dismay at the increasing intensity of its high tides soon to turn into floods. And in Pontedera, the river Era burst its banks and flowed up to the nearby factory walls. The factory gates eventually gave way under the enormous pressure of water and mud. The watchmen on night shift raised the alarm but there was little that could be done to avoid the worst: the smelting molds were extinguished; a truckload of quicklime was moved to higher ground to keep it away from water that would have made it explode. Then it was every man for himself.

A tidal wave of mud poured into warehouse and factory, over machinery and spare parts, ruining half-finished and online units, files and offices—in short, the heart and soul of the company—leaving in its wake nothing but desolation and damage of over 5 billion lire ($3 million).

"I got to Pontedera on a Monday morning," said Umberto Agnelli. "For the first time I could see firsthand the catastrophe that, fifteen years earlier as a child, I'd seen in photographs of the flooding in Polesine at the estuary of the river Po. Two days had gone by since the wall of mud and water had hit the town. But when I saw the offices I felt as if I was looking at a sort of modern-day Pompeii."

The extraordinary dedication of thousands of workers for whom the factory represented survival enabled part

After the disaster, the company turned its attention to the emerging youth market and increased its share capital from 3.15 billion to 5 billion lire ($1.9 million to $3 million) in the spring of 1967.

Moreover, on the decisive ruling by "Dr. Agnelli," Piaggio & Co. canceled the result of the previously held national design competition and took on the hexagonal logo designed by Emilio De Silva of Turin.

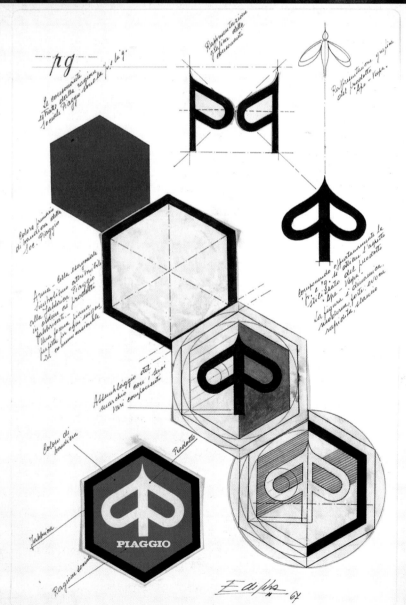

> "The consonants taken from the Piaggio company name—'p' and 'g'—when stylized and placed back to back … gave a bee-wasp insect outline [see upper right], which then evolved into the Ape and Vespa product logo. The figure is dynamic, modern and strong: it evokes speed and ebullience.
>
> "The outline frame," its designer continued, "is a beehive, or six-sided cell, a fitting symbol for the Piaggio factory and the products it manufactures. A flat shape, perfect for every commercial requirement."

of the line to be started up again only four days after the flood. "Exactly one month later, on 6 December, the factory was back on full power: its recovery accomplished in exactly half the time originally planned."

A little recapitulation is in order here: reconstruction was a distant memory, the start-up after World War II, then came the flourishing of Italy and then the first crisis, the catastrophe of the flood and finally the profit posted as early as the 1967 balance sheet. All this was due to the hard work and sacrifice of a lot of people. It was also made possible by the continued success of the leading lady of the piece: twenty years had passed since Vespa was born and her sales were starting to climb again thanks to the mini-scooter that could be ridden in Italy without a driving license: a focal point for the new teenagers.

NO LICENSE PLATE

From a TV advertising short on Vespa and youth (1965) a color film was developed for the cinema. In 1960, Italy already had more than 2,000,000 TV sets as compared with the 1,500,000 in France. Germany, however, had over 4,000,000 and the United Kingdom 11,000,000.

Guys and bobby-soxers, youths, adolescents, boys and girls, or more simply the younger generation—the teenagers—these were the new protagonists, sometimes not fully aware of the importance of their role in an all-encompassing revolution in social habits that started to happen in the early Sixties.

In search of youth

Life expectancy in Italy had doubled over the last century but was still little more than fifty just before the war. Despite this and the population boom, young people were still in a minority compared to the rest of the population. It was also true, however, that the members of this rising industrialized Western society didn't age;

a long adolescence and a never-ending period of youth was awarded to the progeny of the new consumerism. Peace seemed to reign eternal in this new Europe and of the millions who could enjoy its fruits, many were in their late teens or early twenties. Not everybody was willing to play by the rules of the game, however, but at first sight it looked as if there was enough to satisfy everyone.

Junior high school became compulsory in Italy in 1962, creating an impetus for widening the education system already in existence. High school enrollment doubled over a ten-year span to 1.2 million in '65. Also, many more young people were already working, and though neither age group—teens and young workers—had much purchasing power, two-wheeled autonomy was the first step towards freedom, so long as one was allowed to take it.

The scooter was often used in advertising: its rounded contours and shape reinforced the youthful message of the most varied advertisements, from Beat music to Coca-Cola, and satisfied all kinds of styling requirements that television and glossy magazines put forward when moving into this increasingly colorful, free-and-easy, anti-conformist world of adolescents.

Language tried to keep up with images but didn't find it easy. "How would you like your girl?" "Powerful, zippy, easy to handle, strong, quick on the uptake" would be "their" reply, in a TV ad, following in their fathers' footsteps. This comment wasn't much more credible than the stilted atmosphere in which the brand-new Vespa putters around the boulevards of the residential part of

Born in 1963, the new 50 cc Vespa made its mark showing the controversial world of youth in a positive light. A few years later "while her peers were manning the barricades in France, the daughter of the great Tyrone Power was paving her way to stardom."

At the end of the "line," Umberto Agnelli, the new chairman, gets to know the no-plate S version.

Promotion was by means of a luxuriant Ursula Andress in the 1965 calendar showing the Vespa 90, primarily aimed at foreign markets.

town under Mom and Dad's indulgent gaze.

What happened was spontaneous resonance, love at first sight and the instinctive adoption by thousands of youths the world over of this two-seater magic carpet.

Money and time

The Highway Code—which came into force after the Single Text of 1959, when there were already three million cars and more than four million motorcycles on Italian roads—defined a moped as a vehicle "having an engine, if of the internal combustion type, of a capacity not exceeding 50 cc and able to travel on a horizontal road at a top speed of 27 miles per hour."

In particular anyone over the age of fourteen could drive one—without a license—thus opening broad new vistas for a whole generation and for a whole sector of industry too.

In the category of "microscooter" able to "combine the refinement, comfort and practicality of the scooter with the features of a moped," *Motociclismo* magazine lumped together the Giulietta produced by Peripoli, Beta's Cicogna, a small Laverda, the Como made by Agrati and Gilera's G 50; the last two in particular made no secret of their direct descent from the machines made at Pontedera.

The no-license-plate prototype of the Lambretta that had been presented at the Milan Motorcycle Show with fanfare when the new law came out the year before didn't get into mass production until '64. This left the field clear for the new 50 cubic centimeter Vespa

EPOCA

15 Maggio 1968 - A. XIX - N. 982 Arnoldo Mondadori Editore

"J'ai 16 ans.
J'entre bientôt en apprentissage.
L'indépendance et ma première paie !
Je veux en profiter tout de suite.
Mon rêve ? Avoir le permis F.
Et m'offrir une Vespa 50 N Junior toute blanche.
Elle est super.
Elle a une ligne dingue !"

CREATION3

PIAGGIO SERVICE
PIAGGIO
GILERA
BIANCHI

Sweet sixteen for the F driving license in Switzerland, whose driving laws were among Europe's strictest, and for a first job and professional training session: sweet sixteen for one's first pay check and the dream of owning a Vespa.

The Vespa 90 in a German brochure; but there was a 100 cc version too besides the 50 S vintage that was successfully sold in Japan until 2001.

The 50 SS engine on a Schenck test-bench to ascertain specific consumption and the power curve. The engine's power had more than doubled by comparison to the first 1963 version.

to lead from 1963 when it came out with four thousand units sold. The specialized press saw its launch as "undoubtedly one of the most important events to take place in our line of business in the last ten years."

Putting it into production, once the prototype had been defined after going through all the stages of its development, was no mean feat.

A memo dated January 1962, sent to Francesco Lanzara, talked about "putting up two new buildings: one for the big press molds and the other as a workshop for maintenance and as a machine tool store" as well as enlarging existing buildings; the existing plant for the bodywork paint shop and engine testing workshop was still to be used but, naturally, a new assembly line would have to be set up. The cost of machinery,

apparatus and molds varied between 1 billion and 2.8 billion lire ($600,000 and $1.7 million) depending on whether "one hundred units are to be made in sixteen hours with traditional machinery" or "three hundred units with special machines." The new, semi-automatic machinery seemed to involve the hotly disputed "coupling"—attributing varying stages of the production process to a single worker.

Each Vespa would need 14 hours and 51.8 minutes of work and effort, a saving of 3 hours and 33.62 minutes on the 125 cc. This meant less time spent on the engine and bodywork and much the same on everything else from the suspension through the electronics to final assembly. With these figures, the most important hand of the game was to be played, in the

hope of a positive response from the market. And respond positively it did. Up to 23,000 units were sold in '65 with forecasts guesstimating some 48,000 for the year after.

That figure represented the rest of production, exports excluded, to be spread over seven models in four different engine sizes, from the 90 cc with its bizarre and greatly envied 90 SS to the 125, the ideal balance "for those approaching motorized transport for the first time," through the 150 Super "the most classic scooter" up to the 180 Super Sport that could easily overcome the 60-mile-per-hour barrier. It was, however, the small Vespa the "Vespina," for the fourteen-year-olds, that brought best results when Piaggio started to get going again after the flood.

The special metal body shell with integrated side cowlings called for all the experience the panel working technicians and staff could conjure up. There was a particularly high risk of defects and imperfections in the point of maximum curvature.

The equipment in the assembly line of the "Vespina" was continually updated. This photograph dates to the early Eighties.

The "Rumi Formichino" ["Little Ant"] (1954–59), unmistakable because of its aluminum body shell; the front, single-arm suspension was abandoned in mass production.

Facing: a good aluminum casting was used for the body of the Molteni T50 incorporating the headlight, glove compartment, fuel tank and saddle support.

The first M V scooter that enjoyed popularity was the CSL 125 in 1950–51.

The correspondent of *Motociclismo* magazine reported from the 1951 Paris Motor Show: "The extremely fortunate line of Italian scooters, such a happy combination of good looks and practicality, represents an embarrassing standard for comparison; all too easy to copy but all too difficult to improve."

Scooter: not to be driven with no hands

In the same year, the May issue of *Motorcycle* published an article by Dr. Frej, a famous designer and ex-general manager of the Czechoslovak manufacturer Jawa, about new directions in design. We won't go into the author's ideas which introduce the Ami prototype—a cross between a motorcycle and a scooter resulting in a

An English advertisement sings the praises of Vespa: good protection from the elements, excellent engine accessibility, ease of wheel change, gear change on the handgrip and integrated clutch. However the laterally placed engine, which some believe adversely affects the riding trim, is an issue that can't be hushed up. In the end, the sales management joined the fray and sent a memo to the sales agents refuting the word "lateral" and emphasizing that in centrally-placed engines "only the piston-cylinder assembly is central while all other heavy components are laterally mounted, which moves these engines' center of gravity sideways too." With the rider on board, the Vespa "leans between 1°30' and 3° while vehicles with 'centrally'-mounted engines lean between 1°45' and 2°" —insignificant trivialities.

The Zundapp Bella on a '97 Oasis LP cover—*Be Here Now*—almost 45 years after the 125 cc version came out at the Frankfurt Fair.

The German manufacturer Bastert produced some 1,200 Einspurautos: very unwieldy scooters with an aluminum body shell, engines with 150 cc and 175 cc and a highly streamlined look.

superbly unharmonic hybrid that he'd presented that year at the Geneva Show—as a two-wheeler "for everyone." But he showed remarkable pragmatism in considering the limits of low-wheeled vehicles, a pragmatism with a decidedly motorcycle-favoring slant.

With its side-mounted engine, small-diameter wheels and unusual weight distribution (estimated at 72 percent on the back wheel with the driver on board), the Vespa "tends to zigzag and is very difficult, bordering on impossible, to ride without hands." Blithely ignoring the Piaggio racing team that won the season's competitions and the Pontedera acrobatic team, it was affirmed that "the normal scooter rider is usually a beginner in two-wheeled motorized transport and doesn't even feel the urge to go fast." It was only partly true, however, and it

MILANO-TARANTO 1951, 1400 Km.

ANCHE QUEST'ANNO LE MV 125 STRAVINCONO NELLA CORSA DI VELOCITA' E RESISTENZA PIU' LUNGA DEL MONDO, ARRIVANDO I II III IV V

The shape of the Ducati Cruiser (1952–54) came from the refined car-designing pen of Ghia; four-stroke engine, automatic transmission, electric starter, and a built-in mechanical fragility.

The result of a collaboration with Aermacchi, the Topper (1960–65) doesn't really seem like a Harley Davidson: fiberglass body, ripcord ignition, slow enough to do without a front brake.

A closer look reveals that the idea of the scooter was interpreted better by companies outside the motorbike world. A means of transport, to all intents novel, seemed to emerge best from the drawing boards of highly qualified designers with no preconceived ideas. Such resources were available in the aeronautical companies behind Unibus (and Vespa) or, in another case, the big iron and engineering complex behind Innocenti. The most prestigious names in motorbikes—Indian in the United States and Moto Guzzi in Italy—failed to see the scooter's enormous potential, and major, traditional manufacturers like Harley Davidson and Ducati failed to reproduce the magic formula: absolute practicality, ease of use and maintenance, maneuverability and enjoyment in riding.

After the first series (1953–56), in which an original looking fixed wheel-guard carrying a spacious luggage rack was combined with a highly Italian-looking rear end, Peugeot decided on a full-out copy of the Lambretta in this C series.

An Italian engineer, Vincenzo Piatti was the originator of this little Belgian-produced scooter (1952–54) later taken up by a British manufacturer in 1957.

became increasingly less so, seeing the challenge of breaking the purely Italian barrier of 100 km per hour on the fastest models. It was, however, true that only through advanced-level planning and major industrialization could mature products come into being.

Scooters from all over the place

Italian production was mainly centered on two major manufacturers—unless, that is, we're talking about merely dressing a moped. A galaxy of small, semi-industrialized companies were jostling behind the second row taken up by Moto Guzzi with the Galletto and by Isothermo with first the Furetto then the Isoscooter that enjoyed later success. After them there came Agrati, then MV Agusta with all its prestige and a never-ending indecision between monocoque and tubular frame, switching back and forth between the two in just a few years.

There were only six French manufacturers at the 1951 Paris Show but this figure doubled four years later after the French government called for initiatives to deal with the "Italian invasion." There was room for everyone, with almost a million new motorcycles registered in '54, and only forty-thousand above the 200 cc level.

The French producer Motobécane, all-powerful in the market of mopeds and bicycles with auxiliary engines, presented a beautiful scooter in 1951 that was tremendously "Italian" enough to be defined as "Milanese, *à la Lambretta*." Even the Elegante scooter that Peugeot launched in '63, was a painstaking imitation not of Vespa but of Lambretta.

A likable little miniscooter perfectly suited to London-based model Pamela Blaise's miniskirt in this picture of 1966. A few years earlier there was quite a different message in the advertisement for the Sunbeam, a scooter from a famous family but nothing great to look at. The prestige of British motorcycling tradition did not shine here.

Germans loved powerful scooters that were technically sophisticated and reliable: real long-distance cruisers. One was the 1960 Zundapp Bella 204. It had a two-stroke, 198 cc, 12-horsepower engine, electric starter, pedal gear-change and 12 inch wheels and weighed in at more than 350 pounds dry: not the most maneuverable of machines. NSU, which had already produced Lambrettas under license decided to go it alone and gave birth to the first Fünfsterns: "five-star" scooters, though they didn't look it.

Even the United Kingdom, the home of classical motorbikes—the stomping ground of black leather riders—had difficulty producing a winner. Most British scooters were heavy, bulky, vaguely asthmatic, semi-artisan products with little reliability. The majors had

somewhat more success, however, such as the BSA-Triumph group's glossy Sunbeam, presented in 1960.

Where scooters took hold and multiplied with no complexes about the Italian models was in Japan. The Fuji-Subaru group set the ball rolling in 1946 with the Rabbit, while in '47 Mitsubishi followed with the 100 cc Silver Pigeon. Already in the Fifties the two-wheeled Honda empire was turning out thousands of scooters, the first series with a sheet-metal frame and plastic shield and the second, its descendant, with a tubular frame and plastic bodywork.

Aimed at the domestic market, they soon spread all over the Far East and Southeast Asia, gradually finding their way into Europe ... but some decades later and in a situation that had by then changed completely.

The idea developed by Honda in response to the Italian model was the "cub," an inelegant but efficient "no-ped" with, as its description suggests, no pedals but three gears, an automatic clutch and a white plastic shield.

The heir to the Japanese throne on a Silver Pigeon: In May '48, Prince Akihito zips around the grounds of Tokyo's royal palace during the Tango No Sekku Children's Festival.

YOU MEET THE NICEST PEOPLE ON A **HONDA**

Mopeds and scooters immediately became the symbols of belonging to the world of youth. With the Ciao (1968) a new little classic was born. Noteworthy were the shoe brakes like a bicycle's, typical of the first series.

Revolution in the streets of Canterbury in Kent, and in the dress of the pump attendant and the style of the young Mods in the summer of 1965.

Nearly sixteen million teenagers came under close scrutiny as voices of the times, new social subjects, potential consumers. The youth scene at the end of the Sixties was no longer stable. It hadn't been for some time and it was to stay that way: unstable and in ever more rapid headlong flight. Attempting to photograph the situation, it would have been hard not to blur it, things were moving so fast.

The strategy held to be most appropriate for dealing with such a vast, compound public was to avoid the extremes, not take sides and stay attractive. It certainly wasn't easy to find common ground without falling by the wayside, falling prey to ideological limitations and factions that fought among themselves as the emotional climate in Italy became white-hot.

Young people were affected by pernicious Beatlemania or marching against the Vietnam War; blue-collar youth from the south of Italy, working at Alfa Romeo, Magneti Marelli and Fiat, were the true avant-garde of the worker movement ready for conflict. Students resisted the police on the steps of the Architecture Faculty at Rome University. Baton-wielding youths marched alongside right-wing politicians in double-breasted suits or tried to break into the state university that was under student occupation. Young workers and students marched in protest after Italy's 1969 "hot autumn" of social conflict, after the general strike for housing and just a few short days after Parliament passed the Divorce Law. Then December 12, 1969 happened: the Piazza Fontana Massacre, in which a terrorist bomb exploded in a Milan bank killing 16 and injuring 90, raised the curtain on a long, black period.

At that time, three hundred thousand young people were at Woodstock and psychedelic beat was the style seen in downtown shop windows. Twiggy made *Time* magazine's cover, and posters of Angela Davis shared countless bedroom walls with Che Guevara, acknowledged star of posters and T-shirts, who would last another fifty years. Some lost themselves on LSD while others took the Milan-Como main road for another Highway 61, albeit a bit faded.

Devourers of paperbacks, torn between novels, poetry and dutiful, high-brow essays, they listened to 45s played on portable battery-powered record players and would soon flirt with deluxe purchasing and hi-fi sets. Keen on all things foreign, especially if they were American, many

MARCH 1968   PIAGGIO

Ironic, but touching an open nerve, "the ideal mother test" seemed to be in tune with the times.

Riding a GS along the streets of Soho, the scene from *Absolute Beginners* was timeless: swinging London, the capital of Mary Quant, the Sixties, or the 1986 of the Julian Temple film, or perhaps a vintage for the third millennium.

TEST: SIETE LA MADRE IDEALE?

Vostro figlio ha quindici o sedici anni, ha le sue prime amicizie, i suoi primi problemi, le sue prime ambizioni e, perché no?, i suoi primi complessi. Ed anche voi dovete affrontare nuovi problemi, soprattutto psicologici, per il vostro atteggiamento nei suoi confronti. Provate a rispondere sinceramente alle seguenti domande. Sarà per voi un utile esercizio di autocritica e di controllo. Soprattutto saprete se siete davvero o no una madre ideale.

		SI	NO
1	Continuate a considerarlo sempre il « vostro bambino »?	SI	NO
2	Provate un particolare orgoglio nel vederlo vestito in completo da uomo?	SI	NO
3	Quando riceve una telefonata, gli chiedete di chi è?	SI	NO
4	Quando invita in casa gli amici, voi vi inserite nella conversazione e nella compagnia?	SI	NO
5	Gli date ancora il bacio della buona notte?	SI	NO
6	Vi preoccupa che esterni idee politiche?	SI	NO
7	Gli permettete di fumare qualche sigaretta?	SI	NO
8	Gli avete regalato una Vespa?	SI	NO
9	Scegliete voi le sue cravatte?	SI	NO
10	Vi dispiace se telefona a qualche ragazza?	SI	NO

ORA ASSEGNATEVI I PUNTI:
Domanda 1: SI = 0 NO = 1; Domanda 2: SI = 1 NO = 1; Domanda 3: SI = 0 NO = 1; Domanda 4: SI = 0 NO = 1; Domanda 5: SI = 0 NO = 1; Domanda 6: SI = 0 NO = 1; Domanda 7: SI = 0 NO = 1; Domanda 8: SI = 9 NO = 0; Domanda 9: SI = 0 NO = 1; Domanda 10: SI = 0 NO = 1

SE AVETE OTTENUTO FINO A 9 PUNTI: Regalate subito una Vespa a vostro figlio; lui ve ne sarà grato, voi vi sentirete veramente una madre ideale.
SE AVETE OTTENUTO PIU' DI 9 PUNTI: Complimenti, siete una madre ideale e vostro figlio è felice con la Vespa.

Italian teenagers saw themselves as anti-imperialist. Their new, ideal territory was the city, but their favorite places to spend leisure time were out of town or at the beach, or at worst in the city parks.

They liked to think they were unreachable, swift, all gripped by the craze to go somewhere, get moving, get out of town or even, on the other hand, get to know every inch of it slipping along in the traffic.

Unmistakable shapes and colors with the 150 Sprint Veloce in 1969. The Vespa range was in a growth spurt, but the number of registered scooters on the Italian market had fallen by more than 80 percent since 1960.

Shiny, patent-leather knee-length boots, jerkins and buckled mini-dresses in strong colors or even pure white as well as in the optical designs, in a radically different ready-to-wear fashion trend which counted Elio Fiorucci and his Milan shop among its leaders (1967).

This was when an excellent Vespa communication campaign started which enjoyed widespread coverage abroad too.

Speak their language, but how?

There was no need to get the product known; a survey showed that something like 98 percent of the under-twenties knew exactly what a Vespa was.

What was needed, instead, was a way to get through to these new teenagers, who were often investigated and studied since they were so different from everything around them, captured by so many ideas and moved by so many ideals.

Perhaps they didn't all see themselves as the smiling kids of the poster singing "With Vespa you can! 'Cause the world is singing with us, the forest reflects the sun's thousand hues, an hour of joy has a thousand minutes." In their Vespas they were sure to find "a friend who'll help us meet new friends every day, and make us understand. The Vespa friend is always there to give us new ideas and point towards new discoveries. Tomorrow is brighter with Vespa."

The message was already innovative but of course, not everyone out there shared the same idea.

The January 1969 issue of Piaggio's company magazine calmly stated how much consideration had been given to "grown-ups who so often interfere in or even decide on the purchases of young people: hence the reassuring slant, the obvious respectability of Piaggio's ad."

On the other hand, the call for independence for a community of equals all the same age—a world of its own, almost—separated from everything round about it can, somehow, make it through. In order to reach the new consumers, advertising had to associate every product with the celebration of youth—whether it be toothpaste, aperitifs, cosmetics or underwear. Even Agip's Supercortemaggiore—the "powerful Italian gasoline" from the oil well near the town of Piacenza—was advertised with the slogan, "Run young, Run Agip." But there is a risk in all this: the risk of total refusal.

"Wouldn't they—who were so decidedly rebellious against fathers, masters and erstwhile heroes—have felt themselves brutally manipulated by the Marcusian opulent society?"

We were on a razor's edge, apparently. But a stroke of genius implemented with subtle perfidy righted the counterplay within the system.

It's Vespa time again; Vespa with apples this time.

Lara-Vinca Masini

1969, youth revolt, imagination in power and a new strategy of Piaggio communication were born together with a memorable slogan: "Chi Vespa mangia le mele" ["Whoever Vespas eats apples"] by Gilberto Filippetti for the Leader agency of Florence.

Below: Vespa is ready for a new metamorphosis (original sketch by Gilberto Filippetti).

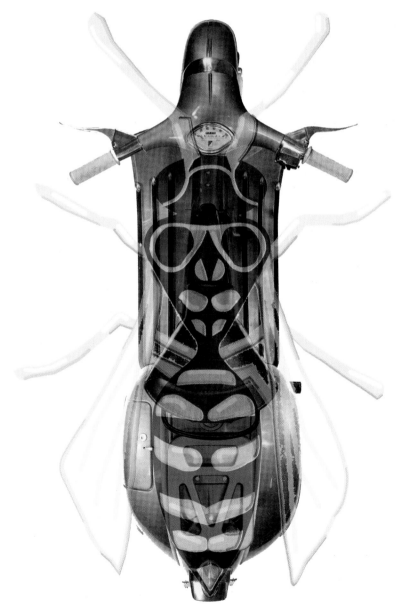

WHOEVER VESPAS...

I think few advertising campaigns have been praised as highly as this one, thought up by Gilberto Filippetti of the Leader advertising agency of Florence for Vespa (whose name, ending in an "A" is feminine), which kept the same up-to-the-minute fragrance and freshness as it had at the outset well beyond the period it was used (1968–71).

This was due to the fact that Gilberto Filippetti always considered advertising work not only as a means of production of consensus for consuming a product, the direct and obvious aim of an adman, but also as an expression of "creativity …, consumption of liberty, 'sociological creativity' since nothing is more socially useful than that which educates the imagination and widens the concept of liberty itself; liberty as a prime necessity which remains an infinity of the mind despite somebody having made a marble statue of it just to confuse the issue…"

In answer to the question "how do you reconcile liberty with the need to generate consumption?," he said in 1984:

"I've always asked myself that question and I think I found the answer in trying to respect people's feelings when I do my job. It may be an illusion but I feel that in advertising products that stimulate people's imagination you give them the faculty of choosing the product that gives them most freedom. This is the way I assess every advertising campaign before launching it so that it corresponds as far as possible to what my conscience dictates, seeking also to safeguard the social aspect of what my profession entails."

He added: "Every new idea has within it something revolutionary. New ideas make you grow old and nobody likes to grow old just as nobody likes to admit that only people who've got ideas are really young. A really new idea can rattle the

The strategy of expressive copywriting in communication concepts included poetry, happiness, colorfulness, likeability, revolution.

The cover of *Il Millimetro* (22 June 1969) which marked the birth event of the new campaign with the title "An apple and a bizarre verb turning creativity on its head."

The key idea was repeated in this sketch, and the wheel-guard of the Vespa carried the distinctive mark of this campaign.

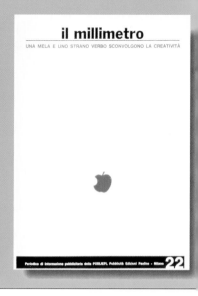

universe ... Just as the repressed represses, people in advertising who can't get on to the same wavelength as the new psychological reality have always tried to stop new ideas crossing out old ones."

This campaign couldn't have started at a better time: Italy was just moving into a period of general well-being, at least when compared to what had gone before. A rural, artisan nation was becoming industrialized and youth was no longer just a transient period in life but now a new "category."

Vespa, initially conceived as a miniature compact vehicle for those who couldn't afford a car, for laborers to get to work but also for small families for their Sunday run in the country, found its most significant collocation in this new world of youth as well as in the one which followed: the feminine world. For youth, the Vespa meant winning new liberties that were expressed in every aspect of life. The hippies were coming on the scene, the flower children: "... be sure to wear some flowers in your hair..."

In the mid-Sixties youth rebelled against the threadbare, degraded world of adults over all the Western world in university students' movements. And it was in Florence in the red-hot climate of "American life" and British and American pop culture that a group of young architects set themselves up as a radical architecture movement (Archizoom, Superstudio, UFO, 9999, Zziggurath) aiming for a renewal of architecture that had been bottled up by speculative building, turning their back on professional practices and moving towards an alternative design that was both playful and strongly critical (the "antidesign" that in the years to come was to set itself up as a "commodity" for both "elite and masses" was gobbled up by the system and became the pride and joy of the new Milan

Below: Marketing now decisively targeting youth inspires the new campaign visuals.

On a double-page spread in every magazine Filippetti's campaign blazons the new slogan.

bourgeoisie after losing its revolutionary impetus).

But by then, youth culture had brought changes to the way we spoke. The movements' slogans intentionally threw the gauntlet before accepted syntax in the name of a recently won freedom.

Filippetti, with refreshing candor, tells his almost "urban legend" story about how the idea came about when "there were some twenty-year olds and some a bit older but it was the first time that only the real twenty-years-olds counted." He was riding on a bus when he saw a boy "completely calm and detached, ignoring the chaos that was happening all round him, munching an apple, he was daubing the wall with white paint with the words 'don't trust anybody over thirty'…."

Whatever the story, it was a stroke of genius and was to create a whole series of slogans of the same kind …

Filippetti's idea in advertising had always been to give words the same importance as the picture, but this time the words came out as a grammatical miracle. The slogan started the phrase with "Chi" ["Who"], used in the senses of "He who" or "The person who" or "Some people." This was a novelty in Italian advertising and was copied in many later advertisements: "Chi Mobil e chi meno," ["Some Mobil and some less"]; the Jesus Jeans slogan, "Chi mi ama mi segua" ["He who loves me follows me"]; "Chi non mangia la Golia è un ladro o una spia" ["He who doesn't eat Golia mints is a thief or a spy"]; "Chi ama brucia" ["Whoever loves burns"] for Pavesini biscuits.

Filippetti's slogan also abbreviated and took grammatical liberties, changing the noun "Vespa" into a verb: "Chi Vespa" ["Whoever Vespas"]. This miracle of transgression and

Berkeley lights up and pulses, clanging like a tilted pinball machine, and so do Paris and Pisa, Trento and Turin. And all over the world fighting words are painted on the walls of the establishment: "We want everything and we want it now!"; "Free Love!"; "Black is beautiful!"; "Women hold up half the sky!"; "Young is beautiful!."

And so put a little zip in your pen and leave all that boring staid marketing behind! Come on with the hot light language of emotion. The young think with energy and optimism, and on paper, as on a wall, they write, "Who Vespas yes, who Vespas no." The pen writes by itself: variant A, "Who Vespas touches the sun, who doesn't doesn't"; variant B, "Who Vespas eats apples, who doesn't doesn't." That's it! We've got it! Yes, that kid wrote it. I called Pico (Tamburini, the owner of the Leader agency) and what did he say? "Great, Gil! Fresh as the rain! But we'll have a hell of a time selling it to the client."

(G. Filippetti, *Fuori disselciano*; see bibliograhy)

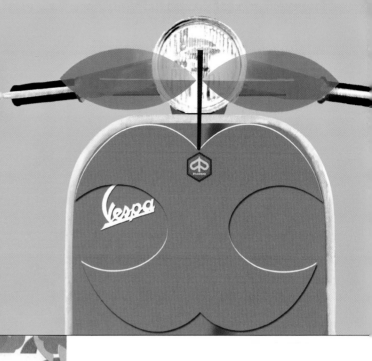

chi "Vespa"
mangia le mele
(chi non "Vespa" no)

un morso alla mela e ... un vroom alla Vespa. Un vroom
alla Vespa e ... lasciati indietro tutti quelli senza fantasia
la mela a stelle si mangia con i fari accesi

LeaDer 8/119B

8 sono i modelli Vespa
da L. 107.000 f.f. in su.
Vespa 50 si guida
senza targa e senza patente
anche a 14 anni.

PIAGGIO

invention unleashed the idea and turned it into something
incisive and totally innovative: "Chi Vespa mangia le mele
(chi non Vespa no)" ["Whoever Vespas eats apples (whoever
doesn't Vespa doesn't)"]. And behind this image—which at
first might seem casual and incoherent—lay an enormous
quantity of recall and meaning that got triggered almost like
a chain reaction.

The apple is a brightly-colored, fresh, natural fruit in the
shape of a perfect sphere with its inherent meaning of
countryside, sun and freedom; but it also has symbolic
significance at the base of eroticism, or love if nothing else—
from the apple of discord, the forbidden fruit debated in the
earthly paradise between Eve and the devious, devilish
serpent, to the apples in the Garden of the Hesperides, the
golden apple that fell from the gods' banqueting table, the
golden apple that Paris attributed to Venus as the most
beautiful goddess of Parnassus, the golden apple that
Hippomenes cast before Atalanta during the race so that
attracted by it she would stop to gather it and lose the race,
and thus become his bride. Not to mention all the iconographic images from Cranach to Lorrain just to mention
a few. The Big Apple symbol of New York City—almost
always linked to the words "I love—" gives the apple strong
connotations, of an erotic nature too.

And if a bite is taken out of each side of an apple, the resulting shape is like that of the front apron of the Vespa, whose
name comes also from its shape "with a waist like a wasp's."

Try placing two images on top of each other as I once did
for fun during a lesson, using two of Duchamp's most
significant works.

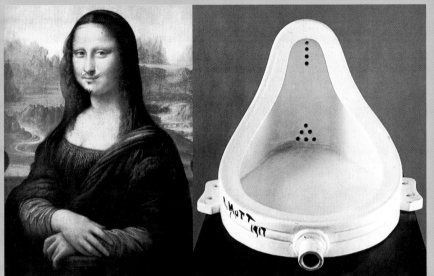

Ideas for analogical collocation between different expressive forms. Freedom of conceptual association in contemporary art: Marcel Duchamp, *La Joconde* (1919) and *Fountain* (1917).

In '17, Duchamp presented anonymously the well-known men's urinal entitled Fountain *"by R. Mutt" at the first exhibition of the American Society of Independent Artists, who obviously turned it down.*

John Thompson described it as a functional object, oddly shaped and drawn from an exclusively male domain. A urinal: a toilet for men that is so feminine and seductive in shape that it suggests a whole series of provocative associations: a mouth or a vagina or the imprint of their opposites, the female that perfectly fits the male.

Katherine Dreier, a friend of Duchamp and a society member, agreed that the elegant and sinuous strength of the urinal was quintessentially feminine.

So, on top of Fountain *I laid* La Joconde, *Duchamp's image—as has been done here with Leonardo's* Mona Lisa—*and lo and behold, the two pictures matched perfectly …*

Putting the apple with two leaves (that match the scooter's handlebars) over the image of the Vespa could conjure up the idea of a lovers' tryst perhaps slightly risqué (but then again didn't we say the Vespa was female? And wasn't the apple always the object of desire, the forbidden fruit?). It is, however, a reminder of the liberty young people then had gained of being able to meet. Weren't those the days when everybody dared to go around preaching free love? This game of superimposing the bitten apple image upon the image of the Vespa does not yield resonances of the same mental, alchemic and conceptual complexity as the two works of Duchamp. Nevertheless, it can offer another interesting interpretation of a work that, in my view, has significance that goes well beyond its original, less sophisticated intentions.

Graphic variations enrich the campaign and increase its success, summarized by the phrase "... the new standard of those seeking an Italian avenue in advertising" by Luca di Montezemolo (16 Nov. '85).

In 1970, the campaign became costume and influenced fashions over a multitude of products. Upim department stores and Esso (Exxon) produced objects and gadgets with the new symbol.

With the phrase *Melacompro la Vespa* (1973), the three years of a campaign unequaled in effectiveness was brought to an exemplary conclusion.

In any case, the most simple reading sees this campaign linked to Pop Art—a type of Pop Art, however, less realistic than normal in the abstract tension of the flat graphic surface that gradually becomes richer in internal figurations, all images of young couples on vacation with new captions after the one that had filled out the first, flat image without the bites.

"The apple is a red heart with a green leaf / It's beautiful and good, you eat it alone or in company but always with the wind in your hair. When it's really red a big bite tastes like sunset / a light blue apple tastes like the spray of the waves, an apple with freckles has upturned leaves and gives you a wink ..." (It's interesting to note that from now on the Vespa, which was originally gray, is now in the liveliest colors: red, green, light-blue...). Later on in the campaign there was the striped apple, the daisy apple, the one with stars, then the heart-shaped one and the one that sang ... and the "very

le sardomobili vivono il caos
liberi "chi Ciao"

PIAGGIO
cambia il mondo
in 2 ruote

The "sardomobile" idea
heralded ecological and
environmentally oriented
campaigns. The language
of the product was carried
over in the new campaign
and was extended to other
products (Ciao and Boxer)
becoming company language
that was to distinguish
all Piaggio communications.

rare musical apple the best of all to eat." This text retains the reference to transgression and adds a visual transgression to the imagined erotic one. The apple really does turn into a daisy, a satellite, a mouth, a heart. It divides into rhythmic degrees conveying a sense of speed moving from Pop Art to Pop-optical (1970).

It should be remembered that that was also the time when besides Pop Art, there was Kinetic, Programmed and Optical Art and the two trends that declared war on each other (irrationality that wanted to do away with the linearity of rationalism, by then out of date) but which often blended together into an enjoyable synthesis especially in the graphics. The number of captions grew: "Whoever Vespas eats apples … and gives a kiss to whoever he pleases."

And again, in 1971, "Melacompro la Vespa" ["I'll buy

myself a Vespa"]. This last is a clever play on words: "Mela-compro" means "I will buy myself," but its first two syllables ("mela") form the Italian word for "apple."

In 1972, in the Leader agency the graphic fantasy and imagination of Filippetti gave birth to the "sardomobiles," brightly-colored sardines with four wheels that packed themselves shoulder to shoulder in the garage, never enjoying the sun, breathing each other's air, challenging each other, never loving each other, always honking their horns, stealing time"… while "whoever Vespa'd" drove on in triumph to "shine," "breathe," pray for peace, be respected by others, "murmur" instead of yell , "get there first"… even if the sardomobiles (obviously "the automobiles") took up ever more room in their ranks not just in the posters, but in the cities too polluting the air and rupturing the silence …

"So, riding along on the crest of the youth revolt was a choice of convenience?"

"Not exactly. It was undoubtedly convenient for the company which had to keep step if it wanted to sell but as far as I was concerned it was a deeply felt conviction. I was young too and I felt part of it all."

(Gilberto Filippetti, *Fuori disselciano*)

le sardomobili non godono il sole
splende "chi Vespa"

WHY VESPA ENDS IN "A"

Standing on the gigantic Vespa exhibited at the 29th Milan Fair in 1951, astride the new 1953 125 or, facing, one of the pretty silhouettes of '58, well beyond the actual importance of the female clientele, the image of a woman was the perfect testimonial to the modernity and great simplicity of use of the machine.

The female factor is already part of the DNA of this softly curvaceous scooter with its pinched waistline; it's as accessible as a woman's bicycle as Corradino D'Ascanio himself emphasized. Every part of the design was developed to the maximum with an eye to it being used by a non-expert, without any physical effort. The unspecialized vocation of the vehicle would seem to make it particularly suitable for the newly emerging women's market. Indeed the attention paid to women purchasers from the very start was surprising, and this policy was not limited to researching possible direct purchasers.

The purse strings

"A recent survey shows that the woman manages the family budget in almost 40 percent of households" announced an item published by the *Piaggio* magazine in Spring '69. "Furthermore, when there are expenses to be made for the family as a whole, it is the woman who decides in 46 percent of the cases. It should also be noted that this percentage rises to 52 in the North, so considering the woman decides not only what she'll spend on herself but also what will be spent on the family unit in almost one family in two it stands to reason that a significant part of the national budget in consumer goods is decided on by women."

So who were these women?

Some of the statistics about them might come as a surprise. No more than 9.2 percent of Italian women could speak a foreign language and exactly twice as

many, though still less than a fifth of the total, said they read books; this statistic may even err on the high side considering how cultural consumption was thought to be prestigious. Sport isn't worth mentioning, for only 2.4 percent of Italian women played some kind of sport in the late Sixties. Despite the number of university students having doubled in just five years, only 200,000—about 40 percent of the total—were women. Perhaps less natural is that fewer than two million women in all of Italy had graduated from junior high school. But then only something like 80 percent of Italians had a primary education.

In this new world, the no-license-plate "Vespina" swiftly dissipated any macho ideas that had been associated up to then with the scooter. Even more so did the Ciao, whose godfather was Umberto Agnelli at its launch held on 11 October 1967 under the huge dome of the indoor sports arena at Genoa's Maritime Exhibition where a procession composed almost exclusively of women riders wove along the runway specially set up for the occasion. It was no coincidence that the riders were women, and the resounding success of Piaggio's first moped can be attributed to its almost exclusively female consumer base.

Having said that, you just need to take one step back and you will find something hackneyed, awkward and old-fashioned.

On the verge of the new world

"There was no way to turn it down without seeming scared. But I hadn't given a thought to what I'd look like … towards sunset, she got me to sit on the pillion seat and then climbed on in front and set off weaving through the cars, sidling alongside vans as tall as houses and rocketing off in front of everybody else if she was at the head of the line when the light turned green … a woman schlepping a man like a package. I don't think I've ever been in such an embarrassing and humiliating situation before in my whole life."

Giuseppe Prezzolini, the passenger on this particular Vespa, was not perhaps the most progressive thinker, but he did express the male sense of pride and the deep-seated national bias regarding women drivers.

"I could see myself written on everybody's face when we stopped at a red light; everybody's barely concealed

During the Ladies' San Remo Rally of 1953 (below) the annual election of Miss Vespa was held and the winner rode around on her Vespa to the delight of the photographers.

At the 1955 Miss Italia contest (left) the showcase was obviously much more important, the promotion much more effective. The winner was Brunella Tocci, Miss Calabria but then living in Rome.

On the streets of Nairobi on a brand-new Vespa followed by the gaze of interested onlookers. The year was 1961, just a couple of years before Kenyan independence and imports from Italy were few and far between. The scooter was kept for the shopping sprees of the ladies of the European colony, and the leisure-time trips of their consorts.

amazement and reproach." Anything's possible—it was still only 1962—but this took place one winter's evening in Manhattan between Forty-second and Broadway— Times Square in other words—and in all probability he was never even noticed among all those lights.

Camilla Cederna, Italian journalist and scrupulous social commentator, wrote about girls on Vespas in the *Espresso* newsmagazine in 1957.

People read about them in foreign magazines too, as women often talked with evident satisfaction about their Vespa experiences. Many women drove and succeeded in arduous enterprises, stimulated by the initiatives organized by the Vespa Clubs, including the traditional, non-competitive Vespa rally first held in '52. Promotion for this had already been going on for

Mary Williamson of Melbourne, Australia certainly deserved to make the cover picture of the weekly magazine in the name of the all-female staff of the city's postal delivery service. The year was 1961, light years from Italy.

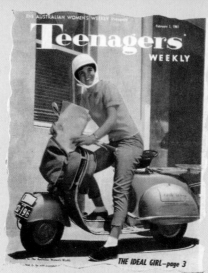

"A tear or two, understandable enough for the disappointment in not quite making it, immediately covered up by the ever-present powder-puff." It was still only 1955, one might say to excuse the tone of this article in the June edition of the Vespa Club d'Italia newsletter. And already, in contrast with the prestige of the Thousand Kilometer or the Three Seas Rally, the Procession of Lady Vespa Enthusiasts on the Côte d'Azur and the International Ladies' Vespa Audax were gaining in importance, testifying to the special attention given to the female public and clientele. Today, the president of the Fédération Internationale des Vespa Clubs is a woman, Christa Solbach.

some time and in the summer of '62 the company magazine came into the open with the headline "Scooters aid female emancipation."

"In English-speaking countries, women's lib was already old hat. Vespa therefore played no part in it in America. In Europe, and especially in Latin Europe, the scooter did play a fairly important part in this area."

It almost looks like Piaggio was trying to keep up with the times and some of the images conjure up a smile after so many years.

"A working girl," for example, in 1960 at the port of Genoa, looking good "so men'll look at us," zips across town; after four hours in an office out she comes, off on the scooter to do a little shopping then back home in time for lunch—"Ciao Mamma! Everything OK?" then she marches to the table to devour her pasta.

Also for strong stomachs was the model used in "Impressions of Rome": gamin hairstyle and trousers on the Spanish Steps or maybe skirt and high heels, with just enough time for a short stop on the Appian Way to down a flask of local wine, draped in a ladylike way over the Vespa saddle.

Excuse me, may I ask you a question?

The next step takes us ten years forward and we are in another world. A fourteen-year-old schoolgirl is being quietly interviewed. Just for the record, her name was Mavi Soldatini.

"You've got a Vespa 50. Are you happy to own a two-wheeled vehicle?"

"You bet."

"What made you chose this kind of vehicle?"

"To be more free to get about, to be able to go with my friends, to be more independent. And the Vespa gives me a feeling of safety and I liked it better too: a lot… the way it looked."

"What does it feel like driving a two-wheeled vehicle?"

"Well, you know, it makes me feel happy, it gives me a buzz, it makes me feel great. I like it a lot, I really do. It's a great little thing. And it makes me feel completely free, free from everyone, away from the city, away from the usual boring things."

"What do your male friends really think about you running around on a two-wheeled vehicle?"

"Well, it's pretty normal nowadays. I'll tell you, its

Get one for all the family to use, suggested an American advertisement, especially for the lady of the house who didn't have to work but "just" look after the home and family: reliable, functional and economic … But for "him," too, Vespa meant first of all "fun transportation."

Another kind of woman: free, creative, open to the world, independent economically and in getting about thanks to the Vespa (featuring a guest appearance by Valentine, the Olivetti typewriter designed in 1969 by Ettore Sottsass).

Agostina Belli holds her own against the approaches of Marcello Mastroianni who plays a detective investigating the case in *Doppio delitto* (1977) directed by Steno.

The image of a new, positive, more aware type of woman was emerging. As always, the ads, here taken from the Piaggio calendars of 1974 and '76, reflect a sweetened but representative version.

not easy to get into a crowd if you've nothing to … You know, to begin with everybody in my crowd had a moped, something to get around on easily. They'd always go off on their own and I was always, like, left out because I had to walk there and there was no way I could do that."

"Do you feel that this two-wheeled vehicle has been a way for you to get more freedom?"

"Well, yes in a way, because beforehand if you saw a girl on a Vespa you mightn't have thought too much of her. You know, motorbikes—I dunno. Well anyway two-wheeled vehicles were, you know, more for boys but that's all past now. Now there's girls on motorbikes too, much bigger ones. Nobody, you know—they're almost looked up to—but nobody thinks badly of them, you know."

"So you could say that it's a kind of women's lib!"

"Sure, I really think so."

Athos Bigongiali

THREE RETURN TICKETS TO PONTEDERA

There were two kinds of flyer with different head-lines. There were the mimeographed ones that the machine churned out with ink smudges all over and the other ones, already lined up in piles on the floor, the printed ones, black letters on yellow paper. The headline was in red block capitals: UNITED WE STAND. But we liked the mimeographs better.

Let's take this one, said Tommaso.

Who's he? asked the man turning the mimeograph handle.

He's the youth secretary, replied Eugenio. The new one.

The other stopped turning the handle and looked at Tommaso.

Goodness, not half curly aren't you, he said. How d'you manage to do your hair?

Tommaso laughed heartily. It grows out of a bushy brain, he said, a real well-ordered one too.

Then he turned to me:

Take a thousand.

A thousand? said the man at the mimeograph. Then he looked back at Eugenio. Don't you think that's a bit much?

No, retorted Eugenio. A thousand. Just like Garibaldi had when he landed.[1]

The man made to spit on his hands. I'm finished, he said, but I'll do it just for you. He leaned over the machine and started turning the handle again. The room was full of smoke. Outside, just beyond the market square, the town clock struck six. By the way, said the man. Do we have to do overtime or not? What d'you reckon?

Eugenio pulled out his watch from his waistcoat pocket with a sigh.

I was the only one of the three who had to phone to say I wouldn't be home that night. I told my father I was going to sleep at Eugenio's. The meeting was going to be long and I had to be at the university early next morning: we were going to study together, after the meeting. But what we did was go and get something to eat at the little restaurant down the end of a dark lane in the old, medieval part of town.

The owner's wife asked: You like cabbage sautéed in sauce?

We'd just finished a big plateful when Tommaso joined us.

It's great, he said. All these arches, that old stone. All this history stuck to the walls with frying oil and smoke. It smells like the Carbonari,[2] it smells like a plot. It really stinks.

He pulled up a chair, took a swig from my glass and said: We're not toeing the line, comrades. Work for the masses, he said, has to be done up front, among the people.

You like cabbage sautéed in sauce? asked Eugenio.

What else is there?

Cod and potatoes.

And cuttlefish with greens! shouted the owner's wife from across the counter.

Ok, Ok said Tommaso. I give in.

We didn't finish eating until late. When we rose, the owner's wife was throwing sawdust on the floor between the tables. You get it, Tommaso told me. We'll square up later.

I lit a cigarette and pulled out my money.

We had to make a racket to wake him up, clapping our hands. He almost toppled off the sofa. Ok, Ok he protested, thanks for the applause. I get it.

Eugenio pulled the covers off him. Come on, get up.

I went into the kitchen to put the coffee on.

I was busy with the machine when I heard him say: What's the time?

Half past three.

I'd like to have a shave if you don't mind.

What d'you mean a shave? Get a move on.

Jesus, that cod! It's sitting right here in my gut.

Will you please hurry up?

We were walking down the hall from the bedroom to the bathroom.

Where's the toothpaste?

How should I know? Look for it.

The toothbrush. Give me a toothbrush at least.

We drank our coffee in silence. Then Eugenio walked over to the window and threw it open. It was pitch dark and peeping through the chimney tops on the roof of the house in front you could see a spring night, cold and starless.

Three to Pontedera, Eugenio asked the ticket office. Returns. The man shoved his glasses up on to his forehead: Whose is the dog?

Eugenio looked round. What dog?

That dog, replied the ticket-seller. No dogs on the train.

He was there behind us, lying by the timetable board. What're you doing here? asked Tommaso bending down to stroke him. What's your name, then?

The dog whimpered and, lowering its head, sniffed his shoes.

Maybe he's hungry, I said.

Maybe not, said Tommaso. Maybe he just wants to cock his leg on me.

We stuffed the bundles of flyers under our arms and went out. The dog stayed where it was near the timetable board. He'd got up and seemed to take a look at the train times, undecided. He wants to leave, said Tommaso. Only he doesn't know where to go.

We went and sat down on a bench.

The dim, neon-lit waiting room was facing us. The platforms alongside the rails were deserted and down the end, where the shelter stopped, a thick patch of fog cut off the rest of the world.

Get a load of him, said Tommaso.

Eugenio was walking towards us, tall in his dark suit with the jacket flapping open to show his beautiful red-and-blue tie and waistcoat with the gold watch chain.

If you didn't know him, said Tommaso, who would you take him for?

A university professor, I replied, a high-up one's assistant.

Tommaso zipped up his jacket and blew into his hands. Remind me to ask the workers, he muttered, starting to whistle "The Internationale."

Then the train came wheezing and whistling along.

It looked like it was in a hurry. It stopped just a minute to let us clamber on, the ticket inspector and us, then with a jerk and a whistle, it set off again fast. But, when it slowed down at the first station, Eugenio opened the window and said: You've got to understand, it's only a local train, an accelerato, *it stops at every station even the tiny ones with*

a couple of houses round the square, the town clock and the Casa del Popolo³, maybe.

We were already in the middle of the countryside.

The odors of manure and hay reached our nostrils across the fog the train was plowing through and we peeled our eyes to see what was behind the hedgerows, the walls and the fences. Was it a well or a fig tree or a farmyard with the dog's kennel in the middle and the farm-buildings beyond lit up by a faint white light? Dawn was starting to break under the black sky.

Have you ever seen it? asked Tommaso.

Seen what?

The Aurora Borealis, he replied.

They say it's caused by the solar wind, he continued, a sort of reflection of the Sun's energy when it gets dark and the Earth thinks it can do without.

People got on at every station. They came out furtively from under the roofing, alongside the carriage, pulled themselves on and got swallowed up by the carriage.

Chilled men; working men.

The train absorbed them one by one and started up again.

It shuffled along, puffing and panting as if, every time, it wanted to shake itself free of the fog that shrouded the view of fields and outhouses.

I was the last to fall asleep.

We started off by saying what we would do as soon as we got there. Not a lot but good. Get to standing in front of the gates before the workers got there, wait for them to come and when they passed by give them each a flyer. Nothing to it, no explanations needed, not even to the workers we knew. Hi. Well, look who's here. How's it going? How do you think it's going, haven't you seen the paper?

The older ones would have folded the flyer in four and not said a word. The younger ones would have joked a bit. So, what's it all about? A strike?

Nobody was very talkative so early in the morning.

Then after the first shift was in off to the café we'd go just down the road. We'd surely have found somebody willing to stand us a cup of coffee:

How do you want yours spiked? Rum?

Come on, down with it. Does you good..

The way he was dressed they'd have taken Eugenio for a party official:

There's still too many, too many who don't think but just follow on. Too many.

Who're you sending to the meeting tomorrow?

The less wily ones too, clutching the mimeograph:

Eat the boss' apples.⁴ What's that mean?

I thought I was listening to Eugenio explaining it to him when I dozed off before I realized it.

Then all of a sudden I heard Tommaso shouting, We're here!

I thought we were too. On the other side of the tracks a bunch of men were setting off down the underpass.

We clambered down in a rush just as the train was starting up again. The bundle! Eugenio yelled. I jumped back on to the train, raced back to the compartment, grabbed the bundle and leaped off on to the platform.

My heart was in my throat and my legs were shaking. What would've happened if we'd been on the battleship Aurora *asked Tommaso a little later. What would we have done? Set the revolution for another day?*

The ticket office was as empty. The corridor led us out to an open space where it was all dark because of the fog. We saw a shadow cycling along a road beside a railway ballast as high as a river bank. Over on the other side at the end, you could see the raised gates of a level crossing.

Eugenio looked around, mystified.

Down this way? Tommaso queried.

Down where?

The road, answered Tommaso. Can't you see it, the road?

Sure, but I can't see the underpass.

What d'you mean?

Can you see it?

The fog swept around us.

There's supposed to be a tunnel, said Eugenio. I remember it clearly.

He turned to me: Do you see it?

No.

Maybe we came the wrong way, he said. We should've come out the other end of the underpass.

That's it, said Tommaso. Come on, everybody, get back.

Later, above the station entrance, we just made out the name of the town in bas relief painted black. Time had faded it like the names of the dead on really old tombstones in the graveyard.

I can't believe it.

Me neither.

So they started to bicker. It was you, I was sleeping. Oh

yeah? But your eyes were open enough when you got off. And you, earlier? Dreaming were you? Do me a favor will you and shut up.

They started on me right afterwards:

You were awake dammit.

Awake? I was about as awake as Sleeping Beauty.

We'd got off at the wrong station and there was nothing we could do about it. But Tommaso kept on:

What's the time?

Quarter to five.

You sure it's right?

Sure.

Tommaso watched as Eugenio fiddled with his watch:

I don't trust that thing.

So who cares.

They started squabbling again. Next time I'm coming on my own. Yes, but in the car. I'm coming on my bike. Good for you! You think I won't? You bet! There's only one man up front!

They sat down on the curb in the meantime. The fog started to lift and we could see the houses on the other side of the square and beyond and above the roofs, the loggia of a bell-tower.

The first person we met was the priest. We were hurrying along when we came across him on rounding the first corner. A black cassock in the small church square, he was carrying a broom holding it upright by the handle.

He looked like a guard.

Will you speak to him?

What for? To tell him we got off at the wrong station?

Their feathers were still ruffled.

I'm not going to speak to him.

Me neither.

You're the secretary.

And you're the head of propaganda.

At that point the priest realized we were there. Good morning.

He set the broom against the doorpost and asked:

Are you here for the funeral?

He observed us from under his glasses. He was an old priest with gray hair and ruddy cheeks. You're here earlier than I expected, he said.

Tommaso went closer.

Oh yes, said the priest, you'll be the grandson. Remarkable likeness!

At that precise instant a woman wearing a headscarf stuck her head out of the vicarage window. She looked as if she'd had a fright.

Good heavens, she squawked, who're they?

Fig? You're sure it's fig?

Taste this, its raspberry.

No no, retorted the priest, it's blackberry. We gather them here ourselves with the Sunday school kids in autumn.

Tommaso stuck his spoon into the jar.

Shove some here, on the bread.

The kitchen of the priest's house was warm and well lit.

Eugenio had shed his jacket and had placed himself at the top of the table with everybody else around him. The woman was standing in front of the cooker.

Here we go, it's almost boiling!

I got up and held my cup out.

As we were eating, the priest said: I must be off but please, take your time. I like having folk in the house when I'm reading mass.

Then he took a flyer from the bundle we'd unwrapped earlier to show him.

I read everything, he remarked. I like to. It makes me feel less ignorant.

Tommaso dipped his bread in the milk with a smile.

---

1. The number of Garibaldi's redshirts at the launch of his military campaign to unify Italy in 1860.

2. A nineteenth-century Italian nationalist conspiracy.

3. The Communist Party leisure center.

*4. "Apples" in Tuscan dialect also means "buttocks" so, aping the apple/*mela *advertising idea, "chew the boss's ass off."*

CLOUDS ON THE HORIZON

The thirty-year anniversary of the end of World War II coincided with a highly delicate period: besides the fierce domestic social tension, the nation looked as though it had become the terrain for a broader conflict to be played out.

Things were changing but change is not always for the better. The anti-conformist revolt had partly seeped through habits and had reached the point of contaminating the taste of young people and adults in fashion and in general the consumption of the average Italian.

It looked like everything was up for sale.

The world of students and young people took on a rigidly political orientation and increasingly took to the streets to celebrate its young martyrs who had died a violent death. It was as though a progressive closing up, a falling back into the private sphere had taken over but, on the outer fringes, there were some who were set on raising the level of strife. The composite galaxy of feminism, with its ability to keep from getting fossilized

and keep away from violence, was a rare exception. The early Sixties were the years of the Piazza della Loggia (in Brescia) and Italicus train massacres (in both cases caused by bombs later proven to have been laid by extreme right-wing terrorists), of continuous exhausting tension, and of fear. The phrase "Compromesso Storico [Historic compromise]" between the Christian Democrats and the Communist Party—which gave external support to the government by agreeing to abstain from voting—was coined in October 1973, just after the coup d'état in Chile.

However, Italy was able to produce other and better things. The conquests of two years of trade-union struggle were enjoyed by all of society: from the law on female labor in the factory, to accident prevention, up

January and February '76: the modesty about showing so much bare flesh, apparently thought excessive, that stop-pressed this calendar month so that a cover-up could be added, makes us smile nowadays.

Bright and breezy, by contrast, this ad by Gilera is obviously by the same hand that had invented the slogan "Whoever Vespa's": "Yes, hello... there's a guy outside who's been looking for an hour... seems like he's never seen a Gilera before."

_...si pronto!
...c'è un tizio
qui fuori
che guarda da un'ora;
sembra
non abbia mai visto
una Gilera._

TELEPHONE

to the 150 hours that workers could utilize to attend further education while working. The worker's statute of 1973 was to be a beacon for the new-born, unified CGIL-CISL-UIL trade-union confederation. Underpinning a new civil conscience was the '74 vote denying a referendum proposal to abrogate the divorce law.

Inflation doubled in a twelve-month period and rocketed to 20 percent. Clouds started to appear on the horizon: Gross Domestic Product was soon to crash from 6 percent to minus 4 percent over two years.

The oil crisis had the face of a hostile Arab turning off the oil tap. An English word, "austerity," came into common parlance to describe the fearful reduction in energy, forced not only on Italy but on the whole industrialized Western world.

The transformation was traumatic with effects clearly seen on the markets. Piaggio suffered a brusque halt in domestic sales in 1973, though exports flourished thanks to the weakness of the lira, literally doubling in two brief years.

After the Ciao phenomenon, the Boxer and Bravo mopeds came out in quick succession from the production lines in Pontedera, which had, in the meantime, become unrecognizable to all but the most assiduous visitor. The new 2R shop was automated and electronic innovations widely incorporated from the manufacturing departments to warehouse management, with over six-thousand personnel between technicians and blue-collar workers and a productivity rhythm of 1,700 units per day. The watchword was diversification, entailing a brusque change after thirty years of Vespa and Ape.

High wheels or low wheels?

The scooter world was feeling the effects of the increasing interest in trail bikes and some of them fell by the wayside. Innocenti's colossal factory ground to a halt in '71: the Lambretta production lines were sold to the Indian government while Leyland later took over the Lambrate factory. Youngsters wanted "real motorbikes" and the female consumer preferred the high wheels that brought agility to mopeds. Moreover, not a few of the mainstream left their car in the garage for something more maneuverable and economical in city traffic.

These were some of the reasons that had induced Piaggio to purchase Gilera, the prestigious company in Arcore near Milan, in 1969 and set about restructuring

The energy crisis involving the whole Western world set a ten gallon per auto limit at this pump in Connecticut in 1974. Increased resources were fed into research on low-fuel engines and alternative energy sources in this period.

GAS SHORTAGE! Sales Limited to 10 GALS. OF GAS. PER CUSTOMER

Still some uncertainty on how to ride this Ciao electric look-alike with a top-speed of just 13 mph but a respectable range of 25 miles at constant speed and 22 miles in urban traffic. The final technical report envisaged a real speed regulator but this would have further penalized performance so an on-off switch was incorporated instead that functioned according to the situation. This, in turn required an automatic clutch, a flexible drive coupling and some caution in riding. A fuddled solution but, for the time being, the only one practicable.

The hydrojet propulsion unit powered by a Piaggio engine and a Berkeley turbine were launched in 1973 just as a short-lived expansion in the nautical segment was happening.

The TIII was an original two-stroke little tractor whose engine was developed from the Ape's. Production continued from 1969 until 1975 with some forays made in export markets also.

and relaunching it. There was no overlapping because product philosophies were so different but commitment was heavy in terms of advertising and communication.

Faithful to the Vespa cause, the "sardomobiles" multiplied over billboards, newspapers and TV ads pointing to the obtuse insensitivity of four-wheeled vehicles in this period of restricted means. In the meantime, the 50 Elestart testified to the company's effort towards product updating. It also meant a letter from the new managing director, Nello Vallecchi, to general manager Francesco Lanzara: as early as April '69, in which he threw a blanket of secrecy over the development of a new, continuous gear-change because it was "of special interest to us, in view of the designs presently being developed." The so-called variomatic would soon be incorporated on mopeds but Vespas without a gear-change still had to wait seventeen years to make their appearance.

Research and development was also hard at work in electric propulsion. Great interest was shown in the experiments conducted by General Motors and Ford and a couple of prototypes saw the light. All that remains of those days are prototypes of the *Ape* Elettrocar and an early, battery-run moped which never made it into production. The road towards large-scale manufacture of an ideal product was long: the electric moped would become a reality only towards the end of the Millennium.

The harmony between the Vespa and the spirit of the times deserves emphasis here: Vespa follows developments in social custom and evolves in accordance with market needs, breathing the air of the times, whether it is good, bad or indifferent.

VESPA50

208

The introduction in 1962 of a law requiring all vehicles with engines larger than 50 cc to carry license plates was a serious blow to the scooter industry. Piaggio's answer to this was immediate: in '63 the Vespa 50 was launched. This new scooter, which required no license plate and could be used without a license, effectively circumvented the crisis caused by the new law and was an immediate success.

Very young users, who had up till now represented only a small portion of Piaggio's clientele, were rapidly acquiring more social and economic importance in society. They now became the hub of the company's sales policy and the most

This was the first model to use the completely new engine with the cylinder canted at 45°. This configuration was later used on all subsequent "small body" Vespas.

The advertising campaign was centered around the needs of the very young user for getting to and from school and for leisure time.

The configuration of the Vespa 50 echoed, albeit on a smaller scale, the overall structure and the styling and functional cues of its bigger sisters. At its debut it cost 102,000 lire ($62).

The saddle support plate could be opened, after loosening a knob, to access the carburetor.

Due to the shape of the body, the only room for the spare wheel was behind the leg shield.

VESPA50

enthusiastic customers of this new vehicle that could be ridden at 14 years of age without a license and with great ease, thanks to its small size and low weight. This was also a major attraction for female customers.

This model, weighing 145 pounds, had a single seat saddle, a three-speed gearbox and a very narrow chassis with the cowls incorporated in the body shell pressing. The very small handlebars were made from a single die-cast element, open underneath and predisposed for the installation of a windscreen fitting. On top, there was a cylindrical hole sealed off by a plug for the installation of the (optional) speedometer. Raising this scooter onto its wide based center stand with rubber feet required very little effort. These were some of the features that made the "Vespina" such a successful part of the Piaggio range (in 1968 the range was further added to with the Ciao). In '63, the Piaggio range consisted of six different models, catering to a large and widely varied market.

The Vespa 50 was available in a variety of colors (metallic paint was also offered as an option) and fitted with either the standard single seat saddle or the longer "Turismo" saddle. This was fitted as standard on the Lusso version, which also had chrome-plated ornaments and more vivid colors.

The engine was a 49.77 cc rotating-valve single-cylinder two-stroke, with a bore and stroke of 38.4 x 43 mm. This unit had three particular characteristics that made it particularly "friendly"

Smaller dimensions gave the Vespa 50 an even slimmer and more harmonious appearance. Note the raised profile of the side cowls which, on this model, were integrated into the pressing of the monocoque body.

This view from above shows the rubber edge trim around the whole footplate, secured by small rubber wedges. The outer strips were fixed at the ends by two rivets incorporated into the profile.

VESPA50

The engine cover was secured by a latch and could be removed to give instant access to the spark plug and to the other engine parts. While on one hand this feature facilitated maintenance, it made the cover itself rather susceptible to theft.

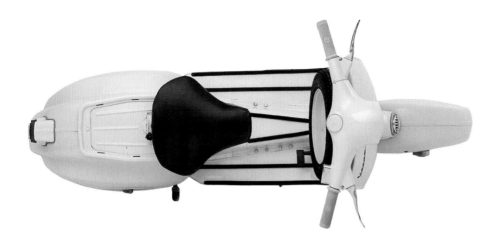

This rear view shows
the narrow cowl moldings
and the remarkable
compactness of
the whole scooter.

The rear light was
made from painted cast
aluminum with a reflector
incorporated in the lens.

The fuel cap, with the
characteristic screw
fastener, was located on
the same surface as the
parcel rack, which was
made from pressed sheet
steel and followed the
contours of the tank.

This model also had an offset front wheel, fitted with a small, 9" tire. The floating outside-link-type suspension used a simple rubber damper.

The legendary "Vespina" was the most popular vehicle used by teenagers and in 1969, with the launch of the 50 Special, it became a legend in its own right. This version differed in having a trapezoidal shaped headlight and a four-speed gearbox.

VESPA50

to use: quiet mechanical elements and exhaust, elasticity (it could even move off from a standstill in second, making things easier for learners) and easy starting, thanks to the powerful magneto flywheel and the rational design of both the kick-starter pedal and the toothed sector it connected to.

A single kick was sufficient for cold starting, whereas a light touch, without even pushing the pedal all the way down, was enough to start the engine when warm. The scooter was easy to start even while the rider was seated. The fuel tap and the choke knob, both located under the saddle, were also easily reached from the riding position. Other strong points were excellent stability, due to a perfectly located center of gravity and good weight

The three-speed gearbox control, with painted half bars and with a highly polished clutch lever.

The round headlight
was incorporated into
the handlebars and had
no surrounding trim.
The "Vespa 50" badge was
made from a thin strip of
adhesive-backed aluminum
painted dark blue.

VESPA50

*distribution, its small
size and effective suspension. These
characteristics made the scooter extremely safe and
highly maneuverable—which a wide turning circle
and short wheelbase also contributed to.*

*The Vespa 50 ran on 2 percent two-stroke pre-
mix, helping cut fuel costs considerably. This
model managed on average 140 mpg and its
tank held 1.6 gallons. The filler cap was located
on the same surface as the large luggage rack.
This was made from pressed sheet steel modeled
to follow the design of the tank. The saddle was
fixed to a removable panel, which also served as
a cover for the plastic tool compartment container.
This container was removed to access the 14 mm
Dellorto carburetor mounted inside the chassis
and connected to the engine by a long intake
header. The round headlight was incorporated
into the handlebars and had no surrounding trim.
The rear light was made from painted cast aluminum with a reflector incorporated in the lens.*

*The birth of the Vespa 50 was a milestone in
the history of two-wheeled motorized transport
in terms of technological and industrial developments as well as sales: it managed to interest and
convert to scooters people who had previously been
indifferent, if not actually hostile, to the concept.*

*The Vespa 50 was to be Corradino D'Ascanio's
last project before retiring. This model, albeit modified through the years, became a constant fixture
in the range.*

VESPA90SS

214

During the automotive boom in the mid-sixties, Piaggio occupied a leading role, offering several models and new versions of the Vespa. These versions were characterized by youthful, cheerful, fun styling and bright colors, and became synonymous with adventure, freedom and independence.

The 90 Super Sprint version was a very special sports model, built with minute attention to detail and with extravagant, original styling.

The first 90 cc Vespa had already been presented in 1963 as a derivative of the 50 cc version which offered a series of appreciable advantages resulting from the adoption of a larger engine

This very particular model was intended for the sports enthusiast who appreciated fast vehicles. Being a Vespa, however, it still appealed to the female user even in this guise.

The most suitable settings for the Super Sprint are the circuits where Vespa Clubs from around the world organize events and races.

The Super Sprint was specifically created for young sports-minded users: it could be ridden by 16-year-olds and was intended for the customer looking for something special in the light motorcycle market.

This front view shows the narrower leg shield tapering towards the top to reduce aerodynamic resistance.

The handlebars, narrower and slightly lowered, housed a speedometer with a scale reading up to 100 km/h (60 mph) against a white background.

VESPA90SS

and was not subject to laws imposing speed restrictions and forbidding carrying passengers on non-license-plated vehicles.

In November '65 a special series was launched. This was the Super Sprint, derived from both the 1963 50/90 cc Vespa and the "new 125" from 1965 (the same year as the SS). In this version, a series of innovations were implemented to improve performance, functionality and comfort. These were accompanied by styling and functional solutions designed to attract younger users.

These different models all shared the same bodyshell design with the side cowls integrated in the body pressing and engines derived from a common project with its cylinder inclined at 45°.

The Super Sprint was marketed as a scooter of high technological content which was powerful, nimble, with strong performance and original styling. Its distinguishing characteristics were apparent even at a glance. This scooter was more streamlined, with a narrower leg shield tapering towards the top to reduce aerodynamic resistance. The hollow space in the mid section of the chassis—a characteristic feature on other Vespas—was now topped by a large, lockable trunk filling the gap between the saddle and the handlebars. This trunk was topped with a padded cushion in the same dark blue as the saddle to allow a racing motorcycle type prone riding position. The design of this feature is somewhat perplexing as it looks like a typical

motorcycle tank and did not fit in very well with the rest of the scooter. Also in the mid section of the chassis, under the trunk, was the spare wheel which, as on the 1955 GS, was mounted on the footplate. The wheel had two hubcaps painted the same color as the bodywork and, in the first series, was secured by a clip and a locking bar at the center of the footplate.

In the first series, the steering column had a larger support that housed the roller bushings carrying the hub pin. The support for the mudguard and shock absorber (mounted coaxially

These views from above
and in front highlight
how extraordinarily slim
this model was; 22 inches
wide and 66 inches long.
The shape recalls that
of the Vespa 98 Corsa
built by Piaggio in 1947.

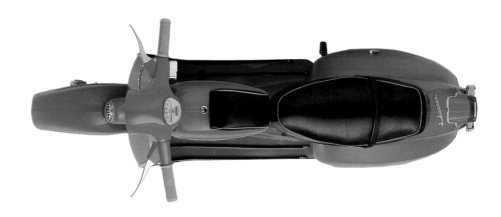

VESPA90SS

The chrome-plated steel
exhaust was specifically
designed for this
model and was
fitted externally.

The right-hand photo
shows a detail of the
fan cover protecting
the underlying
platinum-plated points.

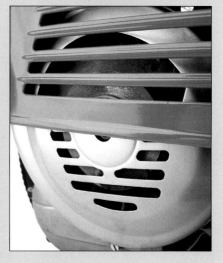

These side views show the unmistakable styling of the SS, characterized by a small dummy tank mounted above the spare wheel with body-colored hubcaps. The front mudguard was much sleeker.

The stickers bearing the script "90 Super Sprint" were, after chassis no. 4545, replaced by transparent plastic badges. On later models, an indentation was made in the dummy tank to keep the badge flush with the bodywork surface.

with the spring) was made in cast aluminum and had an original shape. The handlebars were narrower and slightly lowered (maximum height of the scooter was just over 3 feet) and incorporated a speedometer with a scale reading up to 100 km/h (60 mph) against a white background. The design of the leg shield, which was (as mentioned earlier) now very tapered, and the narrow, sleeker mudguard were radically new.

The sports style riding position was backed up by the performance of the 88.5 cc engine which took the little Vespa up to 56 mph. Nonetheless, the unit retained the typical smoothness of other Vespa engines, with its Dellorto 16/16 carbure-

tor in the same position as on the standard 50 and 90 cc versions. Some of the extra power was the result of using an expansion exhaust specially designed for this model and fitted externally on the rear left. The chrome-plated steel exhaust emitted a characteristic sporty metallic sound and its styling gave this model a more aggressive nature, further emphasized by the 3-inch-by-10-inch tires and the four-speed gearbox.

The small and pleasantly sporty dark blue two-seater saddle was hinged at the back, opening in the opposite direction to the saddles on all other Vespas (this was the only model ever to use this arrangement) and gave access to the plastic tool

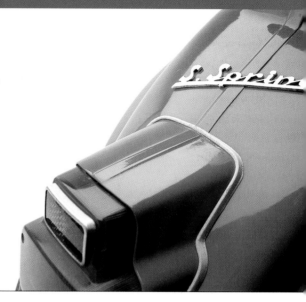

The words "S. Sprint" were
written in full at an angle
on the back of the scooter.

VESPA90SS

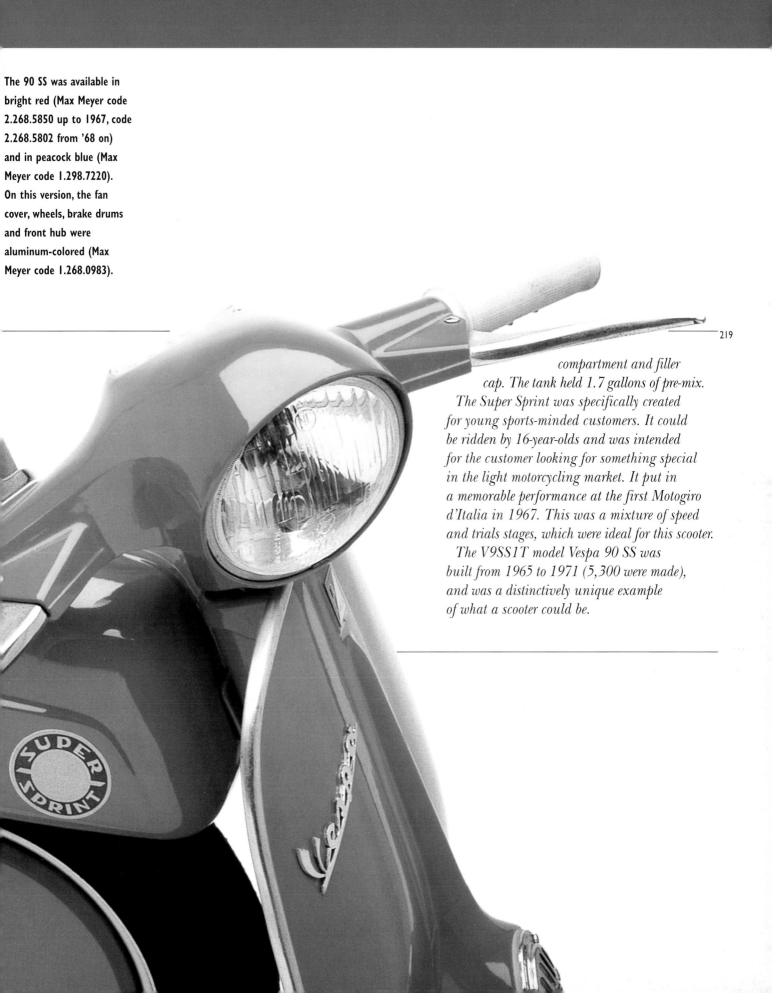

The 90 SS was available in bright red (Max Meyer code 2.268.5850 up to 1967, code 2.268.5802 from '68 on) and in peacock blue (Max Meyer code 1.298.7220). On this version, the fan cover, wheels, brake drums and front hub were aluminum-colored (Max Meyer code 1.268.0983).

compartment and filler cap. The tank held 1.7 gallons of pre-mix. The Super Sprint was specifically created for young sports-minded customers. It could be ridden by 16-year-olds and was intended for the customer looking for something special in the light motorcycling market. It put in a memorable performance at the first Motogiro d'Italia in 1967. This was a mixture of speed and trials stages, which were ideal for this scooter.

The V9SS1T model Vespa 90 SS was built from 1965 to 1971 (5,300 were made), and was a distinctively unique example of what a scooter could be.

VESPAET3

After the death of Enrico Piaggio in 1965 and the subsequent chairmanship of Umberto Agnelli, the company underwent a series of slow but far-reaching changes affecting its organization, management and philosophy. These changes were in part due to the new management, but mainly because of the sizeable drop in Vespa sales. This phenomenon, which lost Piaggio millions, was also related to a slump in the Italian automotive industry.

The restructuring of the company started with communication, and involved rethinking the Piaggio brand with an all-encompassing

The young new chairman of the firm talking with Corradino D'Ascanio in 1967, when the company awarded gold medals to its most important employees.

This pamphlet points out a 3-port cylinder, a sports exhaust, chrome embellishments and an original denim-colored saddle which, however, proved to be uncomfortably slippery.

The leg shield sported the new Piaggio logo, and the "Vespa" script taken from the powerful 200 Rally.

The badge bearing the full name of the model was fitted over the rear light, with the "ET3" moniker shown proudly.

The front mudguard with decal decorations. The front suspension was a floating longitudinal lever (outside link) configuration. The dual rate hydraulic damper, colored matte black, permitted a maximum travel of 1.28 inches.

re-evaluation of its image and services.

The research and development division shifted its focus from the Vespa to concentrate on newer products answering the needs of an economy which was shaped by a worldwide depression which in the early Seventies was to be followed by an oil crisis. This perspective led firstly to the creation, in 1967, of Piaggio's first moped—the Ciao. It was enormously successful. Like the Vespa, it became a legend in its own right and is today considered a modern classic.

The Ciao was soon followed by the Boxer, the Bravo and the Sì.

In 1976, the Vespa 125 Primavera, which was introduced in 1968 as an evolution of the "new 125" (made from 1965 to '82) developed into the ET3—standing for "Elettronica Tre Travasi" ("electronic with three ports").

For the first time, the most traditional model in the Piaggio range was fitted with an electronic ignition module. This feature, which had been tried out previously in 1972 on the Vespa 200 Rally, was now also used on the basic models.

The electronic ignition module was mounted inside the bodywork and was accessible via a compartment in the left cowl (introduced on the 1968 version). It was shielded from the heat of the exhaust by an insulating layer of heat-absorbing fabric glued on the inside of the

These views highlight the slimness of this vehicle. Its dimensions were 27 inches by 66 inches; height at handlebar and footplate 40 inches and 9 inches, respectively.

To create a stronger visual impact, adhesive stripes were applied to the side cowl moldings. The conspicuous matte-black exhaust on the left echoes that of the 90 SS.

VESPA ET3

Detail of the engine access hatch and of the matte-black fan cover, two of this model's characteristic features. Even among other Vespa models, the ET3 stood out for its svelte elegance and for the riding pleasure it offered.

The saddle, shown clearly in this top view, was redesigned to provide more comfortable riding even with a passenger.

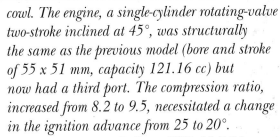

Detail showing the rear brake pedal with its black cover and the characteristic strips protecting the footplate and central rail at the edges of the anti-slip mat.

cowl. The engine, a single-cylinder rotating-valve two-stroke inclined at 45°, was structurally the same as the previous model (bore and stroke of 55 x 51 mm, capacity 121.16 cc) but now had a third port. The compression ratio, increased from 8.2 to 9.5, necessitated a change in the ignition advance from 25 to 20°.

The carburetor, a Dellorto SHB 19/19, was accessible from under the saddle and the new silencer, similar to the one used on the 90 SS, had an expansion chamber and was painted matte black, like the front shock absorber sleeve and the fan cover.

These modifications gave better performance without increasing engine speed (over 7 hp at

Agile, offering great performance, well built and, due to its compact size, appealing also to female users, 143,579 of the 125 Primavera ET3 were built between 1976 and 1983.

The speedometer, with its scale reading up to 120 km/h (72 mph) against a white background, was a bit old-fashioned and had no trip counter.

The 4.6-inch-diameter headlight with chrome-plated surround ring.

VESPA ET3

6000 rpm) and made the Vespa ET3 the fastest 125 cc model to date, with a top speed of 59 mph.

This revised engine permitted long-distance high-speed riding even when carrying a passenger. Fuel economy was excellent: about 120 mpg 2 percent pre-mix, giving a range of 168 miles, and the engine, mated to the four-speed box, offered lively, more accelerative performance and was capable of tackling gradients of up to 35 percent. The excellent handling and agility of the ET3 were due to its reduced trail, short wheelbase, wide steering circle, low center of gravity and a weight of only 122 pounds.

The pressed steel wheels, which were still identical at the back and front, had 2.1-inch rims and were fitted with 3-inch-by-10-inch tires. As on previous models, the wheels were composite to facilitate removal.

Slim, compact and youthful, the ET3 had the classic body shell with incorporated side cowls made from 0.04-inch-thick sheet steel weighing only 33 pounds. Details were well designed and included a very handy hook for carrying bags at the front of the saddle (this had already been used on the 50 L in 1966 and on the 1968 Primavera), a rubber mat in the center of the footplate—where the rider's foot was kept in readiness for using the brake pedal—and a longer, more comfortably shaped saddle. Light blue stripes were applied on the left and right of the rear and on the

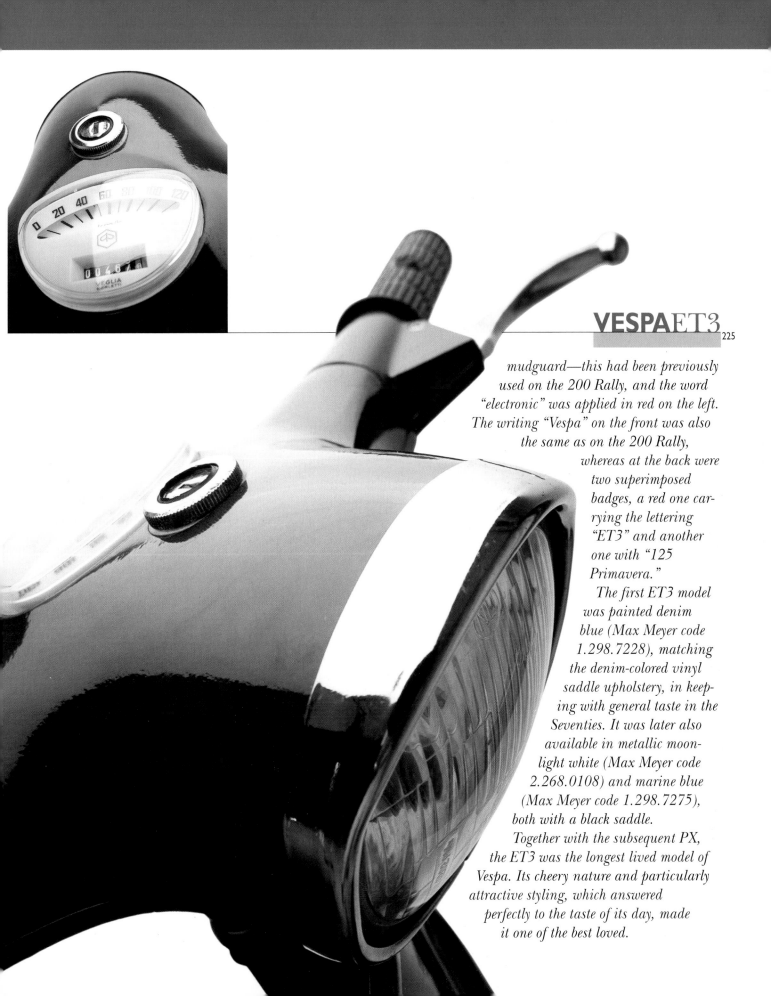

mudguard—this had been previously used on the 200 Rally, and the word "electronic" was applied in red on the left. The writing "Vespa" on the front was also the same as on the 200 Rally, whereas at the back were two superimposed badges, a red one carrying the lettering "ET3" and another one with "125 Primavera."

The first ET3 model was painted denim blue (Max Meyer code 1.298.7228), matching the denim-colored vinyl saddle upholstery, in keeping with general taste in the Seventies. It was later also available in metallic moonlight white (Max Meyer code 2.268.0108) and marine blue (Max Meyer code 1.298.7275), both with a black saddle.

Together with the subsequent PX, the ET3 was the longest lived model of Vespa. Its cheery nature and particularly attractive styling, which answered perfectly to the taste of its day, made it one of the best loved.

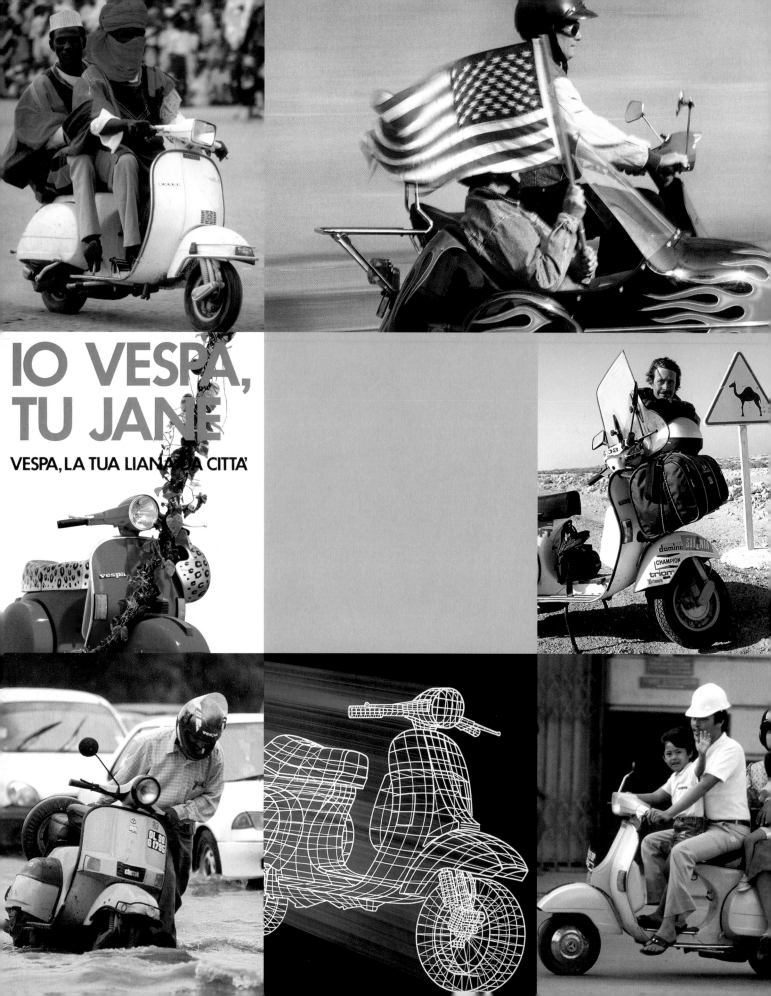

IO VESPA,
TU JANE

VESPA, LA TUA LIANA DA CITTA'

*T*he picture is variegated between light and shade (here we celebrate the glories and the legend, then the crisis follows, and then recovery), but, above all, it is vast and boundless. This little Vespa gets from Europe to India, from Japan to the USA.

1976–1996

A splendid forty-year-old

THE BALANCING ACT

"Boys turn into men" in 1980 but the south of Italy could have been on another planet. The difference between the glossy progressiveness of the new Italy, the new breeding ground for affluence, and street life in Palermo was a yardstick to measure the two speeds of Italy.

"**O**ptimists, and they are still surprisingly numerous, are betting on the Italians being able to get over the crisis." It was clear, in April '76, that this extraordinary country, in the words of *The Financial Times*, "is no longer living on the verge of bankruptcy but is, theoretically at least, already bankrupt."

The see-saw

Events were pushing Italy into the front line. A political confrontation was taking place that seemed big enough to jeopardize détente between the super-powers, and the second half of the Seventies was to prove an especially delicate period. The presidency of the republic seemed to have lost all credibility when its incumbent, overwhelmed by scandal, was forced to resign. But 1978 was first and foremost the year of the Moro kidnapping and murder, the republic's "darkest hour."

The number of terrorist victims continued growing for a further two macabre years while a deeply damaging political and generational split was opening between Italy's communist-based trade union, the largest in the Western world, and the country's youth.

After a good thirty years of unstoppable growth, the first fall in automobile sales occurred when the ratio of 280 vehicles per 1,000 inhabitants had been reached. Fiat of Turin felt it had to resort to the state wage supplementation fund and layoffs of just under forty thousand workers. This triggered a period of trade union

Gennaio, febbraio, Marx, aprile... i ragazzi diventano uomini e Vespa cresce con loro.

Vespa, il mito scooter.

PIAGGIO

One of the strongest messages in this youth-oriented culture was the new centrality of women. Initially it was a result of feminism, but soon it was taken onboard by more and more sections of society.

conflict in autumn 1980. Another forty thousand took part in a silent street demonstration just forty days later but this time the procession was made up of managers, foremen and white- and blue-collar workers demonstrating against the trade union and in favor of calling off the strike. This was the first sign of a new post-industrial reality in which social reform was now no longer driven by political parties and the shop floor.

The unstoppable rise in labor costs in pursuit of inflation, which by now was spiraling out of control, led industry to decentralize, dismantling vertically organized production facilities and distributing individual processes throughout the vast morass of the black labor market in which worker protection was often beyond the reach of the law. The problems facing large-scale

"Participation" was again the key word in 1977 and the advertising campaign developed by the Leader agency for the launch of the new PX had the slogan "Vespa muove la voglia di fare" ["Vespa gets you going"].

industries were now bigger than ever before. And throughout all of this, pressure brought to bear on the entrepreneurial world and civilian society by political parties, "juggernauts of power and clientelism" as the opposition leader called them, was soon to overstep the danger level.

In the meantime, vast swaths of the country had fallen into the hands of the Mafia Anti-State, and these became more vast after the 1980 earthquake in Irpinia, the area surrounding the town of Avellino near Naples. Up until the Capaci massacre twelve years later, in which state prosecutor Giovanni Falcone and his police escort lost their lives to a Mafia bomb, the slide into lawlessness seemed inexorable. The Parliamentary Anti-Mafia Commission in the early Nineties assessed the annual

turnover of the Mob as being greater than Fiat's.

Italian society was riddled with highly visible paradoxes and age-old failings. Despite all this and the sluggishness of the reforms in the late Seventies, the country moved forward. However, 1983 saw the dawn of a new season of incomprehension and ostentation: a ruthless political machine powered by clientelism and, as the popular saying of the day went, manned by "wheeler-dealers, dwarves and chorus girls," was the harbinger of a new consumer drive in which everyone strove frantically to outstrip his neighbor and the morality of the day was insensitive to the values of community spirit.

Debate centered on the controversy surrounding privatizing a number of key sectors while the dubiousness of the benefits inherent in the new media- and informatics-

With one eye looking over his shoulder and the other observing contemporary life, Nanni Moretti, one of the acutest observers of Italian reality, travels the streets of Rome astride a bottle-green Vespa 150. *Caro Diario* won the Best Director Prize at the 1993 Cannes Film Festival.

CARO DIARIO
(JOURNAL INTIME)

un film di
NANNI MORETTI

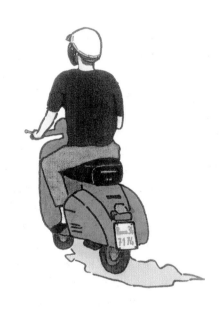

based society became more apparent. In the face of all this, idealism and any kind of underlying reforming spirit were conspicuous by their absence. Politicians showed how inept they were at keeping control of a system increasingly in thrall to the major economic and financial powers, and in the early Nineties the national debt ballooned to 104 percent of the Gross Domestic Product.

And yet the nation seemed ever more split and indecipherable according to the British Sunday newspaper *The Observer* in November 1987:

"As if by magic Italy has become the land of upward social mobility, of young managers and competent capitalists who have put the ideals of the Seventies behind them and now look towards the Holy Grail of profit. Class struggle is démodé and now it's export or die."

A testing station at the end of the assembly line. The New Line Vespa, better known as the PX, turned out to be an exceptionally "long seller." Twenty-five years later it's still in production with very few styling updates.

The rapid succession of images by means of which the changing identity, values and outward appearance of the country could be followed, seemed to be in a time warp stretching, sometimes, beyond belief. Although in 1977 just ten years or so had gone by since the "economic miracle" had come to an end, you would never have been able to tell it just by looking around. Italy was emerging from a long season of discontent during which two-wheeled transport seemed to be in its heyday. Appearances were, however, somewhat deceptive.

Juggling numbers after the "miracle"

A quick look at the numbers shows what was behind the idea of offering two-wheelers as a leisure accessory for a mainly young clientele in terms of overall sales. The market was underpinned and oxygenated by the lowest-powered products—the "mini-50s"—sales of which rose dramatically in 1962 to break through the ceiling of 100,000 units. Numbers rose continuously for almost twenty years: from 207,000 in 1967 to 320,000 in 1970 and 420,000 just two years later, a momentary setback in '75, then up again to 590,000 in '76 to the stupendous, unbeaten 815,000 in 1980. This was the halcyon year in which Italian manufacturers were Europe's most prolific, producing one million brand-new units.

From that point onwards the market imploded dramatically, shrinking to half its size in three short years, then down again leveling out around 450,000 units,

until the Nineties when, in this engine size, the most modern scooters would dominate this market.

Moving up-scale from the "minis" to the more powerful bikes—the 125 and the 200 and up to the mid-level and higher-cc machines—the story was completely different. From the resounding successes between 1957 and 1963, when sales were stable around the 250,000 mark, the fall to an emergency landing was brusque and far from painless—at the end of the decade sales hit a record low of 54,000 new registrations and a long slow climb up was ahead.

At this point, a closer look at the situation is in order.

In 1965, out of a total of 126,000 new registrations, 100,00 were scooters—Vespas and Lambrettas. Five years later, in 1970, 17,000 scooters were a mere third

The new body shell had 37 pounds of 15/10 sheet metal and innovative front suspension. The design staff and technicians at Pontedera, caught between modernity and tradition, seemed to have found the ideal compromise.

For the PX engine, a modern injection system was experimented with, but remained in the prototype stage.

of the total of new registrations of machines under 200 cc. At the other end of the scale, the market of the mini 50s was booming with 320,000 new units.

Later on, the proportions were much the same. Motorbikes saw modest growth of over 98,000 units and the low-wheelers regained some ground, but no-plate mopeds and scooters sold 590,000 units—yet again a rise of 50 percent over the year before. This was in 1976, a year that was to prove a turning point.

The following year, on Piaggio's stand at the Milan Motorcycle Show there was a gigantic replica of a scooter 13 feet high and weighing 1,300 pounds—the New Line Vespa: so described in the company's literature during the extended stages of planning, development and final adjustment, it came to be better

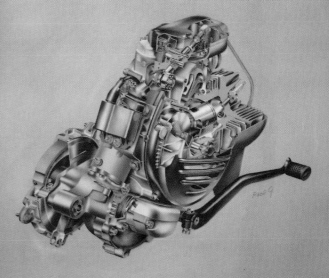

In 1980, two Vespa PX 200s ridden by M. Simonot and B. Tcherniavsky reached the finish line of the Paris-Dakar (the second edition of this desert classic). The French team, organized by Jean-François Piot, was assisted by four-time winner of the Le Mans 24-Hour, Henri Pescarolo.

known as the Vespa PX. Selling over two million units worldwide, it was a commercial milestone, outstanding even today more than a quarter of a century later; a rare phenomenon indeed in this industry.

New, but with the same DNA as always

This "new line" won hands-down on looks, with its volumetric equilibrium between front and back ends and the compactness of the rounded angles.

Two-stroke, cooled by forced air, with direct transmission, four speeds, drum brakes and a spare wheel for good measure: in its exquisite simplicity the formula was more or less the same. The same rotary dis-

tribution had by then fifteen solid years of experience behind it and as a sign of the times the 200 cc model had the optional separate lubrication.

There was however something innovative in the front end, even if it wasn't immediately obvious. If you approached a curve a bit faster than usual or, better still, stopped on a dime at a traffic light, lo and behold: no front-end dip. And to think that up to then it had been so unbecoming for a scooter enthusiast on either a Vespa or a Lambretta to maintain trim in braking.

Coherence, style and a pinch—or maybe a little more this time—of innovation: that was the magic formula the company still religiously applied. The new arrival was soon to make its presence felt: in 1976, scooters accounted for 57 percent in the under 200 cc bracket rising, later, to 68 percent with the PX, and to 74 percent in 1981; for the time being at least the PX had the limelight to itself.

Gradually, but not gradually enough, clouds started to appear on the horizon and the storm broke in full force in the mid-Eighties. The market underwent radical change with new types of product appearing and restrictive legislation being passed which led the company to a critical reassessment of its aims and identity. It wasn't until the late Nineties, in a completely different scenario, but accepting the challenge as it always had done, that Vespa managed to regain all its prestige. Not that it was easy. It took more than forty years, from 1955 to '99, for sales of registered vehicles to return to above the 300,000 unit mark and in the meantime manufacturers had to make do with what market there was—ever-changing and hotly contested by many.

1977-1995: A WINDOW ON THE TWO-WHEELER MARKET IN ITALY

	registrations of motorcycles and scooters				estimate sales of mopeds	total
	< 200 cc	> 200 cc	overall total	scooter total		
1977	81,314	39,673	120,987	55,373	645,000	765,987
1978	72,401	9,564	99,669	52,524	635,000	734,669
1979	93,134	36,318	129,452	68,318	655,000	784,452
1980	112,301	49,249	161,550	81,818	815,000	976,550
1981	149,076	60,675	209,751	109,938	647,500	857,251
1982	161,620	74,768	236,388	118,532	500,000	736,388
1983	138,612	88,106	226,718	88,758	412,000	638,718
1984	123,471	82,061	205,532	63,903	330,000	535,532
1985	121,820	82,100	203,920	58,164	365,000	568,920
1986	94,186	79,836	147,022	35,623	350,000	524,022
1987	58,423	59,537	117,960	12,996	310,000	427,960
1990	44,414	64,390	113,629	10,824	448,391	562,020
1995	32,516	47,677	80,193	24,832	585,398	665,582

(data provided by ANCMA - the Italian Motorcycle Association)

From left: the coil spring on the hub is a mark of the 98 first series (1946); the suspension with the oscillating lever inverted and the coil spring first appeared on the 1948 125; the three elements aligned (1951) revised in '53 were bettered on the 1958 125; the shock absorber with built-in spring, developed for the 160 GS in '62, passed from the 180 SS to the ET3. At center page, the new suspension on the PK ('82).

Below: in the development stages (1975) of the New Line a new front-end telescopic suspension with hydraulic shock absorbers was tried out: "the play rises from 2.8 inches to 3.5 inches and braking recoil is absorbed by the structural components, not by the suspension spring." But its incorporation "depends on other tests where the offset wheel is mantained while solving problems in comfort and braking." Then (14 April '76) the telescopic suspension was set aside "for possible application in the future." Nothing odd here: the new suspension with the oscillating lever has taken shape, a new prototype prepared and "the outcome can be considered brilliant." This was the final choice.

Ο ne of the mainstays of Piaggio's identity was the front suspension, with oscillating linkage and offset wheel. This, along with other planning and production-line choices, distinguished the Vespa, which might otherwise have been lost in the crowd.

First step: the Vespa 98 (1946) opened the series with a feature never repeated. The steering column dropped down the left-hand side and connected to the wheel by a small lever known as the oscillating linkage that pivoted on the steel hub, and the double spiral spring ended astride it. Since the steering column was further back than the hub, braking caused a vertical push that contrasted the inevitable dipping; in technical terms it was called the "pushed wheel system."

Second step: with the 125 in 1948 the suspension moved to the right-hand side of the wheel on the engine side and the coil spring now had more play. This basic scheme, which stayed much the same, tended to snap into full compression during braking, the natural load transfer was added to by the compression resulting from the braking of the wheel where the hub was now further back than the steering column—the so-called "pulled wheel system."

Significantly, there was an additional, torsion spring pivoting between the hub and the steering column to limit this phenomenon on the racing models, subsequently extended as an accessory to a number of outside producers.

Third step: from 1951 to 1953, with some variations of lesser importance, a three-element configuration was developed which put in a line, starting from the hub, the coil spring, the steering column and the shock absorber. This greatly improved stability on uneven roads, around corners and in braking.

Fourth step: inaugurated on the 160 GS of 1962, a single component was placed in the middle, on the oscillating lever between the hub and the steering column coupling. It had two functions: it was also a dual rate hydraulic shock absorber with a built-in spring. This same configuration was used in various models up to the Primavera ET3 of 1976. In each model there was improvement in the size and fit of the various components.

Fifth step: in the 1977 PX the idea was still for improved comfort on rough roads with the pulled-wheel system. However, an innovative, patented anti-dipping system was added by fixing the shock absorber to the brake shoe. In turn, the shoe was free to oscillate on the wheel pivot which was fixed to the oscillating linkage. So the brake moment was absorbed by the telescopic system and no longer hindered the suspension, which gave greatly increased stability.

4 steps forward plus 1

THE FOUR CORNERS OF THE WORLD

Going from Melbourne to Cape Town by Vespa, you might stop at Jaipur in Rajastan and pose, like a normal tourist, on the back of an elephant.

Driving through the Hadramaut desert in Yemen, near the Oman border, with nerves on edge.

Going round the world on two wheels means getting to know every inch of the way, seeing the highways and byways that crisscross the globe etch themselves into your memory (and sometimes onto your body) and seeing a hundred suns in a hundred different sunrises. Going round the world on a Vespa is something else. First you see and then you get below the surface: moving in harmony despite the hardships, and weaving a never-ending tapestry of relationships, thanks to the familiarity and likableness the Vespa exudes. Simplicity—in a word—is her strong point, both in her mechanical reliability and in her ability to make bridges to people.

Over 150,000 miles in ten years, from Siberia to Mozambique, from Pakistan to Venezuela, on difficult roads over impossible terrain, with not a clue about mechanics and no back-up technical service. No fancy leather bike-suits or freeze-dried rations, only a bundle of bags and a big leather suitcase on the luggage rack, a guitar and maybe a chessboard. No tent or sleeping bag, but every night having to look for a place to stay, whether a motel in Iowa or a hut in an Angolan village. That's the way to travel by Vespa in Giorgio Bettinelli's book. Light years away from trans-Sahara safaris that blast through villages like rack and ruin, it's traveling as though it were a calling—and writing, equally important, so as to relive the tale by telling it.

After a long sojourn in Indonesia, the meeting with a Vespa was purely coincidental, and riding along from Bali to Singapore the idea gradually took hold of

"Sometime I'm really glad I'm Italian because of the enormous number of swearwords in our language. When you're really up against it and you press on for a month or maybe two on the trot in dire conditions, every day it's a great comfort … … and yet these are the things, the hardest things, that stick in your mind: Congo, Angola, Ethiopia or Pakistan … perhaps the hardest countries."

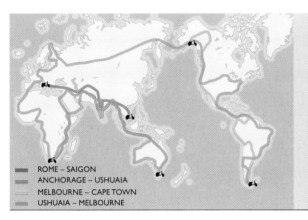

"With the Vespa I surprised, and raised more a feeling of tenderness than anything else as well as offers of help. This was also true for the intrinsic features of the vehicle … a likable vehicle … in an unlikely place … how many times did I call myself an idiot seeing myself from the outside, maybe in the middle of snow, or struggling over a river bed, or clambering over dunes in the desert … you know the Vespa makes you really feel soft-hearted!"

making an enterprise of the journey back to Italy: a trip from Rome to Saigon in 1992–93 embarked on with sublime nonchalance and maybe even just a pinch of foolhardiness. Six months into the seven-month-long trip and 12,000 miles of road and track, mountain passes and desert trails later he discovered, one fine day, that there was "another kind of oil besides the stuff you put in with the gasoline mixture" for the sump: the engine oil, y' know!? the horrified mechanic in Bangkok kept on saying. Time to change it!! Amid gusts of laughter!

Soon after, there were some other extravaganzas on a PX developed like a 150 cc and supplied by Piaggio within the framework of an early sponsorship: Alaska-Tierra del Fuego, 21,600 miles in nine months (1994–95), then Melbourne-Cape Town, 31,200 miles

in 364 days by way of Asia and East Africa (1995–96). Then there was the madcap plan to do 90 countries over five continents taking advantage of the natural "bridges": the Worldwide Overland Odyssey between 1997 and 2001, on a PX 200.

In many places all over the world the Vespa is almost a household object, despite it being seen as Italian, and so people can relate easily to it as in India or Pakistan thanks to the millions that rolled off the Bajaj line at Kurla. Elsewhere it's a total rarity, as in the United States or Canada, where the Vespa Club networks, personifying the dream of many a young enthusiast, were set abuzz by Bettinelli.

Sometimes he was like a raft adrift on the sea, through Africa from Morocco to Cape Town and then back up to Ethiopia in thirteen months: Along the desert trail in Mauritania, through the minefields on the Moroccan border and nine days of tribulation in dunes where the little wheels disappeared into the sand and where the record high, sweating blood, was 5 miles a day; then to Burkina Faso, impoverished but friendly, the chaotic streets of Lagos and the beauteous wonder of the rest of Nigeria, towards Biafra and the forest of Cameroon. Then, just over the Congo border it looked as if the end had come. Three days of hell, the Vespa sequestered like every other piece of property, and Mr. Vespa imprisoned in a hut with no food for three days, watched through the crosshairs of a Kalashnikov, his life, in the end, saved by a whisker. The trip was eventually resumed with another machine, identical to the first, and from July 1999 to May 2001 the final leg to Tasmania was completed.

Below: fixing it "on the road," according to local custom in Mozambique during the Worldwide Odyssey.

Lower left: at the end of the last stretch in Hobart, Tasmania, after more than three years and 150,000 miles since the start in Tierra del Fuego.

A GOOD RECOVERY BUT...

In 1980 Piaggio-Gilera was manufacturing scooters, mopeds, motorbikes, commercial vehicles and hydrojets with an annual turnover of 542 billion lire ($331 million) of which 150 billion ($92 million) came from abroad. This is not considering Bianchi—one of Italy's most famous brands in bicycles and the stable of such famous names in Italian cycling as Costante Girardengo and Fausto Coppi—which entered the Piaggio orbit in 1979.

"Ladies and gentlemen shareholders, we are pleased to announce a profit for the financial year 1977. Despite the worrying overall situation your company has come out well thanks to two favorable sets of circumstances: the energy crisis which has undoubtedly encouraged the demand for low-consumption vehicles; and the availability of vehicles that were already accepted in the marketplace and duly planned for enabled us, in particular, to improve our market share."

These years from 1976 to 1981 were good ones: the Piaggio and Gilera mopeds sold best, reflecting the way the market was developing, and the new Vespa held some 75 percent of market share of license-plated vehicles under 200 cc while the mini non-registered ones

kept up despite their years. The big 2R (as in "2 Ruote" ["two wheels"]) factory was working full time just as the new 3R one was readying to manufacture the Ape.

These were golden years in which sales grew steadily, doubling in the four years between 1978 and 1981. Factory absenteeism halved in three years and after the collective contract was renewed in 1979 strikes dropped dramatically. A new factory was opened in Pisa; the trade union approved but called for greater participation in company strategy.

Production, in the late Seventies, was equally divided between Italy and abroad when the big push for expansion abroad was fostered by the joint Sguazzini-Vallecchi management but settled back to a more normal two-thirds in Italy and one-third abroad.

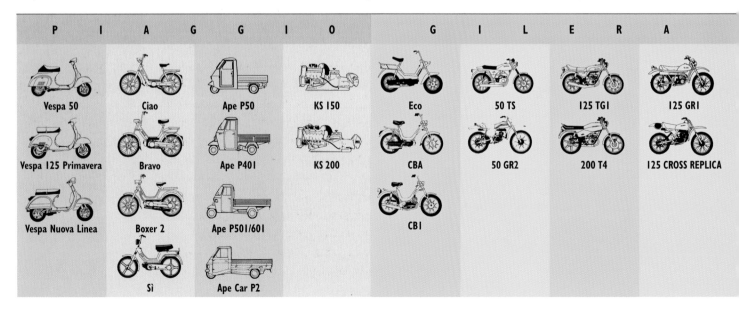

P I A G G I O				G I L E R A			
Vespa 50	Ciao	Ape P50	KS 150	Eco	50 TS	125 TG1	125 GR1
Vespa 125 Primavera	Bravo	Ape P401	KS 200	CBA	50 GR2	200 T4	125 CROSS REPLICA
Vespa Nuova Linea	Boxer 2	Ape P501/601		CB1			
	Sì	Ape Car P2					

In 1981 the workforce reached an impressive all-time high of 13,800 more than 10,000 of whom were employed in blue-collar posts and another 4,750 in the fifteen manufacturing facilities abroad. And 160,000 worked for auxiliary and derivative companies in Italy and abroad.

The 3R (three-wheel) workshops set up alongside the 2R (two-wheel) ones in 1977 just behind the office building. The workshops—built at the time of reconstruction after World War II—are now set aside for engineering and engine assembly but in time the main activity will be moved to the opposite side.

... it looks like rain

As the Eighties progressed the situation worsened especially across the Atlantic. The expected growth in demand for mopeds never materialized: the million units talked about for 1978 petered out into a meager 200,000 forcing the company to take drastic action. The recession progressively worsened with serious consequences on the market for "non-basic semi-durable" goods and the company was obliged to re-import sizeable stockpiles built up by the retail clients of Vespa of America Company in Brisbane, California, near San Francisco.

The Italian scooter was still a highly appreciated symbol of style, but it was having to contend with aggressive Japanese marketing. By now, Vespas were traveling the world's highways and byways, and Piaggio was struggling to keep in fourth place behind Honda, Yamaha, and Suzuki and ahead of Kawasaki, the last of the Japanese. These producers were now flooding the Southeast Asia market where Pontedera up to then had been solidly established. They were also flooding the United States and Europe, where they took the lion's share on both sides of the English Channel.

Vespa GmbH of Augsburg had done its best despite losing some ground to the approaching crisis: sales dropped but its market share rose. Vespa S.A. of Brussels held its own against the competition considering the smallness of the Belgian market.

These "Vespa Jahre" were getting difficult. In 1982 the German market showed a downward turn of over 20 percent but then it evened out. The Vespa 80 cc performed well but the bigger engined versions fell from 5,300 to 4,300.

"Vespa of America Co.—the salient point of financial year 1983" read the communiqué to the shareholders "was the termination of two-wheeled, engine-powered vehicle sales."

In 1983, the year the 80 cc Vespa made its debut, the French market for the scooter of Pontedera grew 66 percent. It was no big deal in terms of absolute value (4,500 units: the same as Belgium), but it was auspicious, when the market went down by 16 percent in twelve months.

The new Japanese scooters looked very different from the old "cubs" that had been churned out by the thousands in the East, in Southeast Asia, and in the developing countries. Already some models were being built under license in Europe, for example by Peugeot.

A Pakistani calendar: developing countries are hard to conquer in competition with the major Japanese producers.

The sister company, Moto Vespa S.A. of Madrid, having to contend with double-figure inflation which played havoc with Spanish purchasing power, managed to win 50 percent of the scooter market thanks to the way its products were tailored to the market and the strength of its distribution network.

Sale-price capping by the government and strong devaluation of the peso paradoxically obliged Pontedera, in 1982, to rein in sales in order to contain the losses incurred on the Mexican market "pending definitive measures."

The Far East licensees were in serious difficulty and those in Africa were being overwhelmed by chronic local instability but after eleven years of blockage the road to India was reopening as we shall see later.

The Japanese domination just over the Alps injected life into the French market, which recovered and evened out after a critical '78. Small-engine machines, powered by 80 cc engines in accordance with legislation passed two years later, paved the way for the new Peugeot which made a lot of noise and sold less than a couple of thousand units, just one tenth of market-leader Honda's figure. Vespa diffusion was alive and well, continually increasing its turnover and market-share and introducing new models.

In 1982, *Moto Journal* magazine set a group of scooter competitors alongside each other: European brands such as Derbi (a Spanish brand later incorporated into the Piaggio group) and Benelli with a nifty little mini-50 whose bodywork was in plastic, some Oriental imports such as the Honda C70 (little more than a moped with part of its fairing in plastic), and some promising-looking Japanese machines tailored for Europe.

The style was nothing to write home about, if the Honda Lead or Yamaha Beluga were the machines to consider, and price point and performance, too, were often less attractive than that of the Vespa 80 cc.

But looking back, the winning streak was already starting to be seen in the Japanese machines' ease of use with an automatic gear change. Ongoing technological product development together with commercial aggressiveness and an ever greater selection of models with attractive finishings and accessories heralded a new era that to begin with at least was putting Piaggio on the defensive.

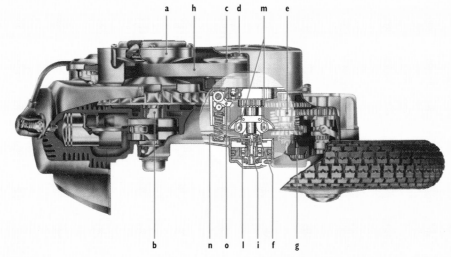

a. First pulley
b. Drive shaft
c. Second pulley
d. Secondary shaft
e. Final reduction gearing
f. Hydraulic piston within the driveshaft
g. Geared pump
h. Transmission belt
i. Cylinder within the driveshaft
l. Sleeve
m. Centrifugal masses
n. Lever
o. Cam connected to accelerator

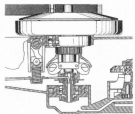

Below: by way of the lever the accelerator-actuated cam modifies the position of the coupling (here) and hence the shaft; this triggers the closure of the pulley and the adoption of a shorter ratio.

The first time in 1983

O ne fine day an "automatic" rolled out of the Pontedera factory and it was a Vespa. Appearing at the September 1983 Milan Exhibition, the PK 125 S A appeared, allowing a glimpse of an odd-looking rounded shielding below the right side panel.

Under the heading "gear change," the technical sheet duly specified that it was an automatic with a hydraulic actuator triggered by a centrifugal sensor.

The idea the technicians had developed was based on a transmission belt between two variable-diameter pulley wheels, both of which were made of conic halves and counterposed, pushed together by a spring. Expanding, the belt worked on the smaller diameter and so varied the ratio, or "the gear."

The first pulley (a), assembled on the driveshaft (b), had a spring with a smaller load to the second pulley (c), assembled on the secondary shaft (d), which drove the wheel through a double step-down gear (e). This difference in forces, when the vehicle was standing still, gave a "short" ratio, good for start-up acceleration with the small diameter pulley at the engine and the large one at the wheel.

When the vehicle was moving, the aperture of the second pulley was determined by the vehicle's speed but it was also governed by the accelerator. Let us see how it worked in more detail.

The internal driven semi-pulley was fixed to the secondary shaft which was hollow and housed a hydraulic piston (f) which was, by contrast, fixed to the external semi-pulley.

The oil pressure generated by a geared pump (g) pushed the piston and thus the external semi-pulley working against the force of the spring and reduced the diameter of the belt take-up (h), lengthening the transmission ratio.

The oil discharge from the cylinder (i) machined into the secondary shaft was regulated by a sleeve (l) by means of a "chaser system" between sleeve and piston (in which every position of the sleeve has a corresponding position of the piston).

The sleeve was set in motion by two centrifugal masses (m) that lengthened the ratio when they opened and by a lever (n), which on being pushed by a cam (o), in turn triggered by the accelerator shifted the sleeve, shortening the transmission ratio.

In short, the difference between this and a moped CVT was that here the size of the gas aperture and the speed with which it was triggered resulted in the best possible ratio from among the infinite range in relation to what was being asked of the machine. So a kick-down effect was obtained, similar to that in an automatic gearbox car when the accelerator is pressed to the floor.

Original and innovative, despite its relative complexity, this system aimed at renewing the Vespa by simplifying its use without any detrimental side effects on performance, which here was even more brilliant than on the four-speed version.

This technical tour de force did not, however, bring the desired results in increased sales. Had it been incorporated on mopeds, it might have enjoyed greater success.

On the other hand, the need to stay within the 1.5 hp legal limit of those days set too many technical obstacles in the way of development of this technology for no-plate machines.

Any revitalization of the scooter, and therefore of the company, can only happen by a radical renovation of the concept. But this time the PX miracle didn't repeat itself. The campaign, run by the RSCG Agency, involved two short films "in a style somewhere between Wim Wenders and a video clip."

"Ladies and gentlemen shareholders, in 1987 the world market for two-wheel motor vehicles … again fell prey to the downward trend that has dogged it in recent years … there has been a fall in sales compared to the Eighties of more than 30 percent." The tune had changed to take account of a difficult situation that saw the United States shut up like a clam, Asia hold its own, thanks to an upswing in India and Taiwan, and western Europe, in particular, have to deal with a slump of more than 40 percent compared to the magnificent year of 1981.

Your company, ladies and gentlemen, is at the top of the list producing almost one third of Europe's total but the cake is shrinking all the time. And although you don't realize it, the worst is yet to come.

Crisis and change

There were stormy seas this side of the Alps and it's not difficult to see why.

The fall in the birth rate reduced the number of potential purchasers nearing their fourteenth or sixteenth birthday by a good 10 percent from 1986.

Frequent outdating of models imposed by Japanese manufacturers as a sales ploy rather than because of technological development sapped purchases and drove clients towards the second-hand market.

New legislation made necessary by statistics enacted in the summer of '86 and obliging riders of registered machines to wear crash helmets had a devastating effect. New machine registration fell by over a third

"Great Britain has no manufacturers left. Germany has got only BMW which manages to survive thanks to funding given to manufacturers who produce in the city of Berlin. In France, Motobécane belongs to Yamaha and the Peugeot branded products are Honda-made. We are now the only European manufacturer in the field: Piaggio has continued to invest heavily in new production technologies and with the 'Cosa' takes a quality leap." —Umberto Agnelli speaking at the 1987 Milan Motorcycle Show.

After the Vespa PK, the latest incarnation of the myth, the new scooter had a lot to live up to and architect and designer Massimo Iosa Ghini managed to lighten the rather squat shape.

in twelve months and the struggle to survive grew fierce. For some time, fashion had been pointing young people toward high-wheel machines and Piaggio responded quite well to this, gaining market share with the Gilera product.

But if it's sensationalism we're seeking then it's to the scooter we must look and especially the Vespa with its absolute monopoly (98 percent of the market in 1987). It was a full-scale collapse. Something like 63.2 percent of 1986 turnover had dissolved into nothing twelve months later and 77 percent over a two-year period.

Corradino D'Ascanio's magic formula was now faced with its greatest threat: backed into a corner it could only entice one purchaser out of ten. The gauntlet was down and the challenge had to be won at all costs.

Redundancies, early retirement and a stop on hiring meant that only six thousand employees kept their jobs while automation was making inroads into the factory. Production was concentrated in Pontedera while the "strategy of linked suppliers" was developed, transferring, for instance, production of spare parts and a number of operations of a mechanical and assembly nature to external companies.

Outsourcing of certain phases took place, "deverticalizing" production—setting up autonomous companies able to operate freely on the market with no ties of exclusivity to the mother company. These were difficult choices that were paid for dearly and caused no little bitterness but were nevertheless taken courageously as the only way towards innovating the production cycle and the product range.

Styer-Daimler-Puch came to Pontedera to renew a product range with brand names already well established in northern Europe; the three-wheeler range was extended to put diesel engines into all the Ape models; new technology such as CAD-CAM-aided design and sheet-metal laser cutting were introduced.

Victory at all costs was the order of the day and a revolution in thinking was about to make its entrance.

Among the more "significant and concrete" results achieved by the present management, ladies and gentlemen shareholders, was "the development and launch of the 'Cosa' a new scooter to replace the glorious number-plate Vespa, now over 40, and which has been designed with a youthful, modern, rational and non-exhibitionist clientele in mind."

The latest in the Vespa lineage was the 50 Rush from 1988 to 1990 which sold a fair number: 61,070.

Getting there wasn't easy after more than forty years of Vespa, and the path was littered with casualties. The "scandal name" was what it was called in the company. There appeared first the name, then the brand, elegantly, which then developed into a complete sentence: "Quella Cosa della Piaggio che cosa la vita" ["That Thing from Piaggio that things your life"].

The launch of the new scooter involved a lot of resources and no effort was spared. Noteworthy was the cover page of *Max* (May, 1988) and an article inside, written by Sting and illustrated by Robert Gligorov, working with the scooter on the set.

The name of the "Cosa"

"Urban, well-educated and well-dressed but not necessarily designer labeled: a trend-setter" was the profile envisaged by Marco Mignani, art director of the agency that won the bid to launch this brand new Vespa—so new that an investment of 35 billion lire ($21 million) had been budgeted, so new that it could do without the name it had always gone by.

Its manifest rationality made it seem not so much aimed towards the teenage group, despite some gestures made in this direction, as towards the young and not so young urban professional classes who, in this two-wheeler increasingly tailored for car users, saw an ideal second or third means of transport for themselves or their families.

Indeed, there seemed to be less of a generation gap in those years for the younger people the market segment aimed at: increasingly they tended to share the tastes, personal hopes and aspirations of their parents who, for their part, fit into no historical pattern, having lived through the Sixties, and were now developing their careers and were fully equipped to take over managerial posts. The bywords were stolid common sense and a pinch of high-tech.

Designers introduced under-body fairing, the wedge-shaped shield and the special outline of the

"I liked 'Modem,' I liked 'Shuttle,'" recalls Marco Mignani. "I eventually whittled it down to about ten names that I wrote down beside 'Vespa' and then I realized that I was on the wrong track. They could only be appendages of the old name type, like 'Vespa-Modem' and 'Vespa-Shuttle,' which was just what the client didn't want. The break factor was missing; no name was powerful enough to beat Vespa in prestige so I settled on the name of all names, the wild card for every topic."

central spoiler, well-joined to the front mudguard, all of which improved aerodynamics by a good 10 percent. These were all arrived at as a result of systematic wind-tunnel testing, but progress was especially high in stability against lateral wind gusts, so important when driving in non-urban settings at constant speed.

Ergonomically good overall, it also incorporated a number of innovations, at least in the models for the European market, such as a compartment below the saddle for storing a helmet. Brakes were hydraulic and integral, meaning that they acted on both drums, back and front, simply by pressing the pedal. There was an anti-skid system that came into play when the front-wheel brake lever was pulled.

Electronic firing, an electric starting motor and an automatic choke were introduced but the shape of this strange Vespa, which surprisingly eschewed its name, was far from the slim elegance of earlier models: it was almost as though the Vespa were going through a mid-life crisis prone to capricious decisions.

The choice not to use the name was courageous but was perhaps let down by a renewal that was not a revolution; this was mentioned only in the agency brief.

Caught between conservatism and innovation, struck by an acknowledged identity crisis, the Cosa failed in its attempt to replace the Vespa, the world's best-known scooter. The slackness in sales did nothing to bolster this ambiguous move towards renewal but made it seem like a rearguard revolution.

The storyboard of a clip to launch the new scooter, which still awaited its final baptism. In this 1987, which was feeling the effect of the compulsory helmet, the real innovation came from far away; a strange armchair on two wheels with a four-stroke engine and automatic gear change. The Honda CN 250 was the daddy of all maxi-scooters.

The first Bajaj "factory" at Kurla: but very soon, wrote Mr. Randich, the on-site engineer, to Pontedera in 1961 "it became clear that it would be impossible to carry on working in the conditions illustrated above."

The vocation to export from Pontedera to the rest of the world was a company ideal from the start-up after World War II.

It is interesting to look back to November '46 when exporting to China was being considered, or to 1947 when a letter from someone in Bangkok who had seen the scooter in *Popular Mechanics* asked, kindly oblige and forward prices for Vespa and Ape rickshaw, underlining the availability for barter payment: scooters for tin, rubber or shellac.

Curious oddities arrived from all over the world, like the requests, dated February 1950, from no fewer than seven separate self-proclaimed "exclusive retailers" in Santiago, Chile, all obviously unknown to the company. That's the price of success. Other contacts led in

One of the technicians and workers who left the Pisa Plain and landed in this strange world sent back regular desolate messages to Francesco Lanzara, the manager: "The smelting plant workers are always new and the old ones don't have the faintest idea about work either because they're not used to it, or because they don't want it, or because it's too hot, or because of the food, or because none of them have got shoes. When the molten metal pours into the molds it doesn't take much for them to get worried about burning their feet … Here there's no hurry; they've no need to learn now; it can wait. Here everybody believes in eternal reincarnation so they've got plenty of time," (May 29, '64).

Thousands of miles from base, the old rivalry started up again. Lambretta was being made by SIL (Scooters India Ltd.) of Lucknow, which when the Lambretta Milan factory closed in 1971–72 took over machinery, stock, documents and projects as well as the worldwide rights for use of the name.

The little guard of a parking lot in Delhi. This is around 1970, but thirty years later scooters and motorcycles represent 70 percent of the over two million vehicles registered in the city, with an increase of 20 percent per annum.

unexpected directions and to surprising results like the export of the Ape rickshaw to Pakistan, a few years later; or in the early Sixties, when Piaggio's intense and controversial adventure in India began.

A second homeland, or almost

"In India, Vespa enjoys enormous popularity thanks to its economy in use and well-known excellence in performance. It is now fully integrated into the landscape both in the crowded city streets and the vast, hinterland plains. Nowadays, eyebrows are no longer raised at the sight of a Vespa parked in the shade of a Hindu temple."

"Nowadays" was autumn '62 when the company magazine celebrated the ten-thousandth Vespa rolling off the production line at the new Bajaj Auto Ltd. factory, which had been licensee for two years for the whole of India. It hadn't been easy up to then and it was to get even more difficult from then on.

From independence in 1947 onwards, industrialization in the subcontinent had been a ticklish business undertaken with massive state involvement. The state had the power to authorize production in the car and motorcycle industries by joint-venture companies in which the Indian partner was licensee of foreign models and technology, and to deny consent for foreign companies to set up shop, let alone organize direct imports.

Start-up was uphill and took place in the old Kurla factory in February 1960.

The building, poorly equipped, was on a muddy lane and made the Pontedera technicians who had been sent there shudder with foreboding. There was an exorbitant number of staff—almost twice what was needed—but a lack of intermediate management and foremen: the diligent company management protested that these weren't necessary. The working procedures were irrational—there were no part holders on the workbenches, packing materials were piled up in the passageways; and quality control was completely inconsistent.

With the new factory—built in accordance with Piaggio's instructions just outside Poona—came a real industrial-labor culture. The Indian government was pushing for external production units to be started so that linked industry would benefit in accordance with the program

In September 1962 from the new factory in Akurdi near Poona rolled the ten thousandth Vespa, blessed by President Kanalnayan Bajaj. The founding father of the company, Jamnalal Bajaj had been a pupil of Mahatma Gandhi in the years of the struggle for independence.

Two-wheeled taxi in front of the Rashtrapati Bhavan, the presidential palace in Delhi. Although it looks a bit odd, this is really an efficient service, which is catching on in Europe too. And the scooter is certainly the best vehicle for this kind of service.

The LML advertising aimed at highlighting quality and technological updating of the product. From 1982 to 1990 the agreement provided for the transfer of technology and licenses, but in the course of these years a joint-venture agreement was signed giving Piaggio a 25.5 percent stake. The understanding, eventually confirmed in '95, involved the installation of a plant for the production of the PK 125 in 1996.

Only Vespa XE is designed along the newest engineering principles to endure the many tests of time.

6 ways to greater durability.

within which the "fourth stage," between autumn 1962 and winter '63, would see the scooter being produced in its entirety in India. Pontedera, however, was advising caution: there was a danger of assembling components still not to specification, and there was a persistently high percentage of production-line rejects caused by low-grade raw materials and poor-quality workmanship.

Despite this, demand was high and sales forecasts were optimistic for both Bajaj and API, Automobile Products of India, the company that had acquired the license to produce Lambrettas. In the first few years, the black market for the "Italian" scooters was booming and widespread, bringing good business until 1971, when large-scale industry, banking and insurance were included in Indira Gandhi's privatization program. Piaggio's license was not renewed and it found itself out in the cold overnight. From then on millions of Vespas have been made by the Indian company which has in the meantime become an industrial colossus employing 18,000 people with a yearly turnover of $936 million able to turn out a vehicle every seventeen seconds. Millions of Vespas now bearing only the Bajaj name made a substantial contribution to putting the sub-continent on wheels, cutting Pontedera dead.

Another "liaison dangereuse"

The balance sheet for the fiscal year 1982 reads: "After 11 years of absence from the Indian market, two license contracts have been signed resulting from negotiations embarked on in 1981. The contracts have been

Forty million motor vehicles circulate in the streets of India. This astronomic figure could represent only half of what the market could absorb. India has about 80 million families, a figure that is constantly growing. Seen in this light, the subcontinent seems more promising than ever.

approved by the Indian Federal Government and our exports to this important market may recommence at the end of 1983."

Lohia Machines Ltd. of Kanpur, originally a producer of textile machinery, looked like the ideal partner for this new adventure. Its welcome exceeded the most unreasonable expectations but a perhaps somewhat short-sighted price policy and a number of technical problems in the first series took the early wind out of its sails.

After setting the production cycle to rights and deciding on a sensible sales policy, LML took off and soared confidently upwards just as the market grew in the early Nineties. Now competing with Bajaj dominance, the strategy called for scooters with good accessories and a suitable level of technology: the new braking system developed at Pontedera, a luggage rack and a padded spoiler backrest were assembled on the standard models. This caused the price to rise and the scooter's inclusion in the mid-to-high market level but it turned out to be a winner. Sales multiplied fourfold in six years, the company was second only to Bajaj boasting 20 percent of market share.

In December 1997, after the untimely death of Giovanni Alberto Agnelli, chairman and CEO of Piaggio Veicoli Europei since 1993, the Indian partnership began to show signs of instability. The Indians maintained that the stock held by the young heir-apparent to the Fiat empire, who had died at the early age of thirty-three and had been very much involved in the initiative, could now change hands and create alliances contrary to the joint venture.

Undoubtedly, the desire for independence had been sensibly growing in the Kanpur offices strengthening the move towards purchasing Indian-made components.

An official request was made in July 1998 to buy out the Piaggio stock—should it be ruled that the Italians had violated the agreement, the Indian partner would have the right to oblige them to surrender their holding at some 30 percent of market value.

A bitter international legal battle ensued between the two erstwhile partners and an out-of-court settlement was eventually reached in 1999 but it cost both parties dearly. However, by then, Piaggio was free to compete on the Indian market with its own brands and products.

I n May 1998, having received plans and designs from Italy for some forty variations for future application to models already in the price list, LML signed a five-year agreement with the South Korea company Daelim to manufacture small- and medium-cylinder motorcycles: the area expanding fastest. It was maintained, besides, that Piaggio had failed to transfer the production technology for the new scooter with plastic paneling already being sold in Europe, an accusation Piaggio obviously denied.

A recent LML poster. Italian scooters had dominated the market up to 1990 but ten years later growth (as much as 37 percent per year) swung towards motorbikes. Despite this the figures are impressive: some 16 percent of the two-wheel market (four million out of a total of twenty-one million units per year) is sold in India.

Tommaso Fanfani

THE CULTURAL PROJECT

A company that can boast more than a century of history and that has been involved one way or another in the manufacture of every means of transport up to the "Vespa" miracle certainly needs a historical archive and a museum to fill in the missing parts and present the documents and the most significant products.

The archive and museum are today a splendid reality, the result of work started in 1992—with research of documentary evidence in the Piaggio Historical Archive, which was named after Antonella Bechi Piaggio—and brought to a conclusion in 29 March 2000, with the opening of the Giovanni Alberto Agnelli Piaggio Museum.

The man behind it all

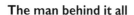

Motivated by interests in the history and sociology of the company in its relations with the surrounding community, the young president of Piaggio, Giovanni Alberto Agnelli, launched a project to recover its past.

Agnelli was profoundly intelligent, highly likable and very friendly. Many were the summers he spent in the woods of Varramista in the villa of his maternal grandmother, Paola Antonelli Bechi Piaggio, during his summer vacation. He made friends with people on the estate and learned to understand and appreciate their wit, openness and sensitivity. Over many seasons he observed the interdependency between Piaggio and its surrounding territory, and, despite spending his time in a rarefied atmosphere far from workers' struggles, he understood the conflicts in industrial relations and the unavoidable dialectic between company and workers.

He studied in Turin and the United States, where he grad-

uated in international relations from Brown University, after which he took his master's degree in business administration. His calling was in the field of social sciences and he loved history. He would spend hours talking about the problems of the south of Italy or the years immediately following the Second World War, when Italy had lived through profound economic change and had laid the foundations for the vigorous growth that followed.

He believed deeply in scientific and technical training. Elected president of Piaggio at a very young age, he had an almost obsessive vision of permanent training for company management and, more generally, for all workers from mid-level management to blue-collar workers.

His view of the importance of the historical and sociological aspects of the relationship between the factory and its locality was not merely functional to the running of the company or complementary to research and development as a means of maintaining and increasing competitiveness in the market place. It ran deeper than that, instilled into every worker in the production process. It was felt—at this level—as an awareness of the individual and an awareness that Piaggio's competitiveness was the latest stage in a long process in which women and men at every level, engineers and laborers, had together made their contribution to development and success through the decades and in the midst of the civil and social fabric of Pontedera and Tuscany, as well as in every other place the company manufactured in. The intimate relationship between the company and the social context of its location had to be cemented not only in the actual physical work of tens of thousands of people inside the factory but also in the sense of interdependence between territory and factory, and factory and territory.

Giovanni Alberto Agnelli, the man behind the cultural project with the ET Vespa. The Piaggio Museum at Pontedera is named after him.

The Piaggio Historical Archive contains more than 150,000 documents and is one of the most representative archives of a company in existence.

Combining these two elements he drew one of the major points of strength for the company in whatever area it was involved in, whatever its core business was. Taking history as its starting point allowed it to trace its roots and endow itself with the added value stemming from its centuries-long experience.

Company and culture, company and territory were the aims he passed on to those of us who were lucky enough to know him, and were taken up by his successor in the presidency of Piaggio and by those who guided the company. This was the starting point for the cultural enterprise, concluded in March 2002, after eight years of work.

The creator of the project was unable to see it completed but it will remain set in stone thanks to his vision of creating a physical setting for the collection of documents and the exhibition of vehicles.

The Archive and Museum Project

Marc Bloch wrote, "The present that becomes the past is imperiously commanded by what has gone before. Taken as such, it can, strictly speaking, describe itself but not understand itself."

The Piaggio Museum and Archive, however, are places in which memory is housed and in which one may come to self-understanding through knowledge of the history of the largest metalworking and engineering company of Italy's center and south. It is a place where you can interact with technical-scientific progress, innovation, development and the stages of creativity in a process in which the past becomes the present and the present the future.

When Piaggio was established in Genoa, Italy had begun its industrial takeoff later than other European nations and new horizons were opening for anyone who had entrepreneurial talent and spirit. Rinaldo Piaggio certainly had these gifts and they enabled him to take his company to ever greater heights and broader scope in production, all of which had something or other to do with means of transport.

The museum tells Piaggio's story, starting with the decades prior to the birth of the Vespa. In terms of creativity, it tells of technical advances born from human ingenuity, able to help the company get over the frequent sticky periods. The company got through each period of recovery thanks to the industriousness and creativity of those innovative engineers, just as today it progresses thanks to the industriousness and creativity

Piaggio technology, from 1884 up to the present day, has brought many impressive innovative projects to fruition. This 1936 train shown at the museum's entrance is an example.

In the central room, the Vespa exhibition opens. The Vespa was the stuff of many people's dreams, and it still has all its charm.

of those capable of holding out, and growing, despite the difficulties brought to markets by globalization.

Our museum recounts every stage in Piaggio's history through a visual itinerary containing actual stories, the tip of a small iceberg of means of transport that will gradually be made available to the public on a rotation basis.

In 1993, Giovanni Alberto Agnelli asked a number of university graduate students to prepare theses on the history of Piaggio. This was the starting point for the first selection of Piaggio's historical documents, which have since been put in order in the archive. This now comprises some 4,000 files containing many tens of thousands of single documents.

The paper chase is not yet over: the personnel archive, with the individual histories of more than a hundred thousand people who have passed through Piaggio's factories in Pontedera and Pisa from 1917 to the present day, has never been touched and is yet to be catalogued. As may be easily understood, this is an extremely significant source for the reconstruction of the social, economic and civil history of Pontedera (and not only of Pontedera).

There is also the enormous stockpile of drawings and designs, some of which are historically priceless, such as the early drawings of the first Vespa, and which have been deemed of particular interest by the state supervisory body for archives, and cultural and environmental heritage.

The archive was therefore the first stage in the move towards

In the shelving, Vespas and mopeds from the past to the future—a unique heritage—from production models to unique versions and prototypes, to be conserved and developed.

Flights of fantasy and actual operational models: the metamorphosis of Ape in the rickshaw version.

253

reconciling culture to company and was the cornerstone for the concept of the foundation and the museum. The foundation was seen as a meeting point between territory and company and was therefore established on the three-way partnership—Piaggio, the municipality of Pontedera and the Province of Pisa—that still runs it today. Its establishing statute states the foundation's aim as being a means of promotion of historical research, of cultural activities and for the realization of the archive and museum which had already been one of Piaggio's declared strategic aims but which was then transferred for implementation to the foundation itself.

Planning the museum continued frenetically and in 1994 it looked certain that the job would be completed in a year or a year and a half at most. However the tragic death of the man behind it brought the project to an abrupt halt.

The death of Giovanni Alberto Agnelli was a severe blow to the progress of the project but the firm belief in its desirability his successors at the head of the company shared, as well as the participation of public partners in the foundation, enabled all difficulties to be overcome.

Built on a design by the architect Andrea Bruno, the archive and museum are living elements in the relationship between company and territory, evocative testimony to the continual process of innovation of a company and also to its creative ability in a context that stretches far beyond the factory walls. In this museum, the story of the company's experience over more than a century is told, and here are collected and exhibited tangible evidence of this history with each prototype as it appeared; here also, studies and images relating not so much to the past but to the present and especially to the future are dis-

seminated. The Piaggio Museum sets out to be a monument to the technical and scientific achievements of the pioneers as well as testifying to the work of hundreds and thousands of regular men and women. The company is a vital part of the social and civil fabric, it is itself the local community and is able to look towards the world market because it is the embodiment of the managerial capacity and concrete ability of generations of women and men who were the undisputed protagonists of the history of their community.

Against this background, the aims of Rinaldo Piaggio, his son Enrico, and Giovanni Alberto Agnelli have now been reconstructed and are now a part of the history of a social dynamics defended strenuously by the company allied with the towns of Pontedera and Pisa and by the surrounding communities of the territory.

So there is a substantial heritage that the museum and archive aims to safeguard: a priceless heritage of culture collected throughout the history of science and technology, and a collection of testimonies that are to be prized not only for the intangible value of culture they represent but also as a collection which, taken together with the narration of creativity, promotes and highlights the image of a company that has contributed not a little to the history of Italy and to the history of modernity of the whole world.

Helping to put post-war Italy back on the road and distributing the Vespa and the Ape in both affluent and developing countries was not just a commercial enterprise.

These testimonies also speak of work and creativity; they should therefore be valued and given the respect due to the highest expressions of civilization.

"In the course of 1991," read the message to the shareholders, "among scooters with plastic bodywork, the Sfera has become Europe's best seller, boasting 58,000 units alongside the other 50 cc versions of the Vespa motorscooters whose supporting bodywork is steel of which 62,000 units were sold"… but the figure for the year before was some 80,000.

At the beginning of the decade, the company was overtaken by a revolution in thought. Public tastes and trends were in flux and moving into new patterns. The very company hierarchy underwent far-reaching change. In 1988, as the total number of vehicles produced in forty years of history reached 10 million, Umberto Agnelli resigned as president. Giovanni Alberto Agnelli, at the tender age of twenty-four, came onto the board of directors and a few months later was elected president of the newly created Piaggio Veicoli Europei, the most important of the many companies belonging to Piaggio & Co., the financial holding company whose headquarters, significantly enough, were moved from Genoa to Pontedera from 1 January 1989.

This was the start of a new season heralding a new line of products and yet another metamorphosis of Pontedera's production facilities—the "infinite factory" as Tommaso Fanfani put it—made to measure to cater to the latest requirements.

Pontedera's heretical scooters

Despite its apparent strength, the brand was starting to give a rather tarnished look to its products, and vice versa. In this period of transition, Europe's biggest scooter manufacturer, with its 40 percent of the continental market for machines under 50 cc and 70 percent of the Italian market seemed, at times, to be suffering from an identity crisis that was filtering through to the purchasing public.

The strong message for change emerged after assessing the new models, which at first sight seemed to renege on forty years of history. Nothing seemed further from the Vespa look than that "so non-Piaggio" two wheeler given the name "Sfera" ["Sphere"].

It had a steel frame, bodywork in rigid plastic, a centrally mounted engine, an electric starter-motor and no choke or fuel tap, both of which were now automatic, as was the gearbox. All this was kept under wraps for two years under the heading "new lightweight scooter."

New robotic production lines launched processes and materials that had rarely been seen before in Pontedera. The monocoque body that the had been envisaged for the Cosa only three years earlier was abandoned, allowing significant savings in manufactoring costs. This was

In the mid-Nineties, attention was eastward-facing too, but the big numbers in European motorbikes in circulation were in Italy (7,800,000) and Germany (4,000,000), followed by France and Spain (3,200,000) while elsewhere the figure was well below the million mark.

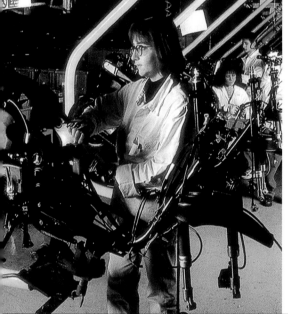

a glimpse of the strategy of wide diversification and product updating that would now be a feature of company life, a line adopted by other manufacturers following in the footsteps of the Japanese motorcycle producers who had perfected it some years previously.

The times were ripe to expand the game plan: the gauntlet was thrown before the Japanese giants and the European-made hybrids, inviting a duel.

The lifetime of each single model was severely curtailed. The market was neurotic, continually enticed by novelties, which forced manufacturers into a frenzy of design and continual technological innovation. "Plastic" scooters mutated, modified in response to their prospective buyers, be they sports riders, young people or adults, of both sexes equally or prevalently women.

At the beginning of the new decade, the Piaggio's factories were producing 700,000 engine-powered vehicles per annum, not counting spare parts: 435,000 from Pontedera, 22,000 from Arcore, 105,000 from Moto Vespa, Madrid and 135,000 from Vespa's Indian partner, LML.

The Sfera which won the coveted Compasso d'Oro design award in 1991 for best industrial design, was, in the 125 version, the first European four-stroke scooter. Zip & Zip tries out the internal combustion/electric hybrid. With Free and then Liberty, high-wheeled scooters were born that would oust mopeds, creating a market in which Piaggio would become leader, selling 600,000 units until 2002. In the early days of the maxi-scooter, a two-wheel Gran Turismo for a mature public, Hexagon topped the European charts for two years running. The Piaggio-owned Gilera models, first Typhoon and then Runner, were noted for their sporty character and led to a single-brand European racing championship.

Che quel giorno fu un grande giorno lo disse
anche il Museo d'Arte Moderna di New York.

Vespa, il mito scooter.

PIAGGIO

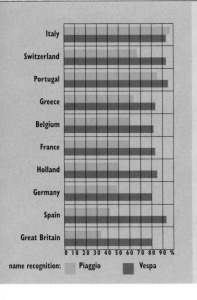

A historical brand for hedonistic consumers

A survey on the images of companies in various European countries over the previous five years (1989–93) revealed some interesting characteristics in consumers: a growing uncertainty about the future, renewed awareness of collective values, less hedonism, greater attention to the material components of well-being such as time set aside for personal matters and personal affection, a growing move towards values and principles and a preference for decentralization—seemingly signs of an ongoing process of maturation.

In consumer attitudes to products, this was translated into demand for high-tech products that were easily available and easy to use as well as attention to "the quality of experience in consuming" rather than attention to the product itself as a status symbol. The pivot and reference point for the entire system was lifestyle quality, for consumers above the twenty-year-old age group.

In fact purchase trends and user habits show the public divided in two groups: teenagers and adults. The former, strongly influenced by the indications of the group of reference, responded in a more emotive way. They asserted their appurtenance, they responded to assertive design, strong emotions and high performance and their aim of use was recreational-exhibitionist, significantly set in relation with the collective model already fashionable in the Eighties.

The adult consumer at the turn of the millennium was more selective, rational, cool and also opportunistic, less prone to brand fidelity.

Consumer vision of what constitutes the Piaggio brand was, in Europe, non-homogeneous and sometimes in contrast with reality. Brand identity for Vespa was strong and widespread in up to 87 percent of potential purchasers and over 60 percent of the general public. In the summer of 1994 it was still "the scooter by name and definition" identifying an "Italian style, classic, original but not innovative" seen as a means of transport "dependable but low-tech" with "relatively low" safety margins and little consideration for the environment.

A unique heritage of product image and value was losing its glitter, credibility and freshness. It was time to start looking for improvements. And for some time Pontedera had been working on it: something really new was taking shape in Piaggio's study and design center.

	0 10 20 30 40 50 60 70 80 90 %
Italy	
Switzerland	
Portugal	
Greece	
Belgium	
France	
Holland	
Germany	
Spain	
Great Britain	

name recognition: Piaggio Vespa

"Today, at European level, Piaggio is seen as both a company and a product brand: Vespa is the company, brand, model and product. Typhoon is a model but nobody knows who makes it." Indeed, the Hill & Knowlton survey on how the company was situated in Europe reveals in the mid-Nineties that there was "a limited perception of Piaggio compared to its actual nature and objectives." At the other end, significantly, "brands like Vespa today represent not only a product but a 'special world' with an extremely high added value to the point that in the more advanced societies it is one of the parameters of a highly valued asset."

1977-83

VESPAPX
PKSA

VESPA PX

The generally unstable political and economic climate between the late Seventies and early Eighties took its toll on the international motorcycling industry and saw Piaggio the largest European scooter manufacturer, in competition with the most prestigious (mainly Japanese) brands.

The company's production process now evolved in the light of two major concepts: the idea of a "system," flexibly and interactively connecting the planning processes of different elements (materials, manufacturing techniques, organization, communication, economics and marketing) to reorganize the production structure; and the

The Fiat Panda was, like the PX, an example of Italian design that marked the period between the end of the Seventies and the beginning of the Eighties.

Details of the New Line Vespa: the cowl anti-theft lock and the air intake hole for the carburetor, housed in a plastic box above the engine.

... with cowls anti-theft device

The new Vespa PX 150 E is equipped with an anti-theft device for securing the two-cowls. This new device, operated by two levers located under the locable seat, prevents the removal of the spare-wheel.

The restyling fundamentally altered the rear of the chassis, now defined by boxy lines. The side cowls were much less voluminous and had slightly indented molded contours running along the flanks in which the indicators (an optional extra) were installed.

Detail of the grille bearing the Piaggio logo on the "nose" of the scooter and protecting the horn.

The engine cowl and the corresponding component on the opposite side were secured by a clip with a return spring.

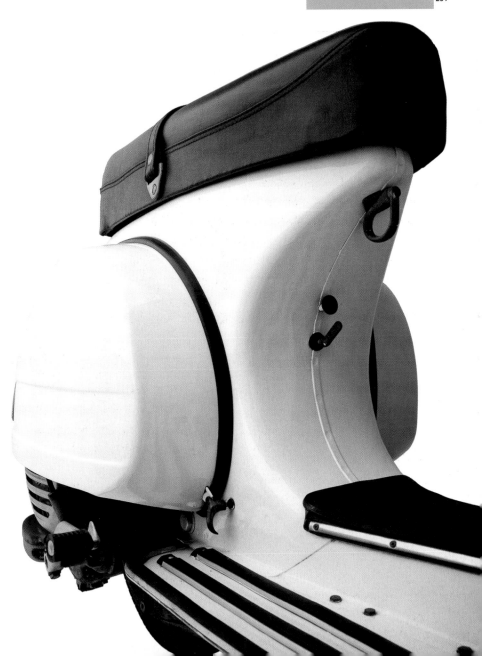

definition of the relationship between human and machine not simply in ergonomic terms but also reversing the priority of mechanicals over electronics.

The introduction of increasingly miniaturized components freed product design from the necessity of accommodating large mechanical elements and permitted more emphasis on aesthetic, emotional and communicational values.

The Olivetti Logos 42 typewriter, designed in 1977 by Mario Bellini, new domestic appliances and work tools, and cars such as the Alfetta and Giorgetto Giugiaro's Panda were examples of mass-produced items designed with deliberately boxy, angular shapes which characterized the style of the decade. The New Line Vespa, launched by Piaggio on 19 October '77, was a product of this era and was built to cater to the needs of a new upwardly mobile generation. This series was available with two engine sizes—125 cc (P 125 X) and 200 cc (P 200 E with electronic ignition)—and the models were almost identical in appearance. Shortly after its introduction, the PX series was given a 150 cc version.

The restyled shape was imposing, sober and elegant while maintaining the original personality of the Vespa. The most obvious changes were the markedly squared off side cowls, now 2 inches narrower which, seen from the side, curved more sharply toward the wheel at the bottom. The side cowls were removable (as on the 1962 160 GS

The front view shows the raised front mudguard to allow for the longer suspension travel. The leg shield is characterized by a central strip, visually balancing the different elements and in keeping with the overall new design.

The general more substantial and compact appearance was given by the narrower side cowls and larger overall dimensions: length, 70 inches; saddle height, 32 inches; handlebar height, 39 inches; leg shield width, 18 inches; maximum width, 27 inches.

VESPAPX

The new speedometer, which was easily legible even at night and was relatively accurate, had no trip counter. The instruments were completed by a headlight pilot, a pilot for any accessories installed and a two-position ignition switch.

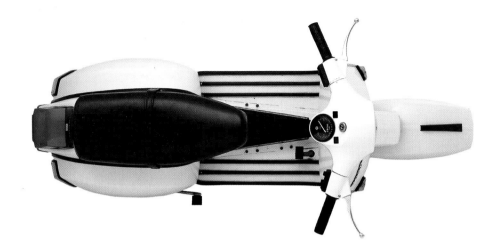

The vehicle was generally more comfortable in part due to improved leg space. The expanded polyurethane foam saddle was comfortable, permitted an ergonomically correct riding position and was more comfortable for the passenger, too.

The rear suspension travel now more closely matched the front (3.2 inches).

The front suspension used a telescopic hydraulic damper anchored to the brake shoe plate. This eliminated diving on braking while also permitting longer travel (3.6 inches instead of 2.8 inches).

The new shape of the front mudguard continuing the lines of the steering column cover on the front of the shield was a characteristic of the first PX series.

The saddle opening button incorporated a lock which opened with a separate key. Despite the lack of a battery, the big rear light provided constant light intensity thanks to the use of electronic regulators.

VESPAPX

and later models) and had fittings for the indicator lights.

The rear end of the chassis was box shaped and raised to eliminate the "beak" profile of the older models. Underneath, the body was closed off by a small black plastic mudguard to offer protection from splashes which gave a more modern appearance to the vehicle.

At the front was a wide, squared off mudguard, sized to stylistically balance the voluminous rear, and a wide leg shield with a protruding central strip modeled following a curve that widened the body at the mudguard attachment and closed off at the front with a grille covering the horn.

The carry-all compartment was larger than on previous versions without encroaching on leg space.

The load bearing body shell, made from 15/10 mm sheet steel and weighing 37 pounds, was manufactured using a new electrophoresis system. This involved an electrostatic body shell treatment process offering greater anti-corrosion protection and a high-tech automated painting process.

While the controls remained unchanged, the handlebars were now raised for a more ergonomically correct riding position. The top side of the handlebars was plastic and easily removable. At the center was a round speedometer next to two indicator lamps and the ignition key.

The 125 was fitted with a horizontally aligned single-cylinder two-stroke rotating-valve engine with an additional third port (as on the ET3).

Top speed was 57 mph and average fuel consumption was more than 100 mpg. The tank held about 2 gallons. The electrical system supplied 12 V—80 W on indicator-equipped versions.

The most important technical innovation was the ingeniously mounted telescopic hydraulic damper, which not only drastically reduced front end dive on braking but also permitted a longer travel. The steering column was still inclined at 25°, but trail was increased from 2.8 inches to 3.1 inches, improving handling.

The PX was the longest lived Vespa to date, and is still in production.

The layout of the controls on the bars remained the same. The switch gear was now grouped together in a newly designed plastic box. Note the size of the locker compartment with lock. The vehicle came with three different (perhaps too many) keys.

VESPAPK

The revision to the product range initiated with the PX series was continued in 1983 with the PK. This was also available with two different engine sizes.

The 50 cc engine was used on the PK 50 (basic), PK 50 S (deluxe, with carry-all compartment and indicators), and the PK 50 S Elestart (with electric starter). The 125 cc version, replacing the Standard and ET3 models of the Vespa Primavera (which was still manufactured for the Japanese market and is the best selling two-wheeled Western vehicle in Japan), was available as the basic PK 125 and the automatic PK 125 S Automatica. The PK 125 retained

Automatic transmission, electronic ignition, both brake levers on the handlebars: the PK 50 A was a very easy scooter to ride.

This ad from the Leader-Filippetti campaign of '82 is a play on words. A line from the Italian national anthem—"L'Italia s'è desta!" ["Italy has awakened!"]— is here transformed into "L'Italia s'è Vespa!" ["Italy has Vespa'd!"].

The handlebar controls were reduced to a bare minimum to make the scooter simple and instinctive to use. On the left was the plastic rear brake lever and the two-position twist grip: 0 is neutral for starting the engine, position 1 engages the automatic transmission when riding and disengages it on its own at low revs. The ignition key, on the right-hand side of the steering column, had three positions and also acted as theft protection. The same key opened the locker compartment, the side cowl covers and the saddle.

Front mudguard and front floating lever suspension with varying spring rate and telescopic hydraulic damper (3.2 inches travel). Tires were 3 inches wide, with interchangeable steel wheels (2.10 inches by 10 inches).

the basic characteristics of the ET3, such as the three cylinder ports and electronic ignition while adopting the technical and styling evolutions used in the PX series.

The design of the PK was characterized by taut almost straight lines, inclined and connected to emphasize the dynamic nature of the vehicle and was the result of advanced new technologies recently introduced by Piaggio.

The chassis was built using a completely new production process, in which the body shell and front mudguard were welded with the edges turned inwards rather then being overlapped. This new system offered significant advantages, especially from an aesthetic point of view, as the weld points were no longer visible.

The cowls were integrated in the body shell and were fitted with indicators near the top (lower on the automatic version) of the molding, which was bent squarely at the sides to form the base. The lower part of the tail was also a closed quadrilateral and had fittings for the engine compartment hatch on the right and the spare wheel compartment hatch on the left.

The battery was fitted at the center of the spare wheel and covered by a plastic disc, which was a similar arrangement to the one used on the 1962 160 GS.

Six inclined slits were cut into these hatches which hinged onto the main body at the bottom. This was a new feature, intended to facilitate

The styling of the Vespa PK was compact, elegant, protective and omfortable. The front shield looked narrower due to the central molding carrying the badges and the horn cover grille.

These side views show the overall design; the saddle extends further into the central space and is fitted with a large, new bag carrier clip at the front end, made of plastic, like the fuel tap underneath.

VESPAPK

Detail of the right hand switch-gear block with switch, selector, red electric starter button and, underneath, the horn button. The electric controls had no markings, which could cause some confusion at first.

maintenance. The size and shape of the hatches were sufficient to allow easy access to internal components and they were now fitted with locks which opened with the ignition key, solving a problem that had arisen on the PX.

The leg shield with incorporated indicators was edged with an easily removable protective molding. The finish details were now modeled with square, angular shapes, such as the carry-all locker, the steering column cover and the trapezoid shaped box protecting the horn whose sound was now, finally, adjustable. The handlebars consisted of a light alloy base with a removable plastic cover and housed the headlight,

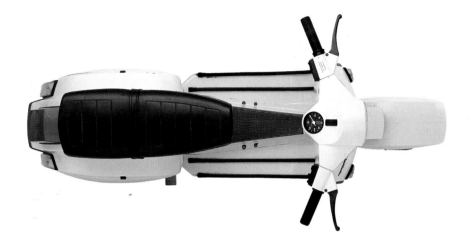

This top view shows that the footplate has no hole for the brake pedal, preventing infiltration of water or dirt.

Apart from the badge on the right under the saddle, the automatic version was distinguishable by the rear indicator lights, which were mounted lower than on the basic version, by the slits shifted further forward along the sides and by the different shape of the engine, which now protruded from under the right-hand flank.

The rear light incorporated a large translucent reflector, to improve visibility at night.

The dash had a very clear design, but still provided very little information. The speedometer numerals and dial were luminous while the odometer now also had a trip counter. The two-part rectangular lamp showed when the indicators and the full beam were on.

VESPAPK

speedometer, indicator lamps and all other instruments, assuming the role of user interface. This was even more the case on the automatic version, where all the scooter's controls were incorporated in the handlebars.

The PK 125 S Automatica was the realization of a goal Piaggio had been aiming at for some time: an "intelligent" clutch-transmission-gearbox unit to make riding the scooter easier.

The introduction of the automatic gearbox, perhaps the most radical change since 1946, offered significant advantages in terms of urban mobility, allowing the rider to focus more on riding and safety. Gone was the twist grip gear control on the left handlebar, as was the rear brake pedal on the right-hand side of the footplate. The rear brake lever was now located on the handlebar like the front brake, taking the place of the clutch lever. All vehicle controls were now included in the handlebars. Together with extreme simplicity of use, enhanced even further with the implementation of electronic ignition, this model also offered interesting performance.

The gearbox was programmed to offer immediate pick-up from a standstill. One problem that this model had was a difficulty in applying the right amount of throttle, and it took some practice to get to know how the auto box behaved and to achieve good fuel mileage. The engine-transmission unit was completely redesigned (with reed valves and a light alloy cylinder) and was

Despite the substantial design efforts that went into this model and the company's expectations, the first gearless Vespa was not commercially very successful.

quiet, vibration-free and untiring, in keeping with the best Piaggio tradition. It was recognizable by a plastic case covering the automatic gearbox pulleys. Top speed was around 54 mph and average fuel consumption was about 60 mpg. To improve comfort, the scooter's dimensions were designed to ensure a correct riding posture and lots of space for both rider and passenger.

This model did not meet with much enthusiasm in younger users, who possibly wanted bolder styling in keeping with the technology used.

The PK 125 was manufactured up until 1987, after the launch of the Cosa. The commercial flop led to the PK 125 FL2 1990, together with an automatic model for the export market.

The new "Vespa" script on the front shield. The range of colors available consisted of white, anthracite and cobalt blue.

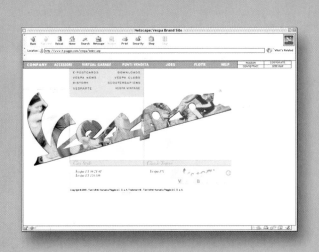

*A*fter more than fifty years here we tell what Vespa is and why. How is it born and how does it take to the world's roads, what are its ways and language, and what does tomorrow hold in this long history?

1996–2003

Talk of the town

NEW FLEDGLINGS FOR THE 50TH YEAR

With 1996 coming up, nothing could be allowed to go wrong. Fifty years of history had gone by and the brand was known in every corner of the world. The PX, which year after year was seen as a benchmark for class and style, was still on the price list. The company's top management had the skills and the idealism necessary to win this match.

New avenues for the new Vespa

The idea that the high-end commuter could become the new standard-bearer of the Vespa tradition was first seen as early as the Autumn of 1990 by "the platform." "The platform" is a term which came into use around 1990 to designate a select body of people working in different departments—marketing, planning, production technology, quality control, purchasing and supplier relationships—involved in the project acting under the coordination of the project head.

Starting, therefore, with the Vespa idea, the first "zero sheet" is prepared in which marketing, in accordance with company strategy, outlines what type of vehicle should take shape as well as who its user should be and what price range it should have. Identifying how development should proceed and what its successive stages should be enables research and development to give their technical and stylistic contribution in the most efficient way. High-tech, avant-garde suggestions in the embryonic stage are then passed to the pilot platform, the first of the five, all of which have been continuously operational in all areas in which the company is active—two wheels, three wheels and commercial vehicles—since 1990. The decision to give full operational status to a number of these suggestions provides the platform with a clearer idea of the article which now is slowly taking shape, both figuratively and in reality.

The little that seeps out beyond the "X" code that the company uses to label new projects leads one to believe that this time the new Vespa would be really new—indeed, spectacularly new in some ways.

It had no gears, to start with, which was enough for a lot of people to take offense both inside and outside the company. Then there was the engine: best not spread the word around too much because anyway, if you don't know, you can hardly see it, but it's … central. It's not lateral anymore: this Vespa runs straight as a die and you

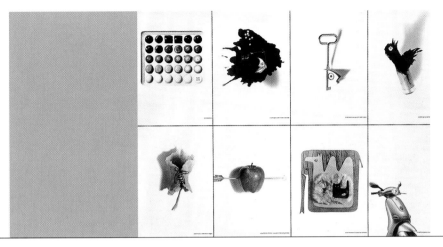

Filippetti's tribute to the young Agnelli on the birth of the new ET: "In the beginning he made sky and stars / made the waters teem therein with fish / made birds to fly high over the earth / then did Eve choose a leafy raiment / and with pointed finger banished evil from Eden / they all lived happily ever after / and on the seventh day he rode off on a Vespa."

get to the engine from above. No, from underneath. Well, from both above and below: you raise the saddle and take out the helmet compartment and there's the engine right below; or, alternatively, off with the lower side moldings just under the body and you get to the engine that way. But it's a four-stroke, not a two-stroke anymore. Aha! It burns less fuel and pollutes less. Four-stroke, no, two. Two-stroke as well but it's the little one, the one with fuel injection. The first time ever, a two-stroke engine with fuel injection.

Such innovations are the result of years of work that a lot of people still have to find out about. From the traffic-light lineup getting an eyeful of the masked prototype, to the production line, everybody has their own ideas about what it should be like, to the "upper floors"

that, anyway, aren't so "upper" at Pontedera; nowhere can you find two people with the same idea about what it should be like.

And yet it works, and it works well; it's got front disc brakes and an instrument panel that doesn't seem like a Vespa, but a Vespa it is, and it shows. The new, "little" heir to the Primavera, within that same product range, accessible, metropolitan, free and easy, and appealing to all as always, is ideal for students, craftspeople and the urban professional classes, the young and not so young, and both sexes with a certain slant towards the female public. It looks small in body but when you measure it it's bigger than the PX. It looks smaller than it is thanks to its balanced looks—balance and style.

On the market and on the roads the ET gradually

Flair and imagination in transforming the typographical representation of "Vespa" into a scooter by Alan Fletcher, the founder of England's Pentagram Studio.

"The problem, then, was not only how to develop the Vespa but also when this should be done" observes Lucio Masut, head of Piaggio's two-wheeler research and development department. "We could have launched it before the plastic scooters came out and they would have seen us as 'them that can only make Vespas'. By contrast, after seeing what happened in that area, and getting confirmation of European sales figures, we decided to present the new Vespa as the best possible option in that category."

VESPA CELEBRATES FIFTY YEARS 1946–1996

After molding with robots and presses of 600, 800 and 1,800 tons the body-work assembly is in part automated but in the manual operations the specialized workers' ability and experience is fundamental.

accelerated, pulling ahead with marked ease: in 1997 and '98 it was the biggest selling two wheeler in Europe and has since proved its staying power, looking like becoming the new classic benchmark.

All down the line

The time was 6:30 pm on a June afternoon in 1996, the 7th to be exact at end of line number 5, the first of the new generation made its appearance—an olive green one-two-five. A commemorative group photograph was taken of the chief of the factory for large-production, two-wheeled vehicles and his staff along with the supervisors of the integrated production center for line number 5 and a scattering of blue-collar workers. They were too numerous, some ninety in all, in two shifts and they couldn't all fit in but they are the ones who physically assemble and finish this jigsaw puzzle of one hundred and eighty main component parts and turn out a completed unit every two hundred and ten seconds.

Its metal body, the only one of its kind in the world, meant the revival of the celebrated molding factory, the nucleus around which production was centered until the Eighties, when every two-wheeled Piaggio, from the PX to the mopeds, was in sheet metal. The season of the "spheroids" didn't affect it all that much; on the contrary, production of four-wheeled light vehicles besides the PX kept the presses busy during this interim period.

The sheet metal assembly plant with one hundred and thirty workers each shift, five robots and eighteen manual work stations put together the eight elements in sheet metal that constitute the actual body of the scooter with 340 welds (all hidden) using 16 inches of welding rod. Downstream, the electrostatic painting process is highly automated. Since February '92, the new OTZ—Operatore Tecnico di Zona [operational technical team leader]—work organization system has been introduced on a trial basis in which a technician is responsible for organizing the work of the team he leads. There are two alternating shifts of sixty workers each, some of whom are involved in maintenance work on the twelve paint stations: six for color application and six for the subsequent transparent finishing coat.

There is said to be a certain amount of pride in those on the production line who feel they are somehow involved in carrying on the special metal-working

A familiar shape starts to appear; in the background it can be seen now fixed with the front apron ready for its first coat of paint.

In the spray booth ET bodies are followed by a disassembled PX, its side bags, handlebar and the steering column housing: 32 seconds of paint spray, 8 of conveyance, and little more to change the colors (to reach greatest productive flexibility).

The next step is installing the electrical fittings and circuitry while the pallets of Line 6 move along. This idea, inaugurated for the fifty-year anniversary of the Vespa, was soon incorporated in all the assembly lines in the factory at Pontedera.

tradition, today more than ever restricted to this particular industry. It's a question of collective identity, workmanship ability, professional updating and, at the same time, links with the past.

The actual assembly line underwent a radical change for the ET with the start-up, in October 1998, of Line 6 in the two-wheeler plant.

It went by the initials TLI meaning a "pallet" line. The conveyor brackets were replaced by simple uprights in the floor supporting the vehicle at the height required and, where necessary, geared to the force required to tilt the piece being worked on. It has also been called "asynchronous" since the pallet can leave the main line and move along a parallel one to enable extra tasks of up to twenty minutes long to be carried out and then rejoin the main flow. Its wheelbase is also variable since the pallet scan can be set to accommodate vehicles up to 50 percent longer than standard.

Line 6 allows its workers to operate in pairs moving around the piece on both sides and leaves the overhead area free which improves illumination a lot. At the end of the line the completed vehicle is discharged from a still position, which cuts the risk of damage to a minimum. The pallet here becomes airborne, returning to the beginning of this nearly 400-foot line with its 67 assembly points to the point where the bodies come down on the double rail conveyor from the paint shop.

In short, this concept has been extended to the other assembly lines—yet another page in the long narrative the many people who work here live out day by day.

Here, we are towards the end of the line and the vehicle is almost complete. The Vespa, metallic by definition, does not eschew plastic in the ET where it is useful such as in the glove compartment to ensure a softer knee contact with the driver.

O ur leading actress starts out in her new role in a very unusual phase, and not just because it's the company's fiftieth anniversary. Recovery at last seems near to becoming reality after the frightening drop during which, only two years earlier, the Italian market had fallen to a quarter of what it had been in 1982, a glorious year if ever there was one.

And now, the wind was favorable in other countries too. The group's strategy was increasingly to sell in foreign markets through its own branch offices and, except Switzerland, Austria and Scandinavia, from the spring of 2000, sales Europe-wide were made through sales points directly controlled from Italy.

Meantime, on the other side of the ocean, in the autumn, "sales of the ET will begin marking an eagerly awaited comeback in response to the high level of awareness that Vespa continues to enjoy in America."

The "premium" for Italian style

"Look at these pictures. They suggest lightness of being. Style. Italian-ness ... and the heady feeling of a romantic escapade."

Behind the CEO, the world's best-known duo of casual Vespa enthusiasts were shown zipping along the streets of Rome. He, Joe Bradley, an American journalist living in the city, was a tall man and the little Vespa looked almost like a toy in his hands. As he leaned over to the left his elbow seemed to be resting on his knee as he drove. She, a young princess in incog-

The 1999 IBM campaign, which appeared in *The New York Times*, *The Wall Street Journal*, *Time*, *Newsweek*, *Business Week* and *Rolling Stone*, selected the object to portray in a campaign promoting Internet as a means of communication and sales.

Possibly the most prestigious name among the many called upon to celebrate Vespa's fiftieth birthday was Milton Glaser, American from New York. A pivotal figure in half a century of graphic and design history he became well-known to the general public for a famous poster showing Bob Dylan in black profile set against his curls portrayed in bright colors.

50 YEARS OF VESPA

bar

nito, was watching the road, peeping over his shoulder, her eyes with just a pinch of apprehension, a sense of adventure, lightheartedness and freedom. The innocent summer madness of this *Roman Holiday* shone through in all its original freshness and enchantment.

In the first Vespa Boutique at 13627 Ventura Boulevard in Sherman Oaks, near Los Angeles, this evening of November 2000 seems imbued with the sweet air of Rome just as Gregory Peck and Audrey Hepburn were feeling in the wall-mounted poster.

"Vespa is not just a product, but a lifestyle." This was the watchword for the start of the new campaign in the United States. The stake was high: the importance and prestige of America required maximizing the company's strategy to conquer such premium markets.

Peter Beard, photographer and artist, anthropologist and writer, and a longtime Vespa enthusiast, recalls a trip he made to Madagascar. A friend of Karen Blixen's, the person who got him interested in Africa, he has done portraits of Picasso, Francis Bacon, Salvador Dalí and Andy Warhol, and is the artist who photographed the 2002 Piaggio calendar.

277

The ET Vespa as seen by Vivienne Westwood, Donna Karan, Givenchy (upper left) and Dolce & Gabbana (lower right). Unique pieces that were auctioned and whose proceeds went to cancer research, these were donated in 2002 by Piaggio Ltd. of the U.K. Below, the ET Vespa according to Agent Provocateur, at the preceding year's auction.

Normally, in countries where there is a high per capita income and in which requirements for mobility have already been satisfied, a campaign must place the accent on intangible values to satisfy "relationship" and "emotional" needs.

One must blend a series of recollections common to everyone, together with values specific to a restricted number of users. This enables the client to identify the product with a characteristic corresponding to his own process of personal selection as well as representing a code of appurtenance to an elite group of those who interpret style. Specifically, this pedigree is necessarily high since we're dealing with the Italian style, but one "cool, hip and smart" just as the Mods said. However, because of their intangibility and evanescence, operations of this kind call for substance and quality in the product.

Emphasis must be placed on the strong attractiveness of the product, or rather of the "Vespa" brand, as well as on a diversified concept, using exclusive sales channels and improving after-sales service, without trying to compete on the same price level as the competition. It is important to keep prices 10 percent higher as evidence of a "differentiation barrier"—and no discounts. It's the no-price competition played out at a different level.

Being in a highly characterized market niche means imports have to be regulated carefully. This reduces turnover but gives more generous margins than average and results in increased customer fidelity. Besides,

The added value of the brand and the sense of belonging are reconfirmed in being shown alongside fashion collections including garments, leather accessories, watches and perfumes, as well as small articles in silver and publications. All made in Italy as are the furnishings that the team of shop-fitters, from Italy obviously, build into the floor-space.

circumstances, at least on the other side of the ocean, have made the niche unavoidable—long distances outside big towns, and urban traffic fraught with problems certainly different from Europe. The scooter has to be perceived as a fashion accessory to nip over to the shopping mall with or to take an evening run downtown more than as a means of getting from home to work and back along the L.A. freeways every day.

"Half vehicle, half toy." With this ringing in his ears, you wouldn't expect an American interested in buying a Vespa to hang around a concessionaire that looked like a Hells Angels garage, where there's a layer of grease that the aficionados love covering everything.

In the Vespa lifestyle, "sales point" gets translated as Vespa Boutique. This is where the customer can expe-

rience real Italian taste, and not just in the espresso he gets at the counter.

The added value of the brand name and identifying with it are underlined by a fashion collection which goes from garments to leather accessories, watches, perfumery, small articles in silver and publications. Everything is produced in Italy down to the furnishing components that a team of specialists— Italian, obviously —fit to the locale selected to house them. This experience is now fast growing in the United States, and Europe is just starting to get used to the idea. Here in Europe, fashion items are bound to sell more than scooters but the formula seems to have good development potential.

"I tore a couple of ligaments and I can't even say I did it with honor on a powerful motorbike—I fell off my Vespa, a Vespa I wanted because I love the film *Roman Holiday*.

"The reason I love the Vespa," comments Steven Spielberg "is because even when I was a kid, I always had a poster of William Wyler, the great director, over my bed riding a Vespa to Cinecittà to direct *Ben-Hur*. He'd been photographed from a second-floor window riding his Vespa down Via Veneto. And since I've always greatly admired Wyler, I always wanted a Vespa to be just like him.

"Last year, my wife Kate gave me a classic gray 1962 Vespa and had it sent to Long Island. In my lifetime I've driven cross-country bikes, dirt bikes, and I'm pretty good—Well, we got the Vespa out of its packaging, I got on and set off towards a hillock in my garden. I did a leap and when I landed, maybe due in part to the small wheels, the impact wasn't very soft. The handlebar suddenly turned sideways and I flew off head foremost! The Vespa's a perfect vehicle but, I have to say, for road riding, not for jumping!"

Bill Buford

URBAN INSECTS

There are, it is said, sixteen million Vespas in the world, but from what I can tell—it's my first month driving one in New York City—there are only two of them here: a dull, dented vintage bike, imported from Italy, which passed me at great speed, hurtling down Broadway this morning, and mine, following along afterwards, driven by me with great caution and at a brisk pedestrian's pace, if only because I was still half expecting to be sideswiped by a hysterical cab driver. I exaggerate of course (about the number of Vespas, that is, not about New York cab drivers): I know there are more than two of these vehicles in this city of eight million, but there don't seem to be many more than two, and, in any case, there are very few in view.

It is, I realize, a privileged moment: the moment before Vespa takes over New York. I could be wrong, but my suspicion is that this moment in New York is probably analogous to a comparable time in Italy—in, say, 1946. Or in France, three years later. Or in England, two years after that. Here, on my motor bike, I am on the eve of witnessing something very big, the vespers of Vespa, a crepuscular passage. I'm experiencing what it must be like to be driving a Vespa for the first time—how many people in the world can enjoy such a moment?

For instance, there is the experience of the red light. I can't stop at a red light without immediately becoming the center of attention. New York is a work city, a busy city, characterized (often oppressively) by everyone needing to be somewhere else very fast. It's not a city for dawdling. But every time I'm waiting at a traffic light, there is always at least one pedestrian who, rushing past me, does a double-take. "Whoa, dude, Vespa!" he'll say (or some variation

thereof). And he stops, right there in the middle of the street, to admire what's between my legs. Once he's stopped, others slow down and stare.

On one occasion (on a freezing January morning, as it happens, when I was very cold and it was starting to snow and I was very keen to get home and get warm), I had five people gathered round me. The level of inquiry wasn't particularly sophisticated ("You like? It's Italian, isn't it?") but the very fact of the inquiry (a crowd in a crosswalk, about to be stranded among the rushing traffic once the light changes) was, in my experience, unprecedented.

But it's not just pedestrians: telephone repairmen (they shout their enthusiasm from high above, suspended from poles), delivery men in vans, taxi drivers, homeless people (one man wrapped in an old blanket mumbled a long disquisition on the genius of Piaggio), and all bicyclists (the cyclists are often messengers, and they whip past at a ferocious speed, do a triple-take, circle back recklessly, zigzagging among the vehicles, and give me the proverbial thumb's-up, recognizing that in me they've got some kind of anti-car ally—that on some level we both share a unique way of traveling through Manhattan).

A number of things interest me in this response to my Vespa—these validations from the pavement, "street cred," if you like, in its most fundamental expression. The first involves the universal recognition of Vespa, even when, at this precious moment in history, there are so few examples of them on New York streets.

The design says "Italy." When Starbucks, the American mass-market coffee chain, packages a pound of coffee beans as "Italian roasted," it puts a silhouette of a Vespa on the outside. When a restaurant in Baltimore wants to indicate the kind of food it serves, it calls itself Vespa. When Joe Bastianich, an Italian American restaurateur, starts to make wine for the first time and is looking around for a name to put on the label, he comes up with Vespa.

The Vespa—the "airplane landing"wheels, the curvaceous metal casing, the accommodating butt (all the qualities that years of Vespa commentators have correctly identified and celebrated)—is as universal and immediate an image as the Coca-Cola bottle or the Volkswagen "Bug," except that, unlike the Coca-Cola bottle and the Volkswagen "Bug," the Vespa is still with us. It is still an active piece of image currency.

In fact, in many ways, it's more active than it was at the height of its popularity, when it was a prop in all those wonderful Italian black-and-white films, if only because, today, it manages to be both contemporary and nostalgic. In effect, the image endures because its message exists in two frames, a past and a present, and the message is the same in each. The nostalgic message is one of simplicity. The design of the bike evokes that time right after the war when a simple thing was required for a time of hardship; but its present message says the same thing, even if it is being said at a different time: simplicity, at a time when so much of our lives is now complex.

Allow me to illustrate by giving some sense of what a Vespa means on a New York street.

The history of the motorbike in the United States is akin to the history of the American car or American sports. It's a history of power. Big, brawny, and dangerous. For instance, the game of football.

In Europe, "football" is the beautiful game; in the United States, it is "a game of titans." The beautiful game involves grace and speed; the game of titans involves brawny expressions of power and violence.

The vehicle of choice in New York is the SUV—the sport utility vehicle. Looking outside my window, I see that the street directly in front of my apartment is lined with SUVs: one after the other—a dozen of these giant things. They're heavy and durable and made to last forever—that's the idea, anyway. They have four-wheel drive, big engines, and innumerable enhanced qualities which allow their drivers to mount any terrain: rivers, mountains, muddy hills, even though they face nothing more challenging than the stop-and-go traffic on Times Square during rush hour. It's hard not to wonder. Why do you need a powerful four-wheel drive vehicle to pass through Times Square? Are you hoping to get through the traffic faster by somehow surmounting the cars and racing across the top of them? People own these things not for they do—could a vehicle be more unnecessary in the city?—but for what they say. "Me, power—you, powerless."

The role of the motorbike is no different. A year after Roman Holiday appeared (where of course the role of the Vespa was like that of a motorized magic carpet—an expression of lightness and love and balmy Mediterranean frivolity), Marlon Brando appeared in The Wild Ones: his bike, a Triumph, was British-made, but his posture was wholly American. Motorbikes, and the life associated with him, represented danger, violence, the outlaw.

The difference is evident in names. In Italy, cars and motorbikes have been named after insects: wasps and bees and crickets and bluebottle flies. In the United States, where the leading indigenous motorcycle manufacturer is Harley Davidson, the bikes are more robustly described. They are called porkers or choppers. Their model names are Indian Chief and Road King. Or Bob-Job, Sportster, and Night Train. And their foreign imitations are even more extreme: Rocket, Hurricane, Trident. These are the names of missiles and bad weather. Again, they make this simple statement of the person riding them. "Me, power—you, powerless."

It is perhaps not surprising that in this overcrowded, overpopulated, cribbed, confined city of towering tall buildings of cramped windowless apartments the pet of choice is a giant dog. A Great Dane, a rottweiler, a muscular Labrador. Again, that recurrent New York statement: "Me, power—you, powerless."

This culture—with all its ridiculous manifestations of itself—is what surrounds me during my waits at traffic lights, where I've pulled up on my cheerfully humming,

perfectly shaped, utterly unthreatening little insect vehicle. No wonder people stop and stare. The Vespa is not simply a well-made motorized vehicle. In its soft, discreet way, it's actually anti-American.

It is feminine rather than overwhelming masculine (the very design suggests a woman's bicycle—easy to get on and off, without having to swing your leg across it like a boy). It says not power but design, and, as such, its message is style. And it also says something else, which I didn't entirely appreciate until my Vespa had been so consistently praised and admired by the city's bicyclists. The Vespa is the world's greatest urban vehicle.

Its history in Europe, I appreciate, is more complex, where it is (in Italy) also a workhorse in villages or (in Spain) the modernized successor to the burro or (in England) a fleet, fly expression of suburban rebellion (Mods and Rockers, and so on). But its natural home is the city. New York, like Rome, needs to be lived on foot to appreciate its infinite mystery—not by subway or taxi or car. But you'll see more of its mystery if you can be motored around it in the open air.

The point came to me while I was waiting at (yet another) traffic light, and confirming to yet another stranger (a van driver delivering fish) that, yes, indeed, I was straddling a Vespa, and yes, he's absolutely correct, it comes from Italy. I was on the corner of Lafayette, downtown, a street I traverse regularly, four, five times a week, when I looked up and noticed that on the third floor of a nearby building was the headquarters of the American Socialist Party. Anywhere else in the world—no big deal. But this is America.

I didn't even know that it still had a Socialist Party, let alone that it had an office in New York. Its windows, which were metal framed and very dirty, were plastered with posters. Inside there were potted plants and stacks of yellowing newspapers. Exactly what you would expect to find, of course; it's only that I'd never seen it. The light changed. I drove on, on my way to midtown, when I suddenly smelled lilacs.

Lilacs in the grimy, gritty city? But of course, I was in the flower district.

I carried on. It was the middle of the afternoon. I spotted chefs sitting outside having a cigarette. It was the time of the restaurant "family meal," and everywhere there were men and women in white aprons resting before the evening service. In Chinatown, I spotted steam coming from a sealed-up window—evidence of a sweatshop at work.

I ended my day by taking the Staten Island ferry, newly charmed by the charms of an unknowable city. That's what my Vespa was teaching me: the city is unknowable, and therefore has an infinite amount to teach me.

By now I'd come to understand the power of my Vespa. It was in its absence of power.

This is not a vehicle about strength. It doesn't intimidate. Its thrills are limited (although there is always a thrill in driving exposed and in the open, the heart of the motorbike experience).

This is the city bike. Its natural habitat is urban. And, as such, this invention from Italy is teaching me more and more about my home in America.

B. B.

...AND FOR THE REST OF THE WORLD

Between trips to the seaside, rallies, historical parades and gymkhanas, the activities of the Vespa Club of Japan are not so very different from its namesakes' some thousands of miles to the West.

The situation in Japan is bizarre—a deep-seated passion for vintage scooters fuels a lively market in second-hand and collectors' pieces to the point of making manufacture of "brand-new used models" worthwhile. But yet again it's a question of style.

Vintage Vespas for the Land of the Rising Sun

The Fiat Bambino—better known in the West as the Fiat 500—is very popular here, where even a good 600 Multipla or Alfa Romeo GT Junior (not to mention a Ferrari) is highly sought after.

A vintage Ape fetches a good price and its quotation is rising fast. Collecting vintage Italian cars is less rare than we might perhaps think in this land, today less far away, perhaps, but where customs, trends and daily life often remain puzzling.

In two wheels, Italy stands first and foremost for Vespa and Lambretta, even more so than for the grand old names of motorcycling, from M V Agusta to Ducati, Guzzi or Gilera. And for a number of years, Vespa was almost only vintage, historical items; a passion which, until 1999, kept a highly specialized sector of the Tuscan factory running: a couple thousand Vespa 50s and Primaveras made exclusively by Pontedera for Japan. These were small but significant numbers, considering three thousand units per year moved through Narikawa, an Osaka importer who has been closely linked to the success of the Italian scooter.

Under signs with Italian-sounding names like "Aranciata" ["orange juice"] (citations in the original language are highly appreciated in the amateur "Pomodoro" racing circuit too) in shops with just a few square meters of floor space that exude the same passion that unites salesmen and customers, shiny, freshly-arrived imported models are lined up alongside restored machines with, here and there, a drop of oil on the floor and some gadgets for the Japanese clients to indulge their passion for "customizing" their machines.

180 thousand yen ($1,540) will buy you a second-hand Vespa 50 S, but a "new vintage" from Pontedera costs almost double that and prices are still rising since production has been recently halted. And even that's not so expensive compared with the 850 thousand yen ($7,274) and more needed to buy a perfectly restored 1955 150 GS.

An innovative and prestigious advertising campaign conveniently shows a typical corner of the Eternal City—the Fountain of the Turtles in Piazzetta Mattei near the old ghetto.

Vespas here are for fanciers: collectors and restorers spare no expense and don't mind getting their hands dirty.

Having said that, if Vespa stands for Italy and its style, art and culture, no less real is the market in which it throws the gauntlet before the major Japanese manufacturers and the pride they take in their world status in two wheels, almost as though there were no one else.

It is in this worldwide context that a second front has been opened with a new distribution channel to sell both the new generation ET Vespa and the top-of-the-line Piaggio scooter products. Here, scope for potential and development are enormous and access to the vast public can be assured, as well as to those who wish to be seen apart from the masses—a paradox in appearance only. On the coattails of the select two thousand who, in a twelve-month period, managed to obtain a factory-made vintage machine, there comes a stream of new users who, besides wanting its style and history, look to all the effectiveness of a means of transport honed specially for metropolitan commuting. The ratio between these two groups, it is estimated, will soon be one to ten and as "secular" as the latter are, they too are "nominal request customers" who have a very clear idea what they're looking for from the shopkeeper in terms of style, prestige and the aroma of an Italian summer, besides total reliability.

Afterwards, inevitably, there came the afternoons in the park with the Vespas lined up by the edge of the grass, the trips to the seaside, he and she on the beach with the Vespa by their side, three days of procession

ABSOLUT ROME.

Shigeo Fukuda, one of Japan's greatest graphic illustrators, measured himself against the Vespa in 1996 and the result is here shown in this highly elegant interpretation.

The Honda Cub 50, a tireless four-stroke workhorse whose frame was in press-molded metal, and small front apron in plastic, had a three-speed gearbox and automatic clutch, and it is estimated that twenty-six million units were produced over fifty years.

for the Christmas festivities, and the Vespa rallies. So Japan isn't so far away after all.

New realities in emerging countries

It is likely that needing to fit the Vespa into the more or less exotic settings of developing countries called for quite a review of the original ideas. Things have changed radically since the Fifties and Sixties. The need for individual mobility for millions, from Southeast Asia through Latin America to some areas of Africa is in many cases met by products of other kinds.

A family of three, four or even five people speeding along the boulevards around Mexico City or the streets of Karachi or slipping through the noisy, smelly traffic of Bangkok will, in all probability and with a good spirit of adaptation, be riding a scooter built not in Ponte-dera but in India; derived from old (if not "ancient," dating from the early Fifties) Piaggio license contracts. And thus they are a perfect counterpart to cars such as the Padmini—an old Fiat 1100—or motor-cycles such as the Royal Enfield Bullet, vehicles that elsewhere find a worthy place in museums.

The "Indian way to the Italian scooter," in its various models, is measured rather by the sturdy workhorses produced in Taiwan or in the People's Republic of China: simple vehicles, almost rudimentary, built according to standards unacceptable to European users and in "Chinese" quantities (within the span of one

When the major Japanese manufacturers talk about their own backyard, they mean the vast area of Southeast Asia and round the China Sea. The photograph shows a Taiwanese couple on a scooter.

A choice that other major manufacturers did not share was to market the entire "European" range in all foreign markets without resorting to the progressive running-down of obsolete production units in developing countries.

year China and India absorb something like ten and four million, respectively, new two-wheelers).

The Chinese market is an extremely difficult one, distinguished on the one hand by enormous volumes of overproduction by the numerous state-owned companies, and on the other—to the detriment of the foreign producers who have set up their own plants in the People's Republic—by the numerous, and often perfect, counterfeits that make their appearance in the shops a few weeks after the launching of the "original" vehicle.

Today the purchaser of the "genuine" Italian scooter, in Lima as in Singapore, in Jakarta as in Hanoi, is an upwardly mobile member of the well-to-do middle class, an admirer of foreign things, motivated by the desire to display his own status.

The window of the Piaggio Center in Ho Chi Minh City, today a city of over four and a half million people, has the same standards as any European sales point, and after selling the first four hundred ETs in 1999 now sees its sales growing to around two thousand units per year.

In this scenario, progression from a non-differentiated demand towards a "more highly segmented one in which subtle requests emerge" can be seen. Public orientation changes daily as though the sectors of reference, which elsewhere have been crystallized for a long time, were here just being sketched out. It's as though the real market were just beginning.

In this context, whether a country's middle class is strongly rooted or not, it is by and large the category most aware of "our" model of culture and consumerism and, besides, the one with the necessary spending capacity.

The "niche of hopefulness" is small. All necessary pointers confirming the exclusivity of the customer's selection are there: emphasis on brand prestige, single brand coordinated sales points, total reliability and high technological content of the vehicle; efficient and as personalized after-sales service as possible. It is foreseeable that subsequent economic development of the country will contribute to a gradual lowering of the product's accessibility threshold as the relative cultural and consumer model gradually takes hold.

Coming home from Europe or the United States, riding around on a Japanese clone of the prestigious Italian scooter is one way of showing off. Here it is in the market, in the city still remembered today by many as Saigon.

INSIDE AND OUTSIDE THE NET

The American example was fundamental in deciding to go on-line in 1995. In the United States, the percentage of customers who go on-line to get information before buying a new car has grown tenfold in five years—in 2002 over 60 percent. Less frequent (14 percent but growing) was starting the purchasing procedure on-line.

A significant overlapping exists between the spread of the Internet and that of Italian customers of two-wheeled vehicles. In the 14 to 44 year-old age group are found 81 percent of Internet users and 91 percent of "two-wheelers." Also, 53 percent of clients and 25 percent of users are between 14 and 24; 23 percent and 22 percent respectively between 25 and 34, and 15 percent and 34 percent respectively between 35 and 44.

On 10 January 1995—in Italy, the Stone Age on the time scale of Internet communications—Piaggio's first electronic mailbox was opened. By virtue of its background and youth, the new company management was highly motivated toward this new tool. Giovanni Alberto Agnelli wanted the company to adopt the American experience in using Internet for internal communications, but making the company's voice heard outside was also of paramount importance.

Many years later this aim is being pursued with continuously progressive acceleration, the primary objective remaining the same: promoting Piaggio's image with as much information as possible on product and company, and getting in touch with users to determine their profile according to their hopes and requirements. On-line selling, the latest step forward, takes on extremely significant added value in terms of a means of acquiring residual information.

The first three years, then rebirth

The first website in Europe for two wheels—for this it was—was inaugurated in 1996 in the form of company pages giving Piaggio's history, range of products, press-kit information and in-house magazine. And then, in particular, the "contact us": the magic formula enabling immediate and direct feedback from the public. The means for customers to communicate interactively with the company had great promise and it didn't take long for the information to start flow-

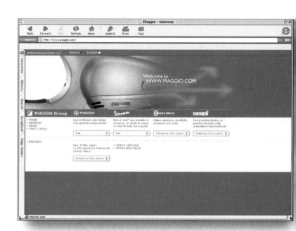

ing. American customers, with their longer experience of using computers, were particularly active showing themselves to be surprisingly fond of the Vespa, a name much better known than Piaggio, and kept pressing the company for three things: vintage pieces, clubs and organizations, and availability in the U.S.A. of new, innovative products.

The liveliness of this exchange was one of the main reasons for Piaggio's decision to get back into the U.S. market, or at least to weigh carefully times and strategies for launching the ET there.

In the three-year running-in period, confirmation of the wisdom of this decision repeatedly emerged, and the finer points of the new website, set up in 1999 on the basis of experience garnered up to then, made

it a milestone in terms of its importance as a point of reference for its market segment.

The "corporate" home page comes up first, outlining the company's profile with details on how it is organized, its history, then the Piaggio Museum, the Archive, the Engine Division and then the Press Area. Thus at least two distinct areas are established, one dedicated to the three brands—Piaggio, Vespa and Gilera—and the other focusing on marketing and presentation of various products on a rotation basis.

The Vespa Boutique on-line enjoys a high profile. Elsewhere, other auxiliary services are available some of which, set up as games, are aimed at obtaining user information and profiles.

The great novelty of this business to consumer

The Vespa Club d'Italia website shows the historical brand-name with three types of Vespa. This styling, with a thousand variations, was adopted by clubs all over the world.

Among the various promotional activities advertised on the Web at www.vespausa.com is the possibility of hiring a Vespa for touring Chianti on two wheels.

The United States boasts more than 3,000 Vespa Club members and more than 100 of the 700 Internet sites worldwide that act as meeting points for Vespa enthusiasts. However, more important are the 30,000 Vespas, half of which are ridden each day by their owners. The Vespa Vintage Restoration Shops grant collectors and restorers access to officially recognized specialty shops where they can get their machine restored or buy the original spare parts that Piaggio manufactures for each model starting from the 1946 Vespa 98, and that are also sold on-line.

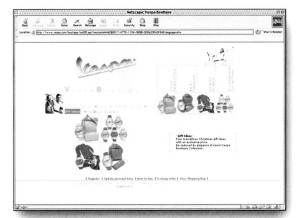

The on-line Vespa Boutique puts the same collection of clothing and accessories on show as the sales points all over the territory.

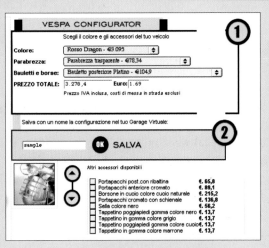

The Virtual Garage configurator which can be used to assemble the machine in detail and obtain a working example of it at the sales point.

(B2C) channel is in the diversification of direct selling procedures.

It's easy to foresee potential difficulties in attempting to reconcile two such different market realities with each other, one off-line and the other on the Internet, a network increasingly used for selling on a par with the thousands of authorized sales points both in Europe and worldwide. The relationship with those involved in promoting and selling Vespa on the ground is crucial: this leads to the strategy "on the Net for the network"—redirecting the flow of potential clients with their now marked product orientation, towards Piaggio sales points.

In "referral" or indirect sales, the visitor to the site may configure his vehicle with the available options down to the smallest detail with the price indication to the last cent shown at every turn. Leaving the Virtual Garage, and sending in the request, you get the right to see a product corresponding to your personal specification at the concessionaire nearest to you, and with whom you can finalize the deal. This in a positive spin-off, also supplies the company with statistics on public taste, divided by set categories such as age, sex, occupation, prior usage of two-wheeled machines and more still.

Potential Vespa enthusiasts get a face and leave a rough portrait of themselves, their tastes—almost a trail of their aspirations.

There is also an intro-
duction to the museum
bearing the name of
Giovanni Alberto Agnelli
and its collection.

Vintage on-line

Direct selling, by contrast is the linchpin of www.ves-
pavintage.com, a real treasure trove where collectors
and enthusiasts alike can, for example, visualize a fuel-
mixture tap for a 1951 Vespa 125, record the relative
catalogue number, order it and have the spare delivered to their home by express courier in any corner
of the globe. Behind this showcase of brand-new,
cutting-edge goodies there stands spare parts production for the whole range, from the first 98 to the
latest four-stroke, as well as a concept of selling in which
customer satisfaction is the aim.

Vintage customers are, by and large, competent and
demand personalized service; they ask questions that
are not always easy to answer and often need to go
into technical detail in some depth. They are not
always familiar with Internet technique but their
enthusiasm often borders on the maniacal and so has
zero tolerance for uncertainties in service or assistance or delays in shipment.

On the other hand, "fidelity" is a weak euphemism
to describe their tenacious relationship with the product and the company.

Whether they live in a fisherman's cottage in the Po
Delta, in Tijuana or on the seventy-fifth floor of a
Hong Kong high-rise, they need to see the same total
dedication to the cause in what the person speaking
to them says and in the quality of service coming up
on their computer screens.

Vespa Vintage is a B2C
(business to consumer)
sales initiative almost
unique among its kind
and, thanks to its
specificity, an ideal test:
an exclusive product
with high added value
for a niche market.

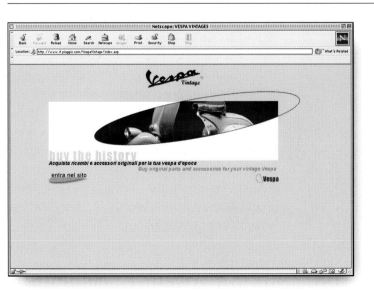

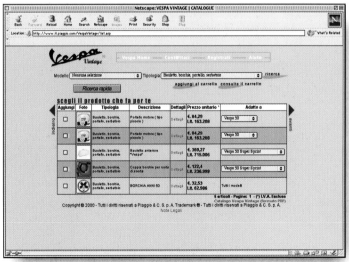

We're at the credit titles, or almost. We have seen what became of that idea sketched out one day by Corradino D'Ascanio's pencil half a century and more ago.

A lot of water has gone under the bridge and that same object has changed shape, seemingly in a process of natural evolution while in fact it has been handed down undergoing transformation as new people have taken the project on.

With each passage, the response has been different according to the market demands.

This history is an ongoing process of progressive refinement with, sometimes, unexpected shifts in direction when the name Vespa was given to vehicles of proven orthodoxy but which were somehow newer compared to what had gone before.

A designer edition in millions of units

"You could actually talk about it for a long time; we ourselves have done so and we still do, with help from outside too, about the details of what 'makes a Vespa.'"

"We" are the "we of the Styling Center," a team of in-house designers. In continuous contact with marketing and planning, the center gives rein to its creative resources to ensure that the demands and trends of the market take firm and final shape in the "new" model in order that it make its mark.

"By its nature, Vespa is rarely subjected to stringent market rules. It is certainly a long seller and it has

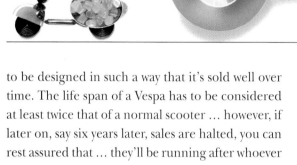

to be designed in such a way that it's sold well over time. The life span of a Vespa has to be considered at least twice that of a normal scooter … however, if later on, say six years later, sales are halted, you can rest assured that … they'll be running after whoever made it."

In the final analysis a Vespa has to be metallic: that's the bottom line. Then, one of its design features is just that imbalance between front end and back end.

"The Vespa has always had this rather maternal backside, very enveloping, and a somewhat slim, bony-looking front part rounded just right but still made out of a single metal sheet with great industrial savvy. But actually, the ET is already the embodiment of something new in this direction."

Something equally basic, and "not easy to do with today's engines," is the splay below the saddle, and then there's the position of the headlight. On the front wheel guard in the first series, it now has to be on the handlebar. This too is what makes a Vespa.

On the front suspension, it's worthwhile to recall the Cartesian definition given by Lucio Masut, the technical director: form equals function.

Behind the offset wheel of aeronautical origin lies the idea of being able to remove it easily, not so important in these days of tubeless tires.

But that, in turn, brought about the single-arm front suspension "more effective than a traditional fork which here would fit less well because of the much shorter joints compared to a motorbike's."

Facing page: Javier Mariscal, a Spanish artist and illustrator and a specialist in the use of different techniques and materials, gives his interpretation of the Vespa myth and memory.

Above: from the 1998 Piaggio calendar (AReA Strategic Design, Antonio Romano), Vespa identity and shape—a theme on which, every so often at least, some irony is welcome.

A basic two-wheeler for individual mobility, Corradino D'Ascanio's scooter gave good protection to its rider and assured low fuel consumption and low maintenance costs: the ideal means of transport. It gave back freedom of movement to millions but was so well worked out that it became a symbol of design all over the world.

Vespa is today more than ever a synthesis of form and function: it can no longer afford to be mere design—never different from itself in essence and never exaggerated, it must evolve in this precise direction.

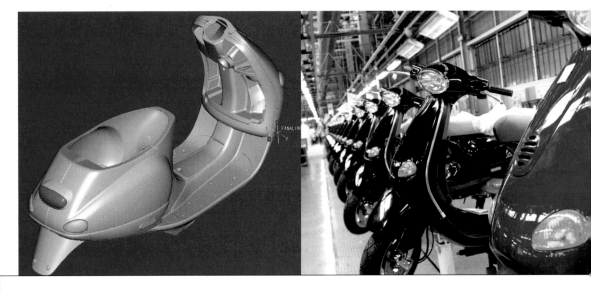

Already, in designing the ET body shell, here integrated in the smallest detail, one can see the effort in keeping a proper balance between front and rear volumes.

The symbol of the nation has low wheels

"The Vespa is a very tricky issue because it involves the very identity of the company … it's a bit like a national symbol more than a project for whoever does it. It's an enormous responsibility, not a nightmare but almost. You might think you can only do worse: the images and the books show that the high point was reached at the end of the Fifties …"

The decision to do a new Vespa has to be shared by everyone, it has to be at company "gut level."

The Styling Center starts it the same way it starts every project: doing sketches and exploring ideas, especially in the concept of what it's supposed to be.

On the basis of the brief summarized in the "zero sheet" the next phase leads to the definition of a first mockup which undergoes substantial integration by what comes out of the planning department—in other words what kind of engine should it have, what kind of wheels, what brakes should they put on it … then again how modern should the new Vespa be … how metallic should it be … how much should it try to follow the evolution of modern-day scooters?

Now, proceeding along industrial lines, development continues with the preparation of one, two, three or as many mockups as are needed. At this stage

After almost half a century of history and a major crisis that made it divide the unsplittable combination of name and object, the Vespa has come back making a strong identity statement. For the values that it now stands for in the public eye, it is looked on as an icon for the present day: the paradox of a mass-produced article that strives to achieve the dignity of a unique item. This was the idea developed in "Pezzo unico" ["Unique Piece"] by Nicola Di Carlo, winner of the Vespart competition held in 2001 among the major Italian design studios and Piaggio's Styling Center. Paolo Maria Iemmi came second with "Mucca pazza" ["Mad Cow"], while Raffaele Dergano & Andreas Wachtler came third with "The Metal Project."

The manufacture of what is now the only metal-bodied scooter in the world has, in the course of time, created a unique company culture in which workers, technicians and designers of Pontedera are fully steeped.

Design time has become much shorter: the whole procedure is accomplished in the 15 to 18 months between deciding the mockup and sales of the first mass-produced Vespa units and working in parallel on the necessary calculations as well as on preparing the services that will be required. The most costly part is upstream: product design, acquiring the reasonable probability of it turning into a winning Vespa. This can take years.

cost, compared to investment called for in production, is almost irrelevant. The Vespa is the final outcome of a process that calls for more investment than the "tupperware" scooters, as American Vespa enthusiasts call the tubular-framed plastic machines.

"Recognizability does not necessarily mean an old-fashioned look, but rather respect for a number of formal standards. A nostalgic idiom is not needed. It can, however, be followed and there's no doubt that a product of this kind would sell: these are all aspects that the company has the duty to explore, in harmony with what's happening in the automobile field too."

Market testing is the norm for every product but Vespa is particularly painstaking about it: in Italy and abroad, especially in France, Germany and Great Britain, "even though the tastes of the latter are particular." Only when public appreciation is perceived can the real work of planning and detail refinement begin, leading to the next stage of industrialization, especially complex in a metal vehicle.

"The dream of those who work on a project like this is that one day when they're walking down the street, somebody will look and say:

'Wow! … there's the new Vespa.'"

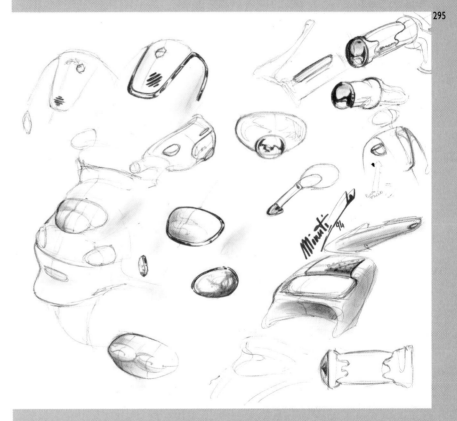

In the sketches and the mockups many avenues are explored: classic, old-fashioned or avant-garde. And, when the job is done, one feels amazement at the coherence of the process, as though the logic and value of the project came back as a leitmotif every time.

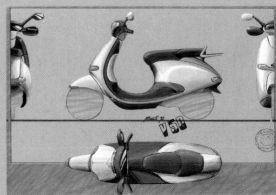

Almost fifty years have passed since the 150 GS came out, here shown between two track-racing cycle champions in team chase events: Guido Messina and Leandro Faggin. Although a sports model it was accessible to many and the "sportsman's Vespa" was a reference point for the new project, initially named X8 by Pontedera engineers and designers.

There were still a couple of years to go before the birth of the ET and already among the Styling Center's papers and hand-written notes could be seen signs, although still vague, of a "new, big-bodied Vespa." It was to be a big, upper-range Vespa based on the four-stroke concept that was soon to come into being.

It is a rather delicate issue to get back on to—we've already said so—with a glorious history and still a lot of prestige.

But this is not a niche product for high-flying styling exercises: the way forward is between legitimate knowledge of one's own uniqueness on the one hand and, on the other, granting undeniable full accessibility to many.

Don't back out of the challenge

Complaining isn't easy these days after four good growth years from 1996 and a scooter that seems to have captured the public image as an ideal means of getting through town traffic and converting automobile owners to two wheels. But the wind can veer without warning: the idea isn't new after all and the scenario is bound to change again moving with the market orientation.

But new owners have had it too good. They want the best of everything. They want a no-plate bike looking like a Grand Prix racer and at the same time a 100-mile-per-hour GT with low wheels, leather upholstery and an electric stand so they can proudly

While the GS series, inaugurated in late 1954 and put in production the following year, must be considered a milestone, another crucial reference point for understanding this new interpretation of the theme by Corradino D'Ascanio is the enduring, hardy PX, which has been in production since 1977 and still today continues to sell in Italy and on foreign markets. In the last few years, in fact, it has become highly appreciated as a vintage scooter inasmuch as it is not only historically perfect but also suits the taste of both young people (24–35) and adults, male customers in particular.

Test drivers astride the 180 SS in 1964; a sporty machine which thanks to its versatility and extreme ease in driving is not so different from the new Vespa Granturismo. It's water-cooled and has a four-valve engine, but there's more—the new big Vespa has a completely new braking system and new suspensions. The Vespa Granturismo, while following in the tradition of innovation established in 1996 with the ET range, is unmistakably new and large. The dimensions are as big as they could be without detracting from the idea of the design and the Vespa "soul."

turn up for work in a fashionable outfit.

In all this perhaps it's time to take a step back and find the sense and dimension of what this is all about. It's time to get back to defining the reasons for the design, the delicate balance, as always, between maneuverability, comfort, ease of use and performance, time to get back to the nub, the pole of attraction and the yardstick for the whole category, and Vespa cannot back out of this challenge.

The general tendency is towards getting larger, getting technologically updated, and explicitly setting a style.

It is significant that low environmental impact and complete mechanical reliability of an engine destined to stay a "black box" are now taken for granted.

Vespa ET4 50. Nuovo motore 4 tempi.
Consuma così poco che potrete fare molti,
ma molti chilometri in più.

Vespa
Liberi tutti.

The development of the new Vespa, whose name evokes the spirit and performance of a touring machine was underpinned by the development of the functions of the ET Vespa, a vehicle prevalently for town use whose customer base cut across categories between adults and youth, male and female.

Perhaps our purchasers are spoiled by too much affluence, and focused on their jobs, but they don't fall into any traps. They have good spending capacity, and especially if the wind looks like changing, you can rest assured many will fight over them.

The road ahead to Vespa Granturismo

In the course of this long preparatory stage, the project has proceeded fairly coherently, seeking at least twice the opinion of a selected sample public: young people and adults, both Vespa enthusiasts and not, and mostly male.

The public was asked for, and gave, its opinion the first time between 1998 and 1999. As much as it is willing to give credit to the brand name and its tradition, as much as it is favorable to Italian design, especially in Germany, it is not willing to be the target of a designer's caprice.

A return to the past must make no concessions to any kind of cheapening and should stay within the bounds of full recognizability. Clients, moreover, are not willing to compromise on a number of fundamental points. So putting the headlight on the wheel guard like in the Fifties, or incorporating a radiator grille (so this time there's no lack of technical innovation) raised a storm of protest.

Extended to a number of European countries, the subsequent test was carried out in summer 2000, this time working more in detail. The X8, for as such was the project now called, still awaiting its final name,

Traveling through time

Ornella Sessa

The fifteen models analyzed were selected as representative of the main development stages in the technology, styling and product of Vespa—a name which, through time, has shown its capacity to rewrite classic ideas in a contemporary style using a language in which product and product type, narration and attitude combine in perfect harmony with the intelligence and masterfulness of the early days.

The survey begins with the MP6, the first prototype and archetype of all scooters and concludes with another prototype taken from the new Granturismo series, launched with the publication of this book.

Comparison of these two models immediately highlights the factors which, over time, have influenced design and production with some features left unchanged while others have undergone radical change with technological evolution and, in particular, as a result of changes in market moods and tastes. One of the unbeaten traditions that underpins the Vespa is its "metal soul," the steel monocoque body which gives both physical toughness and long life—the solid foundation on which the Granturismo project is built.

This project has taken over six years to develop and has been heavily influenced by market trends as well as the burdensome responsibility on Piaggio to create a vehicle above and beyond mere celebration of the myth and moving toward a mature-looking scooter designed in the Vespa idiom and its tradition of evolution.

While the ET is aimed at the fashion-conscious consumer seeking a vehicle combining looks, image and safety (a high percentage of ET4 150s were sold to female consumers who found it suitable to their needs), the PX, on the other hand, is preferred by a more "safety-oriented" consumer, familiar with the consolidated characteristics of riding, reliability and sturdiness.

The Granturismo broadens the range and is Piaggio's answer to the call from the male consumer for a GT-type vehicle for tourism particularly endowed with comfort and safety as well as elegance and style

The ET and the PX are however the reference points (as least as far as the production facility is concerned) for the new Vespa which benefits also from the experience reaped with the Beverly 200, a plastic-bodied scooter with tubular frame from which some ideas have been drawn.

The Vespa idiom is identified in three successful models: the 1955 150 GS, the most beautiful Vespa ever, synonymous with elegance, style and zippiness, the 180 SS of 1964 as a high-performance GT scooter and the 125 Primavera for the compartments lodged within the body.

The final version reveals a vehicle with an unmistakable identity expressed in a language that can reclaim the relationship between past and present, between evoking history and perceiving the needs of today, and place it in its proper perspective.

It once again highlights the special power the Vespa has of getting beyond the idea of a "fashionable product" to something akin to a cult, an interface of the dynamics which link a product to the scale of values which orbit around it.

Need to get away, freedom of movement and openness to the world is the declaration made with more than a pinch of irony in the poster designed by Pierluigi Cerri.

If functionality and style are its characterizing traits, yesterday, just as today, Vespa is for many a two-seater magic flying carpet.

had by now taken shape. Faced with the two final mockups, the sample public reacted very positively but in differing ways. The "English youth" target seemed to appreciate more the homage paid to past tradition, but they were few.

The Vespa Granturismo, for so its name has been decided on, is now ready for the preparation of the styling prototype that will be indistinguishable from the mass produced scooter.

So … so like always there is a flurry of indiscretions prior to its launch: the presentations, the comments, the curious eyes following the first road units, the

more or less credible exegeses on the new, the traditional, the chats over a beer.

A lot is expected of it and whole load of wanting to try it out, take a run, take a day off, be carried along by it. It's like wishing for summer and it doesn't really matter now who's still twenty years old and who's not.

Then there are the memories for many of the days when there was another Vespa, not so many years ago. And looking at this new one now, so big … and yet … yes it's her all right!

The new Vespa's back again.

1996-2003

VESPA ET4
VESPA
Granturismo

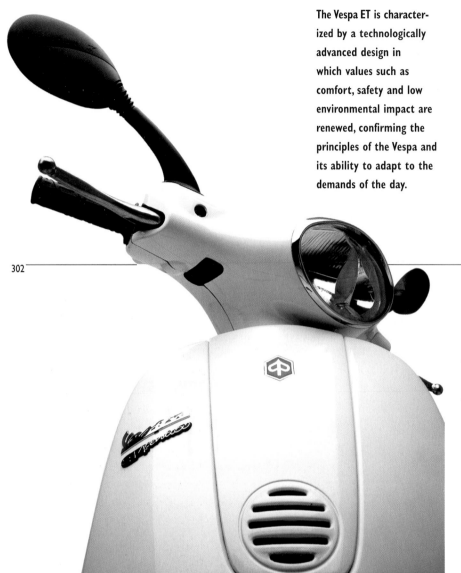

The Vespa ET is character-ized by a technologically advanced design in which values such as comfort, safety and low environmental impact are renewed, confirming the principles of the Vespa and its ability to adapt to the demands of the day.

VESPAET4

To create a plausible product: this was the goal that Piaggio reached with the ET series, introduced in 1996, fifty years after the birth of the Vespa. This model was initially offered in the ET4 variant, with a 125 cc four-stroke engine and the ET2, powered by a 50 cc engine—the first fuel injected two-stroke in the world.

Electric starter as standard equipment, automatic CVT transmission, centrally mounted engine, 10-inch wheels with front disc brakes and electronic theft prevention: these are the main characteristics of the latest generation Vespa. The range was broadened with the two-stroke 50 cc

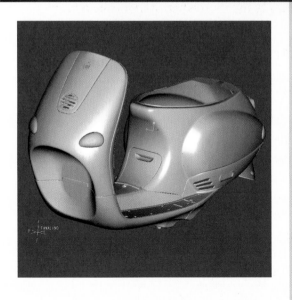

The new Vespa meant a major commitment in terms of production and required substantial investments for its design and development. Radically new yet consistent with tradition, the ET is a reinterpretation of the load bearing monocoque construction using modern design tools and highly advanced industrial production processes.

The rear section is characterized by soft, sleek lines, with drop-shaped cowls molded into the body shell carrying the indicators in their tips. The underside of the body consists of three plastic moldings. The two side moldings are removable with air intake vents and reflectors while the rear molding carries the license plate with its respective illuminating light.

catalyzed ET2, the four-stroke 150 cc ET4 and the four-stroke 50 cc ET4. Its design saw the return of the load bearing monocoque body in sheet steel. This was a decision to return to manufacturing tradition and to offer a more durable product. Steel can be repainted or beaten, and is more logical to use than parts which must be completely replaced when damaged.

The body shell, which required a major effort in design and development, is completely changed and complies with the latest safety and protection standards. Its dimensions were determined through studies to optimize function, comfort, agility and ease of use, while its proportions struck a very happy balance between front and rear.

The organic design takes inspiration from the natural connotations of the word Vespa "Wasp"): gone are the pressed, folded sheets of steel and in their place are surfaces modeled as a whole and assembled to appear like single volumes, with functional appendages which immediately convey a sense of usefulness. So the handlebars are the "head," wearing the mirrors like antennae, the drop shaped leg shield simultaneously engulfs

From the front you can see the soft, contoured shield with the minimal central molding, the horn grille and the characteristic drop-shaped indicators.

The new product is the visible result of a painstaking production program, from pressing—in which a roll of sheet steel enters the in-line presses with four sets of molds at one end and the finished components exit at the end of the line—to the completely robotized concealed-point welding. New automated painting systems applying non-toxic water based paints and a modern liquid and gaseous waste treatment plant substantially reduce the factory's environmental impact.

VESPA ET4

Great care has gone into the design and manufacture of all details: from the mirrors to the internal trim of the leg shield which matches the saddle trim available in black, brown and light gray. There are many standard accessories, such as the quick tire repair aerosol, the bag clip incorporated into the saddle and the special compartment with a tool kit. The range of colors chosen for the body shell emphasizes the "Tuscanness" of the scooter, with Giotto Orange, Olive Green, Livorno Blue, Etruscan Red, etc.

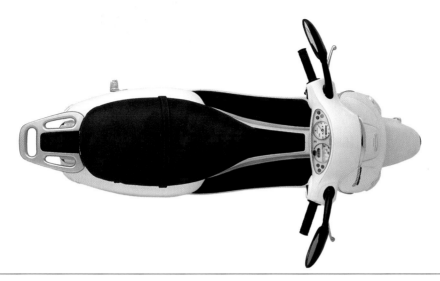

VESPA ET4

the front mudguard and gives form to the spacious locker compartment.

The indicators appear as small luminous eyes and the footplate is no longer straight and flat but is now contoured and robust looking and incorporates the two stands. The rear is made up of two half shells in which the shapes of the side cowls are molded. The cowls, which can no longer be opened, are stiffened by two reinforcement braces giving structure to the hollow engine compartment and completed by three plastic appendages; the two at the sides are removable whereas the third, at the rear, forms a sort of tail supporting the license plate.

Detail of the removable plastic body moldings with reflector and air vent, and of the new catalytic exhaust with chrome plated guard.

The handlebar assembly, with two half-shells united vertically, carries the headlight (with two automotive type 55 W iodine lamps and dual, prismatic reflector dishes in transparent polymer), the indicators, the windshield anchor points, the dashboard and all controls.

VESPA ET4

306

The decision to locate the very compact single cylinder engine horizontally and centrally, maintaining a configuration in which the engine is a load bearing element acting as a swing arm connected to an adjustable preload hydraulic damper not only changes the layout of the rear section, but also revolutionizes weight distribution, lowering the center of gravity considerably and conferring excellent stability. The four-stroke engine, running on unleaded fuel, has two valves and an overhead camshaft driven by a silent chain. It is cooled by a forced air flow and offers excellent performance and very quiet operation; it is cheap to run and very reliable. Fuel

The luggage rack is a trapezoid tapering toward the end. It is painted aluminum color and fitted as standard. Underneath is the oval rear light with chrome plated surround.

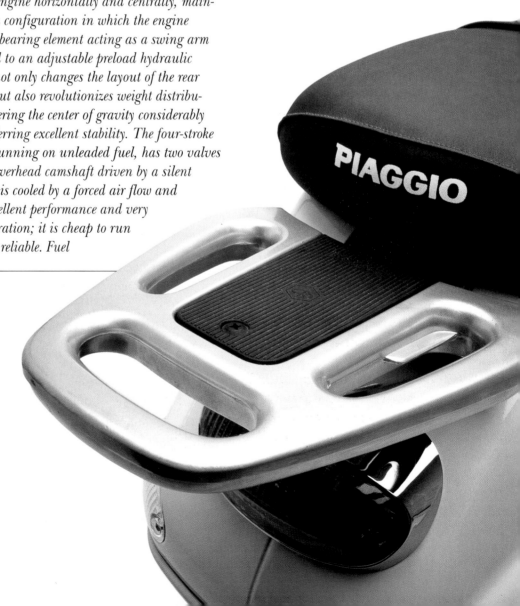

The very modern and comprehensive dashboard includes a speedometer, headlight indicator lamps, indicator function lamps, a reserve fuel level indicator, a fuel gauge and, lastly, a highly legible digital clock.

The front mudguard has an appendage partially covering the suspension linkage, which is vaguely reminiscent of the 1953 model 125 U. The dual rate hydraulic damper and anti-dive linkage ensure excellent stability.

consumption is cut to a minimum while the range is increased even further by the 2.7-gallon fuel tank. It complies with the strictest environmental and noise control laws. The engine is easily accessible by removing the compartment under the saddle, which can be used to hold a full face helmet or other baggage, and accessibility is further improved by the lowered side moldings, which practically expose the engine completely.

The chassis and suspension are also totally new. The support arm is now on the left of the wheel (as on the Vespa 98), and, for the first time, the supplementary kick starter lever is also on the left. The tires are no longer interchangeable as they are now differently sized: 100/80 at the front and 120/70 at the back. The 10-inch wheels are aeronautically inspired to enhance the sporty nature of the vehicle and assure excellent stability and handling on any road surface. The brake system performs well in all conditions and uses a disc at the front and a drum at the back.

The handlebars now carry new electric controls which are more ergonomic and functional (such as the indicator release push button) and incorporates a very modern instrument panel. Theft protection is assured by the electronic "Piaggio Code" system which impedes engine starting without the key and is integrated with traditional measures such as a ring for a padlocked chain and a sturdy steering lock.

VESPA
Granturismo

308

Innovation, creativity and design are the cornerstones of the Vespa Granturismo, the new Piaggio scooter which boasts highly competitive styling and technology. The X8 project, as it was initially named, was a product of the Piaggio Style Center which descibed it as a Vespa with an evolved image in which qualities of safety, reliability, comfort and high performance are in synergy with the very real requirements of individual mobility.

Among the most evident technical novelties is the adoption of powerful four-stroke engines, fitted with four valves and liquid cooling.

Vespa Granturismo 200, the top of the line,

The definition of the overall appearance of the vehicle and of a number of styling details goes through several stages of development and refining.

The inimitable integral steel body shell, the real heart of the Vespa design, shown here in its latest configuration, is the product of tests conducted with the ET.

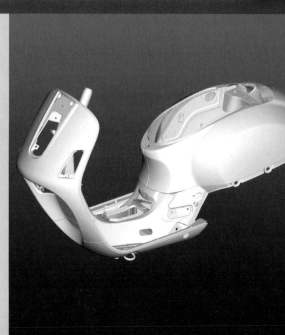

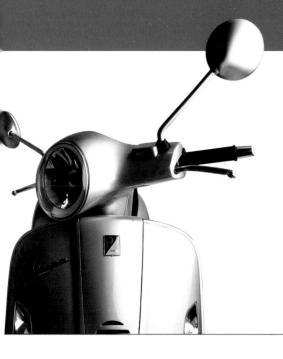

A mockup of the Granturismo, the Vespa's top-of-the-line scooter. The vehicle is targeted mainly at male customers and is intended for touring as well as city use. The design cues retain the unique characteristics of the original Vespa, such as its profile, the integral body shell with integrated cowls and the handlebar-mounted headlight, forming an overall configuration defined by clean, compact lines in keeping with Vespa tradition and status.

The innovative design of the rear light cluster, flush with the bodywork (as are the rhomboid indicator lights), and of the robust, capacious luggage rack.

VESPA
Granturismo

has a maximum power output of 20 hp (14.7 kW) and can almost reach 75 mph. The power output of the Granturismo 125 cc is 15 hp (11 kW).

The decision to use a different cooling system, cetrainly more suitable to a vehicle with the performance of the Granturismo, directly influences noise emission characteristics and power output.

Although traditional air cooling is simpler and cheaper (as it needs no pipes, radiator, cooling liquid, thermostat, electric fan or higher mass flywheel), it results in a less powerful and noiser engine. A jacket of water around the cylinder absorbs a good deal of mechanical noise and contributes to achieving a goal that Piaggio has always considered important—the reduction of noise emissions.

Another important new feature is the rear suspension layout, with two dual rate adjustable preload hydraulic shock absorbers and the use of disc brakes. As a result, the scooter has excellent handling, is very comfortable and offers a high degree of safety.

In keeping with tradition, the integral body shell is in steel with welded structural reinforcement elements: this ensures sturdiness and a longer lifetime and will help keep residual value up over time.

A distinctive element of the Vespa Granturismo is its imposing image, emphasized by its generous dimensions, with the saddle 32 inches from the ground; this is due to the use of 12-inch alloy wheels, which have 120/70-12 (front) and 130/70-12 (rear) tubeless tires.

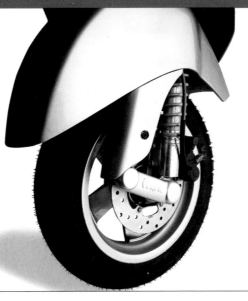

The new Vespa is the largest ever made. The dimensions of the prototype are length, 77 inches; width, 28 inches; and saddle height, 32 inches (dimensions have changed slightly in the definitive production version).

The corporate brief specified a ratio defining the basic configuration of the new prototype (PX : PK = X8 : ET). Piaggio is aiming for a vehicle with highly evolved styling, in part already tested with the ET and now developed further to define a high performance scooter with a strong visual impact and technological content which is at the same time both innovative and essential.

VESPA
Granturismo

The front view shows off the new downward teardrop-shaped headlight, the dimensions of which have determined those of the central strip. The strip itself is wide and short to make room for the large wheel.

The compartment in the leg shield fits flush with the surface of the shield itself.

The body shell is defined by fluid lines which become more terse and muscular around the footplate and tail sections.

The innovative new rear light cluster is fully incorporated into the bodywork, as are the new, rhomboid indicator lights.

The footplate is characterized by a pronounced center tunnel, ensuring maximum stiffness.

The footplate is also slightly smaller than in previous models, and has been optimized to offer a more comfortable foot position for the rider, whereas there are two manually opened folding pillion footrests incorporated in the bodywork for a passenger. The large, faired-in side cowls are

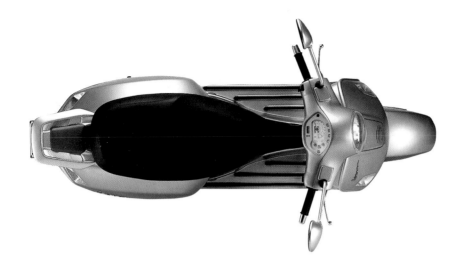

The profile of the body shell incorporates the large side cowls: the footplate has also been upsized for greater comfort and safety.

The rear light cluster is incorporated into the bodywork and is protected by a transparent cover.

Detail of the leg shield showing the engine cooling air intake grille incorporated in its side.

The handlebars incorporate the comprehensive and easy-to-read dashboard. On top are the mirrors and the two brake fluid reservoir caps which, in the prototype, do not completely fit in with the overall design.

Tradition continues through the use of historically tried and tested solutions, such as the single arm front suspension. The rear suspension has been revolutionized with the use of two dual rate adjustable preload hydraulic shock absorbers.

VESPA
Granturismo

The body shell is closed off underneath by plastic, bodywork-colored splash guards; as on the Vespa ET, these are removable to facilitate access to the engine. The catalytic exhaust on the right hand side of the vehicle is fitted with a protective shield following the overall design. The 12-inch alloy wheels are fitted with tubeless tires (120/70-12 at the front and 130/70-12 at the rear).

incorporated in the body shell pressing for both economical and structural reasons, and emphasize continuity with the ET and its links with the Primavera.

The front leg shield has also been substantially transformed as a result of the use of larger wheels and of the inclusion of two lateral air intake grilles. While the shield of the Vespa 98 was made from a single sheet of pressed steel, here, as on the ET, the shield now also has a backing to house the original twin radiator cooling system as well as the locker compartment: this layout confers a substantial appearance to the front, to create a well proportioned visual balance between the front and the rear. The wide handlebars, characterized by a teardrop shaped headlight, are inclined ergonomically to ensure complete control of the vehicle and a correct riding posture and incorporate large, comfortably placed intuitive controls and an easy to read analogue dashboard.

Transmission is again a belt drive system with an automatic CVT. This solution was adopted with the ET (after tests conducted with the PK) and has never been abandoned since.

Comfort and space on the Granturismo are ensured by the very generous saddle which is tapered to make room for the legs and which offers an ideal riding position quite different from that of today's custom maxi-scooters.

The passenger is also well cared for, with a slightly raised seating position and with comfort-able grab handles. Under the saddle, which is opened by pressing a button in front of the rider's legs, is a capacious compartment with room for two helmets; the document locker hatch is completely flush with the leg shield and is opened, when stationary only, by pushing the ignition key into its keyhole. The bag holder hook in plastic, which can be folded away so that it takes up less space, is now located under the handlebars next to the saddle opening button.

The attractive, handy luggage rack is predisposed for carrying the matching luggage trunk.

The functional choices defining the Granturismo can be summarized as follows: growth in size towards the GT, comfort, protection, sturdiness, durability, practicality, complete reliability and safety. Design, on the other hand, is oriented towards a more attractive and fashionable image.

CATALOG

by **Giorgio Notari**

In preparing a catalog of the models that were milestones in the long history of the Vespa, I opted for a layout both practical and easy to understand: the models are first listed by engine size and then in the order of their year of production. I dealt with the sport Vespas separately, then, lastly, the more recent, four-stroke series.

All told, the following are the models that wrote the history of the Vespa in the world from April 1946 when the firstborn, a mere 98 cc, emerged. Two years later saw the first 125, an engine size unchanged to this day. It wasn't until late 1954 that Piaggio started to sell the 150, later brought out in a sports version, the Vespa Gran Sport which in Italy became known as the "Vespone" ["Big Wasp"].

The next year was a crucial one in which the indefatigable two-stroke engine underwent a radical change to adapt to rotary distribution which made it stronger and cheaper to run. All Vespa engines followed this example with the exception of a few sports models.

Two novelties appeared in 1962: the square-looking 150 Gran Lusso and the 160 Gran Sport that had a dual rate hydraulic damper front suspension. The next year was memorable for the launch of the no-plate Vespa 50, highly popular with fourteen-year-olds. The same shell was used for the 90 cc and, two years later, for the first "small" 125, the forerunner of the famous 1967 Primavera. Another '64 model was the 180 Super Sport; the year after saw the birth of the surprising 50 and 90 SS—two sports models sharing an unmistakable shape and an impressive performance. The last models to use 8-inch wheels were, again in 1965, the Vespa 125 and the 150 Super.

The late series—1968 to be precise—saw the launch of the 180 Rally later replaced, in 1972, by the 200, the first Vespa to have electronic ignition. The 125 ET3 Primavera of 1976 was also a convert to electronics.

The Seventies marked the debut of an enormously successful model, still in production to this day: the Vespa PX, launced in the autumn of 1977.

The PK began production in 1982 and, two years later, this model included the first automatic gearbox ever to appear on a Vespa: at the same time the P 125 ETS, a performance-oriented model aimed at the younger market, was being manufactured.

The latest example of sports Vespas is the PX 125 T5 of 1985. Named simply "Pole Position" its sales campaign was set in the world of Formula One racing. With a modified shell and a new instrument panel, it also had a five-port aluminum engine.

In 1996, fifty years after the birth of the very first model, a new Vespa made its appearance. It was wholly new and to a certain extent revolutionary, from its four-stroke engine centrally mounted in the shell, to its automatic transmission and disc brakes: the 125 ET4 was soon flanked by a 150, then a 50 cc two and a 50 cc four-stroke.

In 2003 the Vespa Granturismo arrived. It can be considered the culmination of the stylistic and functional revolution launched by Vespa in 1996, on the occasion of its fiftieth anniversary.

With Vespa Granturismo the range of the world's most popular scooter was completed with its top-ranking model.

Imposing in size, the Granturismo is to the ET series what the PX series was to the PK, re-creating the myth of the "Vespone," or big model, alongside the smaller "Vespina." Its steel bearing body, powerful four-stroke water-cooled engine, disc brakes and elegant, timeless line channeled the technical revolution into the long-established Vespa tradition.

—the Curator

VESPA 50 / 1963
(1963–83 / 658,120 units / V5A1T)

length	1630 mm
width	610
wheelbase	1155
height	980
weight	70.5 kg
tires	2.75 x 9"

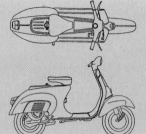

■ **ENGINE:** *V 5A1 M* OTTO CYCLE, TWO STROKE, 2% OIL-GASOLINE MIXTURE; SINGLE CYLINDER 49.77 CC (38.4 X 43), COMPRESSION RATIO 1:7.2; MAXIMUM POWER 1.45 HP AT 4500 RPM; FORCED AIR COOLING

■ **TANK:** 5.2 LITERS

■ **CLUTCH:** MULTI-DISK OIL BATH

■ **GEARBOX:** 3 SPEEDS, SELECTOR ON LEFT HANDLEBAR

■ **SUSPENSION:** RUBBER SPRINGING AND DAMPING ELEMENTS (FRONT); COIL SPRING AND HYDRAULIC DAMPER (REAR)

■ **BRAKES:** DRUM BRAKES, FRONT 125 MM Ø, REAR 135 MM Ø

■ **ELECTRIC SYSTEM:** FLYWHEEL-MOUNTED MAGNETO, 6V – 20W

■ **FUEL CONSUMPTION:** 1.48 LITERS /100 KM

■ **TOP SPEED:** 39.5 KM/H

VESPA 50 S / 1963
(1963–83 / 110,791 units / V5SA1T)

length	1650 mm
width	610
wheelbase	1160
height	995
weight	74 kg
tires	3.00 x 10"

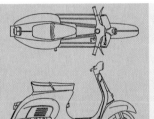

■ **ENGINE:** *V 5SA1 M* OTTO CYCLE, TWO STROKE, 2% OIL-GASOLINE MIXTURE; SINGLE CYLINDER. 49.77 CC (38.4 X 43), COMPRESSION RATIO, 1:7.2; MAXIMUM POWER, 2.6 HP AT 5800 RPM; FORCED AIR COOLING

■ **TANK:** 5.2 LITERS

■ **CLUTCH:** MULTI-DISK OIL BATH

■ **GEARBOX:** 4 SPEEDS, SELECTOR ON LEFT HANDLEBAR

■ **SUSPENSION:** COIL SPRINGS, DUAL ACTION HYDRAULIC DAMPERS

■ **BRAKES:** DRUM BRAKES, FRONT 125 MM Ø, REAR 135 MM Ø

■ **ELECTRIC SYSTEM:** FLYWHEEL-MOUNTED MAGNETO, 6V – 30W

■ **FUEL CONSUMPTION:** 1.67 LITERS /100 KM

■ **TOP SPEED:** 60.6 KM/H

VESPA 50 / 1972
(1972–75 / 94,670 units / V5B1T / 469,283 units / V5B3T)

length	1655 mm
width	610
wheelbase	1180
height	1000
weight	72 kg
tires	3.00 x 10"

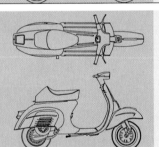

■ **ENGINE:** *V 5A2 M* OTTO CYCLE, TWO STROKE, 2% OIL-GASOLINE MIXTURE; SINGLE CYLINDER. 49.77 CC (38.4 X 43), COMPRESSION RATIO 1:7.2; MAXIMUM POWER 1.45 HP AT 4500 RPM; FORCED AIR COOLING

■ **TANK:** 5.2 LITERS

■ **CLUTCH:** MULTI-DISK OIL BATH

■ **GEARBOX:** 3 SPEEDS, SELECTOR ON LEFT HANDLEBAR

■ **SUSPENSION:** COIL SPRINGS, HYDRAULIC DAMPERS

■ **BRAKES:** DRUM BRAKES, FRONT 125 MM Ø, REAR 150 MM Ø

■ **ELECTRIC SYSTEM:** FLYWHEEL-MOUNTED MAGNETO, 6V – 20W

■ **FUEL CONSUMPTION:** 1.43 LITERS /100 KM

■ **TOP SPEED:** 40 KM/H

VESPA ET2 50 / 1997
(179,794 units – 2002 / C38100)

length	1780 mm
width	710
wheelbase	1275
height	1010
weight	90 kg
tires	100/80-10 (front) 120/70-10 (rear)

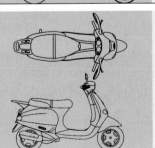

■ **ENGINE:** *C381 M* OTTO CYCLE, TWO STROKE, 2% OIL-GASOLINE MIXTURE; SINGLE CYLINDER 49.3 CC (40 X 39.3), COMPRESSION RATIO, 1:11; MAXIMUM POWER – ; DIRECT FUEL INJECTION; FORCED AIR COOLING

■ **TANK:** 9 LITERS

■ **CLUTCH:** AUTOMATIC CENTRIFUGAL DRY

■ **GEARBOX:** CVT (AUTOMATIC CONSTANTLY VARIABLE TRANSMISSION)

■ **SUSPENSION:** COIL SPRINGS, DUAL ACTION HYDRAULIC DAMPERS

■ **BRAKES:** FRONT, 200 MM Ø DISK, HYDRAULIC CONTROL (RIGHT HANDLEBAR); REAR, 110 MM Ø DRUM (LEFT HANDLEBAR)

■ **IELECTRIC SYSTEM:** FLYWHEEL-MOUNTED MAGNETO, 12V – 140W; 12V BATTERY; ELECTRONIC IGNITION

■ **FUEL CONSP.:** 2.5 LITERS / 100 KM

■ **TOP SPEED:** CODE

VESPA 90 / 1963
(1963–83 / 285,526 units / V9A1T)

length	1650 mm
width	610
wheelbase	1160
height	995
weight	74.5 kg
tires	3.00 x 10"

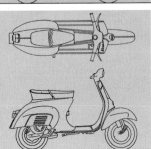

■ **ENGINE:** *V 9A1 M* OTTO CYCLE, TWO STROKE, 2% OIL-GASOLINE MIXTURE; SINGLE CYLINDER. 88.5 CC (47 X 51), COMPRESSION RATIO, 1:7.2; MAXIMUM POWER, 3.6 HP AT 5250 RPM; FORCED AIR COOLING

■ **TANK:** 5.2 LITERS

■ **CLUTCH:** MULTI-DISK OIL BATH

■ **GEARBOX:** 3 SPEEDS, SELECTOR ON LEFT HANDLEBAR

■ **SUSPENSION:** COIL SPRINGS, DUAL ACTION HYDRAULIC DAMPERS

■ **BRAKES:** DRUM BRAKES, FRONT 125 MM Ø, REAR 135 MM Ø

■ **ELECTRIC SYSTEM:** FLYWHEEL-MOUNTED MAGNETO, 6V – 30W

■ **FUEL CONSUMPTION:** 1.76 LITERS /100 KM

■ **TOP SPEED:** 69.2 KM/H

VESPA 98 / 1946
(1946–47 / 17,078 units / V98)

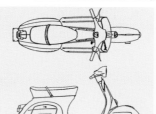

length	1655 mm
width	790
wheelbase	1160
height	860
weight	60 kg
tires	3.50 x 8"

■ **ENGINE:** *V 98* OTTO CYCLE, TWO STROKE, 5% OIL-GASOLINE MIXTURE; SINGLE CYLINDER 98 CC (50 X 50), COMPRESSION RATIO 1:6.5; MAXIMUM POWER 3 HP AT 4300 RPM; FORCED AIR COOLING

■ **TANK:** 4.75 LITERS

■ **CLUTCH:** MULTI-DISK OIL BATH

■ **GEARBOX:** 3 SPEEDS, SELECTOR ON LEFT HANDLEBAR

■ **SUSPENSION:** FRONT WITH TWO SPIRAL SPRINGS, REAR WITH RUBBER BUFFER

■ **BRAKES:** DRUM BRAKES, FRONT 124 MM Ø, REAR 124 MM Ø

■ **ELECTRIC SYSTEM:** FLYWHEEL-MOUNTED MAGNETO, 6V

■ **FUEL CONSUMPTION:** 2 LITERS /100 KM

■ **TOP SPEED:** 60 KM/H

VESPA 125 / 1965
(1965–67 / 17,099 units / VMA1T)

length	1650 mm
width	670
wheelbase	1165
height	1005
weight	78.4 kg
tires	3.00 x 10"

■ **ENGINE:** *V MA1 M* OTTO CYCLE, TWO STROKE, 2% OIL-GASOLINE MIXTURE; SINGLE CYLINDER 121.16 CC (55 X 51), COMPRESSION RATIO 1:7.2; MAXIMUM POWER 4.8 HP AT 4500 RPM; FORCED AIR COOLING

■ **TANK:** 5.6 LITERS

■ **CLUTCH:** MULTI-DISK OIL BATH

■ **GEARBOX:** 4 SPEEDS, SELECTOR ON LEFT HANDLEBAR

■ **SUSPENSION:** COIL SPRINGS, DUAL ACTION HYDRAULIC DAMPERS

■ **BRAKES:** DRUM BRAKES, FRONT 125 MM Ø, REAR 150 MM Ø

■ **ELECTRIC SYSTEM:** FLYWHEEL-MOUNTED MAGNETO, 6V – 50W

■ **FUEL CONSUMPTION:** 2 LITERS /100 KM

■ **TOP SPEED:** 83.8 KM/H

VESPA 125 Primavera / 1967
(1967–83 / 216,477 units / VMA2T)

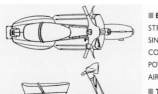

length	1655 mm
width	670
wheelbase	1180
height	1005
weight	78 kg
tires	3.00 x 10"

■ **ENGINE:** *V MA2 M* OTTO CYCLE, TWO STROKE, 2% OIL-GASOLINE MIXTURE; SINGLE CYLINDER 121.16 CC (55 X 51), COMPRESSION RATIO 1:8.25; MAXIMUM POWER 5.56 HP AT 5500 RPM; FORCED AIR COOLING

■ **TANK:** 5.6 LITERS

■ **CLUTCH:** MULTI-DISK OIL BATH

■ **GEARBOX:** 4 SPEEDS, SELECTOR ON LEFT HANDLEBAR

■ **SUSPENSION:** COIL SPRINGS, DUAL ACTION HYDRAULIC DAMPERS

■ **BRAKES:** DRUM BRAKES, FRONT 125 MM Ø, REAR 150 MM Ø

■ **ELECTRIC SYSTEM:** FLYWHEEL-MOUNTED MAGNETO, 6V – 50W

■ **FUEL CONSUMPTION:** 2.01 LITERS /100 KM

■ **TOP SPEED:** 92.3 KM/H

VESPA 125 Primavera ET3 / 1976
(1976–83 / 143,579 units / VMB1T)

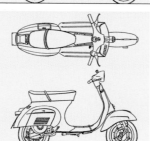

length	1660 mm
width	680
wheelbase	1180
height	1000
weight	78 kg
tires	3.00 x 10"

■ **ENGINE:** *V MB1 M* OTTO CYCLE, TWO STROKE, 2% OIL-GASOLINE MIXTURE; SINGLE CYLINDER 121.16 CC (55 X 51), COMPRESSION RATIO 1:9.25; MAXIMUM POWER 7 HP AT 5500 RPM; FORCED AIR COOLING

■ **TANK:** 5.6 LITERS

■ **CLUTCH:** MULTI-DISK OIL BATH

■ **GEARBOX:** 4 SPEEDS, SELECTOR ON LEFT HANDLEBAR

■ **SUSPENSION:** COIL SPRINGS, DUAL ACTION HYDRAULIC DAMPERS

■ **BRAKES:** DRUM BRAKES, FRONT 125 MM Ø, REAR 150 MM Ø

■ **ELECTRIC SYSTEM:** FLYWHEEL-MOUNTED MAGNETO, 6V – 50W, ELECTRONIC IGNITION

■ **FUEL CONSUMPTION:** 2.14 LITERS /100 KM

■ **TOP SPEED:** 85.92 KM/H

VESPA PK 125 / 1982
(1982–83 / 7,824 units / VMX1T)

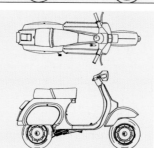

length	1675 mm
width	700
wheelbase	1175
height	1070
weight	87 kg
tires	3.00 x 10"

■ **ENGINE:** *V MX1 M* OTTO CYCLE, TWO STROKE, 2% OIL-GASOLINE MIXTURE; SINGLE CYLINDER 121 CC (55 X 51), COMPRESSION RATIO 1:9.3; MAXIMUM POWER 4.35 KW (5.90 HP) AT 5600 RPM; FORCED AIR COOLING

■ **TANK:** 5.8 LITERS

■ **CLUTCH:** MULTI-DISK OIL BATH

■ **GEARBOX:** 4 SPEEDS, SELECTOR ON LEFT HANDLEBAR

■ **SUSPENSION:** COIL SPRINGS, DUAL ACTION HYDRAULIC DAMPERS

■ **BRAKES:** DRUM BRAKES, FRONT 150 MM Ø, REAR 150 MM Ø

ELECTRIC SYSTEM: FLYWHEEL-MOUNTED MAGNETO, 6V – 50W, ELECTRONIC IGNITION

■ **FUEL CONSUMPTION:** : 2.1 LITERS /100 KM

■ **TOP SPEED:** 84.5 KM/H

VESPA PK 125 S A / 1983
(1977–82 / 8,922 units / VAM1T)

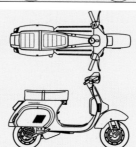

length	1680 mm
width	700
wheelbase	1180
height	1070
weight	90 kg (105.5 kg aut. mix.)
tires	3.00 x 10"

■ **ENGINE:** *V AM1 M* OTTO CYCLE, TWO STROKE, 2% OIL-GASOLINE MIXTURE; SINGLE CYLINDER 121 CC (55 X 51), COMPRESSION RATIO 1:10.5; MAXIMUM POWER 5.5 KW AT 6200 RPM; FORCED AIR COOLING

■ **TANK:** 5.8 LITERS (5.8 +1 LITER AUT. MIX.)

■ **CLUTCH:** AUTOMATIC CENTRIFUGAL DRY

■ **GEARBOX:** AUTOMATIC WITH BELT REGULATOR, HYDRAULIC CONTROL

■ **SUSPENSION:** VARIABLE RATE COIL SPRINGS, DUAL ACTION HYDRAULIC DAMPERS

■ **BRAKES:** DRUM BRAKES, FRONT 150 MM Ø, REAR 150 MM Ø

■ **ELECTRIC SYSTEM:** FLYWHEEL-MOUNTED MAGNETO, 12V – 80W

■ **FUEL CONSUMPTION:** 2.2 LITERS /100 KM

■ **TOP SPEED:** 85.5 KM/H

VESPA 125 / 1948
(1948 / 16,003 assembled units / V1T)

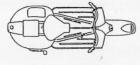

length	1650 mm
width	790
wheelbase	1130
height	960
weight	70 kg
tires	3.50 x 8"

■ **ENGINE:** *V 1 M* OTTO CYCLE, TWO STROKE, 5% OIL-GASOLINE MIXTURE; SINGLE CYLINDER 124.789 CC (56.5 X 49.8), COMPRESSION RATIO 1:6.5; MAXIMUM POWER 4 HP AT 5000 RPM; FORCED AIR COOLING

■ **TANK:** 5 LITERS

■ **CLUTCH:** MULTI-DISK OIL BATH

■ **GEARBOX:** 3 SPEEDS, SELECTOR ON LEFT HANDLEBAR

■ **SUSPENSION:** COIL SPRING (FRONT); COIL SPRING AND HYDRAULIC DAMPER (REAR)

■ **BRAKES:** DRUM BRAKES, FRONT 124 MM Ø, REAR 124 MM Ø

■ **ELECTRIC SYSTEM:** FLYWHEEL-MOUNTED MAGNETO, 6V

■ **FUEL CONSUMPTION:** 2 LITERS /100 KM

■ **TOP SPEED:** 70 KM/H

VESPA 125 / 1951
(1951–52 / 78,779 assembled u. 1951, tot. 155,552 units / V30 - V33VM1T)

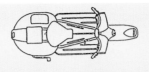

length	1670 mm
width	790
wheelbase	1160
height	960
weight	85 kg
tires	3.50 x 8"

■ **ENGINE:** FROM *V30* TO *V33 M* OTTO CYCLE, TWO STROKE, 5% OIL-GASOLINE MIXTURE; SINGLE CYLINDER 124.789 CC (56.5 X 49.8), COMPRESSION RATIO 1:6.5; MAXIMUM POWER 4 HP AT 5000 RPM; FORCED AIR COOLING

■ **TANK:** 5 LITERS

■ **CLUTCH:** MULTI-DISK OIL BATH

■ **GEARBOX:** 3 SPEEDS, SELECTOR ON LEFT HANDLEBAR

■ **SUSPENSION:** FRONT AND REAR WITH HYDRAULIC DAMPER

■ **BRAKES:** DRUM BRAKES, FRONT 125 MM Ø, REAR 125 MM Ø

■ **ELECTRIC SYSTEM:** FLYWHEEL-MOUNTED MAGNETO, 6V

■ **FUEL CONSUMPTION:** 2 LITERS /100 KM

■ **TOP SPEED:** 70 KM/H

VESPA 125 / 1953
(1953 / 91,787 units / VM1T- VM2T)

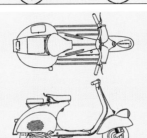

length	1680 mm
width	790
wheelbase	1160
height	960
weight	85 kg
tires	3.50 x 8"

■ **ENGINE:** *VM 1 M - VM 2 M* OTTO CYCLE, TWO STROKE, 5% OIL-GASOLINE MIXTURE; SINGLE CYLINDER 123.7 CC (54 X 54), COMPRESSION RATIO 1:6.5; MAXIMUM POWER 4.5 HP AT 5000 RPM; FORCED AIR COOLING

■ **TANK:** 6.25 LITERS

■ **CLUTCH:** MULTI-DISK OIL BATH

■ **GEARBOX:** 3 SPEEDS, SELECTOR ON LEFT HANDLEBAR

■ **SUSPENSION:** FRONT AND REAR WITH HYDRAULIC DAMPER

■ **BRAKES:** DRUM BRAKES, FRONT 124 MM Ø, REAR 126 MM Ø

■ **ELECTRIC SYSTEM:** FLYWHEEL-MOUNTED MAGNETO, 6V

■ **FUEL CONSUMPTION:** 2.19 LITERS /100 KM

■ **TOP SPEED:** 75 KM/H

VESPA 125 U / 1953
(1953 / 6,000 units / VU1T)

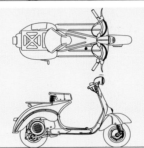

length	1680 mm
width	790
wheelbase	1160
height	950
weight	78 kg
tires	3.50 x 8"

■ **ENGINE:** *VU 1 M* OTTO CYCLE, TWO STROKE, 5% OIL-GASOLINE MIXTURE; SINGLE CYLINDER 1234.85 CC (56.5 X 49.8), COMPRESSION RATIO 1:6.4; MAXIMUM POWER 4.5 HP AT 5000 RPM; FORCED AIR COOLING

■ **TANK:** 6.25 LITERS

■ **CLUTCH:** MULTI-DISK OIL BATH

■ **GEARBOX:** 3 SPEEDS, SELECTOR ON LEFT HANDLEBAR

■ **SUSPENSION:** COIL SPRING (FRONT); COIL SPRING AND HYDRAULIC DAMPER (REAR)

■ **BRAKES:** DRUM BRAKES, FRONT 124 MM Ø, REAR 126 MM Ø

■ **ELECTRIC SYSTEM:** FLYWHEEL-MOUNTED MAGNETO, 6V

■ **FUEL CONSUMPTION:** 2,3 LITERS /100 KM

■ **TOP SPEED:** KM/H 65

VESPA 125 N / 1957
(1957–59 / 115,430 units / VNA1T)

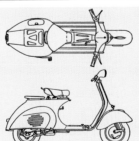

length	1735 mm
width	655
wheelbase	1180
height	985
weight	87 kg
tires	3.50 x 8"

■ **ENGINE:** *V NA 1 M* OTTO CYCLE, TWO STROKE, 6% OIL-GASOLINE MIXTURE; SINGLE CYLINDER 123.7 CC (54 X 54), COMPRESSION RATIO 1:6.5; MAXIMUM POWER 4.5 HP AT 5000 RPM; FORCED AIR COOLING

■ **TANK:** 7.7 LITERS

■ **CLUTCH:** MULTI-DISK OIL BATH

■ **GEARBOX:** 3 SPEEDS, SELECTOR ON LEFT HANDLEBAR

■ **SUSPENSION:** FRONT AND REAR WITH HYDRAULIC DAMPER

■ **BRAKES:** DRUM BRAKES, FRONT 125 MM Ø, REAR 127 MM Ø

■ **ELECTRIC SYSTEM:** FLYWHEEL-MOUNTED MAGNETO, 6V

■ **FUEL CONSUMPTION:** 2 LITERS /100 KM

■ **TOP SPEED:** 75 KM/H

VESPA 125 / 1959
(1959–61 / 88,849 units / VNB1T)

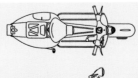

length	1745 mm
width	655
wheelbase	1180
height	985
weight	92 kg
tires	3.50 x 8"

■ **ENGINE:** *V NB 1 M* OTTO CYCLE, TWO STROKE, 2% OIL-GASOLINE MIXTURE; SINGLE CYLINDER 123.4 CC (52.7 X 57), COMPRESSION RATIO 1:7.2; MAXIMUM POWER 4.6 HP AT 5000 RPM; FORCED AIR COOLING

■ **TANK:** 7.7 LITERS

■ **CLUTCH:** MULTI-DISK OIL BATH

■ **GEARBOX:** 3 SPEEDS, SELECTOR ON LEFT HANDLEBAR

■ **SUSPENSION:** VARIABLE RATE COIL SPRINGS, DUAL ACTION HYDRAULIC DAMPERS

■ **BRAKES:** : DRUM BRAKES, FRONT 125 MM Ø, REAR 127 MM Ø

■ **ELECTRIC SYSTEM:** FLYWHEEL-MOUNTED MAGNETO, 6V–30W; 6V 2-4 AH BATTERY

■ **FUEL CONSUMPTION:** 1.91 LITERS /100 KM

■ **TOP SPEED:** 78.5 KM/H

VESPA 125 / 1965
(1965–69 / 24,145 units / VNC1T)

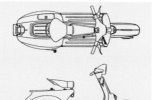

length	1740 mm
width	670
wheelbase	1200
height	1015
weight	93.5 kg
tires	3.50 x 8"

■ **ENGINE:** *V NC 1 M* OTTO CYCLE, TWO STROKE, 2% OIL-GASOLINE MIXTURE; SINGLE CYLINDER 123.4 CC (52.5 X 57), COMPRESSION RATIO 1:7.7; MAXIMUM POWER 6.16 HP AT 5000 RPM; FORCED AIR COOLING

■ **TANK:** 7.7 LITERS

■ **CLUTCH:** MULTI-DISK OIL BATH

■ **GEARBOX:** 4 SPEEDS, SELECTOR ON LEFT HANDLEBAR

■ **SUSPENSION:** VARIABLE RATE COIL SPRINGS, DUAL ACTION HYDRAULIC DAMPERS

■ **BRAKES:** DRUM BRAKES, FRONT 125 MM Ø, REAR 135 MM Ø

■ **ELECTRIC SYSTEM:** FLYWHEEL-MOUNTED MAGNETO, 6V – 50W

■ **FUEL CONSUMPTION:** 2.1 LITERS /100 KM

■ **TOP SPEED:** 86.7 KM/H

VESPA GT / 1966
(1966–73 / 51,581 units / VNL2T)

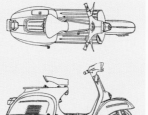

length	1770 mm
width	670
wheelbase	1200
height	1045
weight	95 kg
tires	3.50 x 10"

■ **ENGINE:** *V NL 2 M* OTTO CYCLE, TWO STROKE, 2% OIL-GASOLINE MIXTURE; SINGLE CYLINDER 123.4 CC (52.5 X 57), COMPRESSION RATIO 1:7.8; MAXIMUM POWER 6.27 HP AT 5000 RPM; FORCED AIR COOLING

■ **TANK:** 7.7 LITERS

■ **CLUTCH:** MULTI-DISK OIL BATH

■ **GEARBOX:** 4 SPEEDS, SELECTOR ON LEFT HANDLEBAR

■ **SUSPENSION:** VARIABLE RATE COIL SPRINGS, DUAL ACTION HYDRAULIC DAMPERS

■ **BRAKES:** DRUM BRAKES, FRONT 150 MM Ø, REAR 150 MM Ø

■ **ELECTRIC SYSTEM:** : FLYWHEEL-MOUNTED MAGNETO, 6V – 50W

■ **FUEL CONSUMPTION:** 2.09 LITERS /100 KM

■ **TOP SPEED:** 92.42 KM/H

VESPA 125 TS / 1975
(1975–78 / 28,703 units / VNL3T)

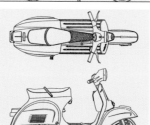

length	1770 mm
width	690
wheelbase	1200
height	1070
weight	101 kg
tires	3.50 x 10"

■ **ENGINE:** *V NL 3 M* OTTO CYCLE, TWO STROKE, 2% OIL-GASOLINE MIXTURE; SINGLE CYLINDER 123.4 CC (52.5 X 57), COMPRESSION RATIO 1:8.2; MAXIMUM POWER 8 HP AT 5600 RPM; FORCED AIR COOLING

■ **TANK:** 7.7 LITERS

■ **CLUTCH:** MULTI-DISK OIL BATH

■ **GEARBOX:** 4 SPEEDS, SELECTOR ON LEFT HANDLEBAR

■ **SUSPENSION:** VARIABLE RATE COIL SPRINGS, DUAL ACTION HYDRAULIC DAMPERS

■ **BRAKES:** DRUM BRAKES, FRONT 150 MM Ø, REAR 150 MM Ø

■ **ELECTRIC SYSTEM:** FLYWHEEL-MOUNTED MAGNETO, 6V – 50W

■ **FUEL CONSUMPTION:** 2.17 LITERS /100 KM

■ **TOP SPEED:** 85.7 KM/H

VESPA P 125 X / 1977
(1977–82 / 197,147 units / VNX1T)

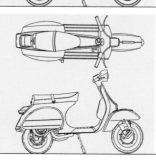

length	1760 mm
width	695
wheelbase	1235
height	1110
weight	104 kg (105.5 kg aut. mix)
tires	3.00 x 10"

■ **ENGINE:** *V NL 3 M* OTTO CYCLE, TWO STROKE, 2% OIL-GASOLINE MIXTURE; SINGLE CYLINDER 123.4 CC (52.5 X 57), COMPRESSION RATIO 1:8.2; MAXIMUM POWER 8 HP AT 5600 RPM; FORCED AIR COOLING

■ **TANK:** 8 LITERS (8 +1.5 LITERS AUT. MIX.)

■ **CLUTCH:** MULTI-DISK OIL BATH

■ **GEARBOX:** 4 SPEEDS, SELECTOR ON LEFT HANDLEBAR

■ **SUSPENSION:** VARIABLE RATE COIL SPRINGS, DUAL ACTION HYDRAULIC DAMPERS

■ **BRAKES:** DRUM BRAKES, FRONT 150 MM Ø, REAR 150 MM Ø

■ **ELECTRIC SYSTEM:** FLYWHEEL-MOUNTED MAGNETO, 6V – 60W

■ **FUEL CONSUMPTION:** 2.17 LITERS /100 KM

■ **TOP SPEED:** 85.7 KM/H

VESPA 150 / 1954
(1954–55 / 15,999 units / VLIT - VL2T)

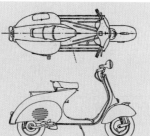

length	1700 mm
width	785
wheelbase	1165
height	1040
weight	98 kg
tires	3.50 x 8"

■ **ENGINE:** *V L 1 M* OTTO CYCLE, TWO STROKE, 5% OIL-GASOLINE MIXTURE; SINGLE CYLINDER 145.6 CC (57 X 57), COMPRESSION RATIO 1:6.3; MAXIMUM POWER 5.4 HP AT 5000 RPM; FORCED AIR COOLING

■ **TANK:** 6.25 LITERS

■ **CLUTCH:** MULTI-DISK OIL BATH

■ **GEARBOX:** 3 SPEEDS, SELECTOR ON LEFT HANDLEBAR

■ **SUSPENSION:** VARIABLE RATE COIL SPRINGS, DUAL ACTION HYDRAULIC DAMPERS

■ **BRAKES:** DRUM BRAKES, FRONT 125 MM Ø, REAR 127 MM Ø

■ **ELECTRIC SYSTEM:** 6V - ALTERNATOR 32 W AND RECTIFIER

■ **FUEL CONSUMPTION:** 2.4 LITERS /100 KM

■ **TOP SPEED:** 82.9 KM/H

VESPA 150 / 1957
(1957 / 98,699 units / VB1T)

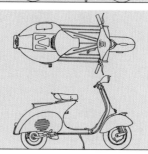

length	1700 mm
width	730
wheelbase	1165
height	1025
weight	98 kg
tires	3.50 x 8"

■ **ENGINE:** *V B 1 M* OTTO CYCLE, TWO STROKE, 5% OIL-GASOLINE MIXTURE; SINGLE CYLINDER 145.6 CC (57 X 57), COMPRESSION RATIO 1:6.3; MAXIMUM POWER 5.4 HP AT 5000 RPM; FORCED AIR COOLING

■ **TANK:** 8.2 LITERS

■ **CLUTCH:** MULTI-DISK OIL BATH

■ **GEARBOX:** 3 SPEEDS, SELECTOR ON LEFT HANDLEBAR

■ **SUSPENSION:** VARIABLE RATE COIL SPRINGS, DUAL ACTION HYDRAULIC DAMPERS

■ **BRAKES:** DRUM BRAKES, FRONT 125 MM Ø, REAR 127 MM Ø

■ **ELECTRIC SYSTEM:** 6V - ALTERNATOR 32 W AND RECTIFIER

■ **FUEL CONSUMPTION:** 2.4 LITERS /100 KM

■ **TOP SPEED:** 82.9 KM/H

VESPA 150 / 1958
(1958–60 / 124,039 units / VBA1T)

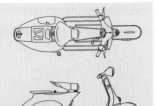

length	1735 mm
width	710
wheelbase	1180
height	1020
weight	93 kg
tires	3.50 x 8"

■ **ENGINE:** *V BA 1 M* OTTO CYCLE, TWO STROKE, 2% OIL-GASOLINE MIXTURE; SINGLE CYLINDER 145.45 CC (57 X 57), COMPRESSION RATIO 1:6.5; MAXIMUM POWER 5.5 HP AT 5000 RPM; FORCED AIR COOLING

■ **TANK:** 7.7 LITERS

■ **CLUTCH:** MULTI-DISK OIL BATH

■ **GEARBOX:** 3 SPEEDS, SELECTOR ON LEFT HANDLEBAR

■ **SUSPENSION:** VARIABLE RATE COIL SPRINGS, DUAL ACTION HYDRAULIC DAMPERS

■ **BRAKES:** DRUM BRAKES, FRONT 125 MM Ø, REAR 127 MM Ø

■ **ELECTRIC SYSTEM:** 6V - ALTERNATOR 35 W AND RECTIFIER

■ **FUEL CONSUMPTION:** 2.2 LITERS /100 KM

■ **TOP SPEED:** 85 KM/H

VESPA 150 / 1960
(1960 / 144,999 units / VBB1T)

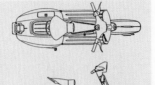

length	1735 mm
width	710
wheelbase	1180
height	1020
weight	93 kg
tires	3.50 x 8"

■ **ENGINE:** *V BB 1 M* OTTO CYCLE, TWO STROKE, 2% OIL-GASOLINE MIXTURE; SINGLE CYLINDER 145.45 CC (57 X 57), COMPRESSION RATIO 1:6.8; MAXIMUM POWER 5.5 HP AT 5000 RPM; FORCED AIR COOLING

■ **TANK:** 7.7 LITERS

■ **CLUTCH:** MULTI-DISK OIL BATH

■ **GEARBOX:** 4 SPEEDS SELECTOR ON LEFT HANDLEBAR

■ **SUSPENSION:** VARIABLE RATE COIL SPRINGS, DUAL ACTION HYDRAULIC DAMPERS

■ **BRAKES:** DRUM BRAKES, FRONT 125 MM Ø, REAR 127 MM Ø

■ **ELECTRIC SYSTEM:** FLYWHEEL-MOUNTED MAGNETO, 6V – 35W; 6V - 7 AH BATTERY

■ **FUEL CONSUMPTION:** 2.12 LITERS /100 KM

■ **TOP SPEED:** 87 KM/H

VESPA GL / 1962
(1962 / 79,854 units / VLA1T)

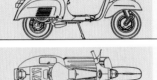

length	1770 mm
width	675
wheelbase	1200
height	1045
weight	100 kg
tires	3.50 x 10"

■ **ENGINE:** *V LA 1 M* OTTO CYCLE, TWO STROKE, 2% OIL-GASOLINE MIXTURE; SINGLE CYLINDER 145.45 CC (57 X 57), COMPRESSION RATIO 1:7.2; MAXIMUM POWER 6.25 HP AT 5000 RPM; FORCED AIR COOLING

■ **TANK:** 7.7 LITERS

■ **CLUTCH:** MULTI-DISK OIL BATH

■ **GEARBOX:** 4 SPEEDS, SELECTOR ON LEFT HANDLEBAR

■ **SUSPENSION:** VARIABLE RATE COIL SPRINGS, DUAL ACTION HYDRAULIC DAMPERS

■ **BRAKES:** DRUM BRAKES, FRONT 150 MM Ø, REAR 150 MM Ø

■ **ELECTRIC SYSTEM:** FLYWHEEL-MOUNTED MAGNETO, 6V – 35W; 6V - 7 AH BATTERY

■ **FUEL CONSUMPTION:** 2.4 LITERS /100 KM

■ **TOP SPEED:** 90.4 KM/H

VESPA P 150 X / 1978
(1977–82 / 346,402 units / VLX1T)

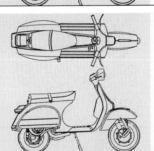

length	1760 mm
width	695
wheelbase	1235
height	1110
weight	104 kg (105.5 kg aut. mix)
tires	3.50 x 10"

■ **ENGINE:** *V LX 1 M* OTTO CYCLE, TWO STROKE, 2% OIL-GASOLINE MIXTURE; SINGLE CYLINDER 149.48 CC (57.8 X 57), COMPRESSION RATIO 1:8; MAXIMUM POWER 8 HP AT 5600 RPM; FORCED AIR COOLING

■ **TANK:** 8 LITERS (8 +1.5 LITERS AUT. MIX.)

■ **CLUTCH:** MULTI-DISK OIL BATH

■ **GEARBOX:** 4 SPEEDS, SELECTOR ON LEFT HANDLEBAR

■ **SUSPENSION:** VARIABLE RATE COIL SPRINGS, DUAL ACTION HYDRAULIC DAMPERS

■ **BRAKES:** DRUM BRAKES, FRONT 200 MM Ø, REAR 150 MM Ø

■ **ELECTRIC SYSTEM:** FLYWHEEL-MOUNTED MAGNETO, 12V – 60W

■ **FUEL CONSUMPTION:** 2.2 LITERS /100 KM

■ **TOP SPEED:** 91 KM/H

VESPA 150 GS / 1955
(1955 / 12,299 units / VS1T)

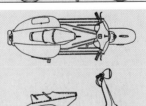

length	1700 mm
width	700
wheelbase	1180
height	1050
weight	111 kg
tires	3.50 x 10"

■ **ENGINE:** *V S 1 M* OTTO CYCLE, TWO STROKE, 5% OIL-GASOLINE MIXTURE; SINGLE CYLINDER 145.6 CC (57 X 57), COMPRESSION RATIO 1:7; MAXIMUM POWER 8 HP AT 7500 RPM; FORCED AIR COOLING

■ **TANK:** 12 LITERS

■ **CLUTCH:** MULTI-DISK OIL BATH

■ **GEARBOX:** 4 SPEEDS, SELECTOR ON LEFT HANDLEBAR

■ **SUSPENSION:** VARIABLE RATE COIL SPRINGS, DUAL ACTION HYDRAULIC DAMPERS

■ **BRAKES:** DRUM BRAKES 150 MM Ø, WITH COOLING FINS

■ **ELECTRIC SYSTEM:** FLYWHEEL-MOUNTED MAGNETO, 6V – 20W; 6V – 5W BATTERY

■ **FUEL CONSUMPTION:** 2.86 LITERS /100 KM

■ **TOP SPEED:** 101 KM/H

VESPA 150 GS / 1958
(1958–61 / 79,999 units / VS5T)

length	1700 mm
width	710
wheelbase	1180
height	1065
weight	111 kg
tires	3.50 x 10"

■ **ENGINE:** *V S 5 M* OTTO CYCLE, TWO STROKE, 2% OIL-GASOLINE MIXTURE; SINGLE CYLINDER 145.45 CC (57 X 57), COMPRESSION RATIO 1:6.5; MAXIMUM POWER 7.8 HP AT 7000 RPM; FORCED AIR COOLING

■ **TANK:** 9.5 LITERS

■ **CLUTCH:** MULTI-DISK OIL BATH

■ **GEARBOX:** 4 SPEEDS, SELECTOR ON LEFT HANDLEBAR

■ **SUSPENSION:** VARIABLE RATE COIL SPRINGS, DUAL ACTION HYDRAULIC DAMPERS

■ **BRAKES:** DRUM BRAKES, FRONT 150 MM Ø, REAR 150 MM Ø

■ **ELECTRIC SYSTEM:** FLYWHEEL-MOUNTED MAGNETO, 6V – 35W; 6V 12 AH BATTERY

■ **FUEL CONSUMPTION:** 2.86 LITERS /100 KM

■ **TOP SPEED:** 101 KM/H

VESPA 160 GS / 1962
(1962–64 / 59,999 units / VSB1T)

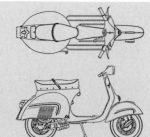

length	1795 mm
width	710
wheelbase	1220
height	1045
weight	111 kg
tires	3.50 x 10"

■ **ENGINE:** *V SB 1 M* OTTO CYCLE, TWO STROKE, 2% OIL-GASOLINE MIXTURE; SINGLE CYLINDER 158.53 CC (58 X 60), COMPRESSION RATIO 1:7.3; MAXIMUM POWER 8.9 HP AT 6500 RPM; FORCED AIR COOLING

■ **TANK:** 9 LITERS

■ **CLUTCH:** MULTI-DISC OIL BATH

■ **GEARBOX:** 4 SPEEDS, SELECTOR ON LEFT HANDLEBAR

■ **SUSPENSION:** COIL SPRINGS, FLEXIBLE DEVICES, DUAL ACTION HYDRAULIC DAMPERS

■ **BRAKES:** DRUM BRAKES, FRONT 150 MM Ø, REAR 150 MM Ø

■ **ELECTRIC SYSTEM:** FLYWHEEL-MOUNTED MAGNETO, 6V – 35W; 6V – 12 AH BATTERY

■ **FUEL CONSUMPTION:** 2.61 LITERS /100 KM

■ **TOP SPEED:** 103 KM/H

VESPA 180 Super Sport / 1964
(1964–68 / 35,699 units / VSC1T)

length	1770 mm
width	670
wheelbase	1230
height	1065
weight	116 kg
tires	3.50 x 10"

■ **ENGINE:** *V SC 1 M* OTTO CYCLE, TWO STROKE, 2% OIL-GASOLINE MIXTURE; SINGLE CYLINDER 181.145 CC (62 X 60), COMPRESSION RATIO 1:7.7; MAXIMUM POWER 10 HP AT 6250 RPM; FORCED AIR COOLING

■ **TANK:** 9 LITERS

■ **CLUTCH:** MULTI-DISC OIL BATH

■ **GEARBOX:** 4 SPEEDS, SELECTOR ON LEFT HANDLEBAR

■ **SUSPENSION:** COIL SPRINGS, FLEXIBLE DEVICES, DUAL ACTION HYDRAULIC DAMPERS

■ **BRAKES:** DRUM BRAKES, FRONT 150 MM Ø, REAR 150 MM Ø

■ **ELECTRIC SYSTEM:** FLYWHEEL-MOUNTED MAGNETO, 6V – 35W; 6V – 12 AH BATTERY

■ **FUEL CONSUMPTION:** 2.475 LITERS /100 KM

■ **TOP SPEED:** 106.5 KM/H

VESPA 50 Super Sprint / 1965
(1965–71 / 2,524 units / V5SS1T)

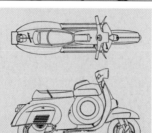

length	1650 mm
width	550
wheelbase	1165
height	1000
weight	80.5 kg
tires	3.00 x 10"

■ **ENGINE:** *V 5SS 1 M* OTTO CYCLE, TWO STROKE, 2% OIL-GASOLINE MIXTURE; SINGLE CYLINDER. 49.77 CC (38.4 X 43), COMPRESSION RATIO, 1:8.7; MAXIMUM POWER, 3.68 HP AT 7000 RPM; FORCED AIR COOLING

■ **TANK:** 5.6 LITERS

■ **CLUTCH:** MULTI-DISC OIL BATH

■ **GEARBOX:** 4 SPEEDS, SELECTOR ON LEFT HANDLEBAR

■ **SUSPENSION:** COIL SPRINGS, DUAL ACTION HYDRAULIC DAMPERS

■ **BRAKES:** DRUM BRAKES, FRONT 125 MM Ø, REAR 150 MM Ø

■ **ELECTRIC SYSTEM:** FLYWHEEL-MOUNTED MAGNETO, 6V – 50W

■ **FUEL CONSUMPTION:** 2.02 LITERS /100 KM

■ **TOP SPEED:** 78 KM/H

VESPA 90 Super Sprint / 1965
(1965–71 / 5,308 units / V9SS1T)

length	1650 mm
width	550
wheelbase	1165
height	1000
weight	81.7 kg
tires	3.00 x 10"

■ **ENGINE:** *V 9SS 1 M* OTTO CYCLE, TWO STROKE, 2% OIL-GASOLINE MIXTURE; SINGLE CYLINDER. 88.5 CC (47 X 51), COMPRESSION RATIO, 1:8.7; MAXIMUM POWER, 5.87 HP AT 6000 RPM; FORCED AIR COOLING

■ **TANK:** 5.6 LITERS

■ **CLUTCH:** MULTI-DISC OIL BATH

■ **GEARBOX:** 4 SPEEDS, SELECTOR ON LEFT HANDLEBAR

■ **SUSPENSION:** COIL SPRINGS, DUAL ACTION HYDRAULIC DAMPERS

■ **BRAKES:** DRUM BRAKES, FRONT 125 MM Ø, REAR 150 MM Ø

■ **ELECTRIC SYSTEM:** FLYWHEEL-MOUNTED MAGNETO, 6V – 50W

■ **FUEL CONSUMPTION:** 2.48 LITERS /100 KM

■ **TOP SPEED:** 95.2 KM/H

VESPA 180 Rally / 1968
(1968–73 / 26,494 units / VSD1T)

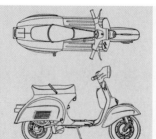

length	1770 mm
width	670
wheelbase	1230
height	1070
weight	106.6 kg
tires	3.50 x 10"

■ **ENGINE:** *V SD 1 M* OTTO CYCLE, TWO STROKE, 2% OIL-GASOLINE MIXTURE; SINGLE CYLINDER 180.69 CC (63.5 X 57), COMPRESSION RATIO 1:7.7; MAXIMUM POWER 10.3 HP AT 5700 RPM; FORCED AIR COOLING

■ **TANK:** 8.2 LITERS

■ **CLUTCH:** MULTI-DISC OIL BATH

■ **GEARBOX:** 4 SPEEDS, SELECTOR ON LEFT HANDLEBAR

■ **SUSPENSION:** VARIABLE RATE COIL SPRINGS, DUAL ACTION HYDRAULIC DAMPERS

■ **BRAKES:** DRUM BRAKES, FRONT 150 MM Ø, REAR 150 MM Ø

■ **ELECTRIC SYSTEM:** FLYWHEEL-MOUNTED MAGNETO, 6V – 50W

■ **FUEL CONSUMPTION:** 2.63 LITERS /100 KM

■ **TOP SPEED:** 104.8 KM/H

VESPA 200 Rally / 1972
(1972–79 / 41,274 units / VSE1T)

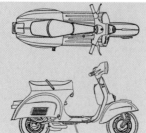

length	1770 mm
width	690
wheelbase	1230
height	1077
weight	107.6 kg
tires	3.50 x 10"

■ **ENGINE:** *V SE 1 M* OTTO CYCLE, TWO STROKE, 2% OIL-GASOLINE MIXTURE; SINGLE CYLINDER 197.97 CC (66.5 X 57), COMPRESSION RATIO 1:8.2; MAXIMUM POWER 12.35 HP AT 5700 RPM; FORCED AIR COOLING

■ **TANK:** 8.2 LITERS

■ **CLUTCH:** MULTI-DISC OIL BATH

■ **GEARBOX:** 4 SPEEDS, SELECTOR ON LEFT HANDLEBAR

■ **SUSPENSION:** VARIABLE RATE COIL SPRINGS, DUAL ACTION HYDRAULIC DAMPERS

■ **BRAKES:** DRUM BRAKES, FRONT 150 MM Ø, REAR 150 MM Ø

■ **ELECTRIC SYSTEM:** FLYWHEEL-MOUNTED MAGNETO, 6V – 50W, ELECTRONIC IGNITION

■ **FUEL CONSUMPTION:** 3 LITERS /100 KM

■ **TOP SPEED:** 116 KM/H

VESPA P 200 E / 1977
(1977–83 / 158,899 units / VSX1T)

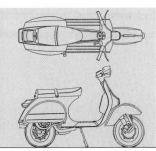

length	1760 mm
width	695
wheelbase	1235
height	1110
weight	108 kg (109.5 kg aut. mix.)
tires	3.50 x 10"

■ **ENGINE:** V SE / M OTTO CYCLE, TWO STROKE, 2% OIL-GASOLINE MIXTURE; SINGLE CYLINDER 197.97 CC (66.5 X 57), COMPRESSION RATIO 1:8.2; MAXIMUM POWER 12.35 HP AT 5700 RPM; FORCED AIR COOLING

■ **TANK:** 8 LITERS (8 +1.5 L. AUT. MIX.)

■ **CLUTCH:** MULTI-DISC OIL BATH

■ **GEARBOX:** 4 SPEEDS, SELECTOR ON LEFT HANDLEBAR

■ **SUSPENSION:** VARIABLE RATE COIL SPRINGS, DUAL ACTION HYDRAULIC DAMPERS

■ **BRAKES:** DRUM BRAKES, FRONT 150 MM Ø, REAR 150 MM Ø

■ **ELECTRIC SYSTEM:** FLYWHEEL-MOUNTED MAGNETO, 6V – 60W, ELECTRONIC IGNITION

■ **FUEL CONSUMPTION:** 3 LITERS / 100 KM

■ **TOP SPEED:** 116 KM/H

VESPA P 125 ETS / 1984
(1984–85 / 11,710 units / VMS1T)

length	1680 mm
width	700
wheelbase	1180
height	1070
weight	88 kg
tires	3.00 x 10"

■ **ENGINE:** V MS / M OTTO CYCLE, TWO STROKE, 2% OIL-GASOLINE MIXTURE; SINGLE CYLINDER 121 CC (55 X 51), COMPRESSION RATIO 1:9.5; MAXIMUM POWER 6.5 KW AT 6000 RPM; FORCED AIR COOLING

■ **TANK:** 5.8 LITERS

■ **CLUTCH:** MULTI-DISC OIL BATH

■ **GEARBOX:** 4 SPEEDS, SELECTOR ON LEFT HANDLEBAR

■ **SUSPENSION:** COIL SPRINGS, HYDRAULIC DAMPERS

■ **BRAKES:** DRUM BRAKES, FRONT 150 MM Ø, REAR 150 MM Ø

■ **ELECTRIC SYSTEM:** FLYWHEEL-MOUNTED MAGNETO, 12V – 80W, ELECTRONIC IGNITION

■ **FUEL CONSUMPTION:** 2.2 LITERS /100 KM

■ **TOP SPEED:** 91.9 KM/H

VESPA PX 125 T5 / 1985
(1985–91 / 36,061 units – 1991 / VNX5T)

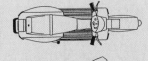

length	1820 mm
width	700
wheelbase	1250
height	1170
weight	115 kg
tires	3.50 x 10"

■ **ENGINE:** V NX 5 M OTTO CYCLE, TWO STROKE, 2% OIL-GASOLINE MIXTURE; SINGLE CYLINDER 123.5 CC (55 X 52), COMPRESSION RATIO 1:11.3; MAXIMUM POWER 9.0 KW AT 6700 RPM; FORCED AIR COOLING

■ **TANK:** 8 LITERS

■ **CLUTCH:** MULTI-DISC OIL BATH

■ **GEARBOX:** 4 SPEEDS, SELECTOR ON LEFT HANDLEBAR

■ **SUSPENSION:** COIL SPRINGS, HYDRAULIC DAMPERS

■ **BRAKES:** DRUM BRAKES, FRONT 150 MM Ø, REAR 150 MM Ø

■ **ELECTRIC SYSTEM:** FLYWHEEL-MOUNTED MAGNETO, 12V – 80W, ELECTRONIC IGNITION

■ **FUEL CONSUMPTION:** 2.7 LITERS /100 KM

■ **TOP SPEED:** 100.7 KM/H

VESPA ET4 50 / 2000
(20,064 units – 2002 / C26100)

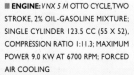

length	1780 mm
width	710
wheelbase	1275
height	1090
weight	97 kg
tires	100/80-10 (front) 120/70-10 (rear)

■ **ENGINE:** C26 / M M OTTO CYCLE, FOUR STROKE, 2 VALVES, ELECTRONIC CAPACITIVE-DISCHARGE IGNITION (CDI), SINGLE CYLINDER 49.9 (39 X 41.8); MAXIMUM POWER – ; FORCED AIR COOLING

■ **TANK:** 9 LITERS

■ **CLUTCH:** AUTOMATIC CENTRIFUGAL DRY

■ **GEARBOX:** CVT (AUTOMATIC CONSTANTLY VARIABLE TRANSMISSION)

■ **SUSPENSION:** COIL SPRINGS, HYDRAULIC DAMPERS

■ **BRAKES:** FRONT, 200 MM Ø DISC, HYDRAULIC CONTROL (RIGHT HANDLEBAR); REAR, 110 MM Ø DRUM (LEFT HANDLEBAR)

■ **ELECTRIC SYSTEM:** FLYWHEEL-MOUNTED MAGNETO, 12V – 165W; 12V BATTERY; ELECTRONIC IGNITION

■ **FUEL CONSUMPTION:** 2.2 LITERS /100 KM (40 KM/H)

■ **TOP SPEED:** CODE

VESPA ET4 125 / 1996
(dal 1996 / 1,180,500 units – 2002 / M19200)

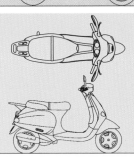

length	1780 mm
width	710
wheelbase	1275
height	1090
weight	108 kg
tires	100/80-10 (front) 120/70-10 (rear)

■ **ENGINE:** M192 M M OTTO CYCLE, FOUR STROKE, 2 VALVES, ELECTRONIC CAPACITIVE-DISCHARGE IGNITION (CDI), SINGLE CYLINDER 124.02 CC (57 X 48.6); MAXIMUM POWER 8 KW AT 8000 RPM; FORCED AIR COOLING

■ **TANK:** 9 LITERS

■ **CLUTCH:** AUTOMATIC CENTRIFUGAL DRY

■ **GEARBOX:** CVT (AUTOMATIC CONSTANTLY VARIABLE TRANSMISSION)

■ **SUSPENSION:** COIL SPRINGS, HYDRAULIC DAMPERS (REAR ADJUSTABLE PRELOAD)

■ **BRAKES:** FRONT, 200 MM Ø DISC, HYDRAULIC CONTROL (RIGHT HANDLEBAR); REAR, 110 MM Ø DRUM (LEFT HANDLEBAR)

■ **ELECTRIC SYSTEM:** FLYWHEEL-MOUNTED MAGNETO, 12V – 165W; 12V BATTERY; ELECTRONIC IGNITION

■ **FUEL CONSUMPTION:** 2.6 LITERS /100 KM (60 KM/H)

■ **TOP SPEED:** 91 KM/H

VESPA GRANTURISMO 200 | 125 / 2003
(M31100)

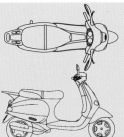

length	1940 mm
width	755
wheelbase	1395
height	1180
weight	138 kg
tires	120/70-12 (front) 130/70-12 (rear)

■ **ENGINE:** M312 M | M311 M OTTO CYCLE, FOUR STROKE, 4 VALVES, ELECTRONIC CAPACITIVE-DISCHARGE IGNITION (CDI), SINGLE CYLINDER CC. 198 (72 X 48.6) | 124 (57 X 48.6); MAXIMUM POWER KW 14.7 A 9000 | 11 A 10000 RPM; LIQUID COOLING

■ **TANK:** 10 LITERS

■ **CLUTCH:** AUTOMATIC CENTRIFUGAL DRY

■ **GEARBOX:** CVT (AUTOMATIC CONSTANTLY VARIABLE TRANSMISSION)

■ **SUSPENSION:** COIL SPRINGS, HYDRAULIC DAMPERS (REAR ADJUSTABLE PRELOAD)

■ **BRAKES:** FRONT, 220 MM Ø DISK, HYDRAULIC CONTROL (R. HANDLEBAR); REAR, 220 MM Ø DISK (L. HANDLEBAR)

■ **ELECTRIC SYSTEM:** FLYWHEEL-MOUNTED MAGNETO, 12V – 165W; 12V BATTERY; ELECTRONIC IGNITION

■ **FUEL CONSUMPTION:** 2,7 | 3.0 LITERS /100 KM/H (60 KM/H)

■ **TOP SPEED:** 115 | 102 KM/H

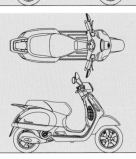

VINTAGE VESPA REGISTRY

The Vespa Historical Register was set up in 1980 in order to safeguard the patrimony of technical, historical and cultural information linked to the Vespa and disseminate the means of conserving vintage Vespas, milestones in the history of two wheel vehicles worldwide. Vespa events, shows and exhibitions made to coincide with special occasions and concours d'élégance set aside exclusively for vintage models have contributed a great deal to keeping interest alive in this area.

The register is a highly useful tool for all enthusiasts, especially collectors. After taking a close look at the vehicle, it may issue a certificate of conformity for all models built by Piaggio from 1946 to 1976.

The register functions through a national technical committee comprised of a curator, Luigi Frisinghelli, a secretary, Roberto Leardi, and a board of six experts (Umberto D'Ambrosi, Carlo Ruggero, Giuseppe Stefanelli, Uldiano Acquafresca, Giorgio Notari and Luigi Bertaso).

Three types of conformity certificates are presently being issued. If the vehicle has been perfectly restored or kept impeccably and corresponds in every way to the original specification, it is an assessed as excellent and awarded a golden plaque certifying First Class. If the vehicle shows some imperfections in restoration, assessment is given as "good" and a Second Class silver plaque is awarded. The third category awards a bronze plaque for vehicles with significant imperfections. The defects are listed in the conformity logbook—if the vehicle is repaired properly it can be resubmitted to the assessment of the commission, which may consent to its upgrading.

To date there are some three hundred certified vehicles.

The International Historical Register was set up in 1994 within the Fédération Internationale des Vespa Clubs coordinated by Luigi Frisinghelli and is operational in Austria and Germany. Its activities will soon be extended to France and Switzerland.

VESPA CLUBS IN THE WORLD

FÉDÉRATION INTERNATIONALE DES VESPA CLUBS
President Christa Solbach
via Flaminia, 259 00196 Roma
tel./ fax (+39-06) 3201060
<fiv@rmnet.it>
Pres. office Lungotevere Flaminio, 80
00196 Roma
tel. (+39-06) 323298

–

VESPA CLUB AUSTRIA
President Andreas Strobach
Webgasse, 36/18
1060 Wien
tel. (+43-676) 5442651
fax (+49-89) 244381440
<vespaclubaustria@
hotmail.com>
<www.vespaclub.at>

VESPA CLUB OF GREECE
President Kostas Kirou
Gamvetta 125
54644 Thessaloniki
tel./fax (+30-31) 0869097
<info@scootershop.gr>

VESPA CLUB DE BELGIQUE
President Jacques Chantrain
Rue Kloth, 58
4720 La Calamine
tel. (+32-87) 657767

VESPA CLUB ESPAÑA
Delegate Manel
Malo López
pl. Les Termes, 16 Bjos.
08204 Sabadell (Bcn)
tel. (+34-93) 7110488/
0034-600.401875
fax (+34-93) 724.30.81
<vespaclubsabadell@
hotmail.com>

VESPA CLUB VON DEUTSCHLAND
President Dieter Mertes
Birkenstrasse 18
66773 Schwalbach
tel. (+49-6834) 51312
fax (+49-6834) 567099
<mertes@vcvd.de>
<www.vcvd.de>

VESPA CLUB D'ITALIA
President Roberto Leardi
via Davide Campari, 190
00155 Roma
tel./fax (+39-06) 2285646
<presidenza@vespaclub.it>
<www.vespaclub.it>

VESPA CLUB OF BRITAIN
President Leslie Smith
The Hawthorns, Vicarage
Lane – Duffield
Derbyshire – DE56 4 EB
tel. (+44-1332) 830404 (uff.)
tel. (+44-1332) 842392
fax (+44-1332) 830202
<vcb2000@hotmail.com>
<www.motorcycle-uk.com/
VespaClubBritain.html>

VESPA CLUB DE FRANCE
President Jean Léon
Blanquart
2, Rue Bassano
21000 Dijon
tel. (+33-380) 369572
fax (+33-380) 369582
<president@vespaclub
france.com> <www.vespa
clubfrance.com>

VESPA CLUB SAN MARINO
President Gino Giardi
via Rio Cerbiano, 46
Murata A-8 – 47031
Repubblica San Marino
tel./fax (+39-549) 997650

VESPA CLUB DANMARK
President Allan Houe
Silkeborgvej 582
DK-8220 Brabrand
tel. (+45-86) 253880
<fam_houe@
mail1.stofanet.dk>

VESPA CLUB NEDERLAND
President Anton Somers
Wad 13
9843 DA Grijpskerk
tel. (+31-594) 212699
fax (+31-594) 213904
<ajsomers@wolmail.nl>
<www.castel.nl/vespavsn>

VESPA CLUB SCHWEIZ
President Patrick Schneider
Schützenstrasse, 7
CH 8963 Kindhausen AG
tel/fax (+41-1) 7411693
<vespatrick@scooterist.ch>
<www.scooterist.ch>
<www.vespaclub.ch>

VESPA CLUB PORTUGAL
Delegate Vasco Alves Carvalho
Refontoura 4610
677 Felgueiras
cell. (+351) 964864222
fax (+351-255) 340389

VESPA CLUB U.S.A.
Delegate Rolf P. J. Soltau
1566 Capri Drive
Campbell CA 95008
tel. (+1-408) 379-1536
fax (+1-310) 604-3989

VESPA CLUB OF CANADA
President Simone Gore
731-916 West Broadway
Vancouver, BC V5Z 1K7
tel. (+1-604) 255-6405
<info@vespaclubof
canada.com> <www.vespa
clubofcanada.com>

FINNISH SCOOTER CLUB
President Heikki Tikkanen
P.O. Box 51 – 33101 Tampere
tel. (+358-8) 3111923
cell. (+358) 50-5751638
<tikkanen.heikki@
kolumbus.fi>

VESPA CLUB SWEDEN
President Henrik Börjeson
P.O. Box 11216
SE 404 25 Göteborg
tel. (+46-46) 2118368
<president@scooter
klubben.com> <www.
scooterklubben.com>

VESPA CLUB JAPAN
President Kouichi Yamanobe
Finess bld. 15-1
Nogikuno Matsudo City
Chiba 270-2243
tel. (+81-473) 733590
fax (+81-473) 733595
<vespacj@ch.mbn.or.jp>
<http://plaza17.mbn.or.jp>

VESPA CLUB NORWAY
President Tom Arheim
Emanuelsvei 6
N-1366 Lysaker
tel. (+47) 67123287
fax (+47) 24125471
<tanked@online.no>

VESPA CLUB PARAGUAY
President Osvaldo Huth
Candia
Avda. Eusebio Ayala, 3321
Asuncion 1203
tel. (595-21) 607-770
fax (595-21) 607-769
<comagro@comagro.
com.py>

VESPA CLUB OF AUSTRALIA
Delegate Nathan Donolato
2/55 Esplanade Park
Parade – Fairlight NSW
Australia 2094
tel./fax (+61-2) 93572794
<vespazari@hotmail.com>

VESPA CLUB NEW ZEALAND
Delegate Götz Neugebauer
17 Ruru Street
Mt. Eden Auckland
tel./fax (+64-9) 3772525
<scootemo@ihug.co.nz>
<www.scooterhouse.conz>

VESPA CLUB D'ALGERIE
President Hamoud
Benyoucef Mosbah
Mont Fleury, 87
16015 Ruisseau Alger
tel. (+213-21) 672860
cell. 0044-7899886345
fax (+213-21) 233334

VESPA CLUB VENEZUELA
Delegate Fabio Serafini
Arcuri
Av. Castellana Chacao
61680 – Caracas 1060 - A
tel. (+58-2) 2634055
fax (+58-2) 2633654
<fabios@telcel.net.ve>

VESPA CLUB LUXEMBOURG
President Marco Frattini
4/4 Route de Longwy
L-1940 Luxembourg
tel. (+352) 091385941
fax (+352) 453714

VESPA CLUBE DO BRASIL
Delegate Rolf P. Adam
Rudolf Steiner Str. 2
28816 – Brinkum
Stuhr – Germany
tel. (+49-421) 8099967
<vespaclubedobrasil@
gmx.net>

VESPA CLUB ARGENTINA
Delegate Salvador Mateo
Ruiz
Urquiza 2535 3 "A"
2000 Rosario (R.A.)
tel.-fax (+54-341) 4372582
<vespaclubargentina@
hotmail.com>

VESPA CLUB OF SOUTH AFRICA
Delegate Ben Vandenberg
P.O. Box 30172
Tokai Cape 7966
tel. (+27-21) 7122661
fax (+27-21) 7122896
<www.vespa.za.net>

INDONESIA VESPA CLUB
Delegate Arfan Joelianto
Jalan Pratista Utara III
No. 7 – Antapani
Bandung 14092, West Java
tel. (+62-22) 7207359
<fivindonesia@yahoo.com>

VESPA CLUB SINGAPORE
Piaggio Asia Pacific Pte Ltd
Pres. office Royston Ho
19 Genting Road
Singapore 349478
tel. (+65) 5474466
fax (+65) 5474277
<piaggios@singnet.com.sg>

VESPA CLUB OF TAIWAN
President Christopher Yang
no.7 Alley 216
Chiah Sing St, 110 – Taipei
tel. (+886-2) 27367265
fax (+886-2) 27364249
<nuart@ms7.hinet.net>

BIBLIOGRAPHY

The company Historical Archive, named after Antonella Bechi Piaggio was the main documentary source for writing and illustrating this book.

Moreover, among the material published by Piaggio:

"Piaggio – Rivista della produzione e organizzazione Piaggio," periodical 1949-80

"Piaggiornale – Periodico di informazione aziendale edito da Piaggio S.p.A.," bi-monthly periodical 1993-95, monthly periodical 1996-

"Vespa Servizio – Notiziario dei Venditori della Vespa," bi-monthly periodical 1955-1965

Various Authors, *Il mito di Vespa*, Pontedera 1995

Boldrini Maurizio, Calabrese Omar, *Il libro della comunicazione*, Pontedera 1995

Calabrese Omar, Livolsi Marino, *Il libro dell'Ape*, Pontedera 1998

Fanfani Tommaso, *Una leggenda verso il futuro. La storia della Piaggio*, Piaggio & C. S.p.A. – Fondazione Piaggio, Pisa (1994) II ed. 2001

Piaggio & C. – 75 anni di attività, Genoa 1960

Furthermore, mention is made of the following:

Bassi Alberto, Mulazzani Marco, *Le macchine volanti di Corradino D'Ascanio*, dicembre 1999 – gennaio 2000 Spazio Giorgetti di Milano, Electa – Giorgetti Spa, Milan 1999

Bettinelli Giorgio, *Brum Brum – 254.000 chilometri in Vespa*, Feltrinelli, Milan 2002

idem, *In Vespa – da Roma a Saigon*, Feltrinelli, Milan 1997-2000

Biancalana Stefano, *La Piaggio nel primo decennio successivo alla fine della seconda guerra mondiale. Nascita e affermazione della Vespa*, Degree thesis defended with Prof. Tommaso Fanfani, Pisa University academic year 1993-94

Biancalana Stefano, Marchianò Michele, *La Vespa… e tutti i suoi vespini*, Giorgio Nada Editore, Vimodrone, n.e. 1999

Crainz Guido, *L'Italia repubblicana*, Giunti Gruppo Editoriale – Castermann, Florence 2000

Dossier Vespa in "Motociclismo d'epoca," n. 2 year II 1996

Due ruote di libertà – Cicli e motocicli. Storia, tecnica e passione, 14 settembre – 16 ottobre 1999 Palazzo dell'Arte, Milano, Electa, Milan 1999

Filippetti Gilberto, "Fuori disselciano" in *Il mito di Vespa* cit.

Ginsborg Paul, *Storia d'Italia dal dopoguerra a oggi*, Einaudi, Turin 1989

Lanza Marco, Marcelli Stefano (eds.), *Quelli della Vespa – Immagini e memorie del movimento operaio di Pontedera*, Pontedera 1996

Leardi Roberto, *Cinquant'anni di Vespa Club d'Italia 1949-1999*, CLD, Fornacette 1999

Leardi Roberto, Frisinghelli Luigi, Notari Giorgio, *Vespa tecnica 1 – 1946-55*, CLD, Pontedera 1998

idem, *Vespa tecnica 2 – 1956-64*, CLD, Fornacette 1999

idem, *Vespa tecnica 3 – 1965-76*, CLD, Fornacette 2000

idem, *Vespa tecnica 4 – Record and Special Production*, CLD, Fornacette 2001

idem, *Vespa tecnica 5 – 1997-2002*, CLD, Fornacette 2002

Leardi Roberto, *Scooters italiani degli anni '40/'60*, Polo Books, Rome 1998

idem, *Vespa – Storia di una leggenda*, Polo Books, Rome 1999

Mondini Alberto, *Un'elica e due ruote: la libertà di muoversi – Vita di Corradino D'Ascanio*, Nistri-Lischi, Pisa 1995

"Motor Collection. Motori da collezione," n. 2 year VII 1977

Passetti Lanciotto, *Tratti di vita – dieci anni di antifascismo e trenta di lotte operaie alla Piaggio*, Bandecchi e Vivadi, Pontedera 2001

Rawlings Terry, *Mod, a Very British Phenomenon*, Omnibus Press, London 2000

Rossi Ezio, Trini Castelli Auro, *Vespa da mito a culto* in "Ottagono" n. 149 April 2002

Sparrow Andrea & David, *Motor Scooters Colour Family Album*, Veloce Publishing Plc, Dorchester 1998

idem, *Vespa Colour Family Album*, Veloce Publishing Plc, Dorchester 1995-99

Tartaglia Daniela, *La Piaggio di Pontedera 1944/78*, La Nuova Italia, Florence 1981

Tessera Vittorio, *Innocenti Lambretta*, Giorgio Nada Editore, Vimodrone 1999

idem, *Scooters made in Italy*, Giorgio Nada Editore, Vimodrone 1993

Walker Alastair, *Scooterama – Café Chic & Urban Cool*, Carlton Books Ltd, London 1999

In particular, for the styling and design development of Vespa as an industrial product:

Aa. Vv., *Storia del disegno industriale*, Electa, Milan 1991

Bürdek Berhard E., *Design, teoria e prassi del disegno industriale*, Mondadori, Milan 1992

CENTROKAPPA, *Il design italiano degli anni 50*, RDE, Milan 1977

Frateili Enzo, *Il disegno industriale italiano 1928/1981*, Celid, Turin 1982

Sampietro Silvio, Scevola Annamaria, *Prodotto industriale italiano contemporaneo*, Edizioni Archivolto, Milan 1999

Segoni Roberto, *Corradino D'Ascanio: nel segno dell'invenzione* in "Rassegna," year VI 18/2, June 1984

Motociclismo, a periodical published by Edisport Editoriale Spa, Milano, was a valuable source of information on market trends and, especially, for the road tests of the various Vespas from 1946 to the present day.

INDEX OF NAMES

PHOTOGRAPHIC REFERENCES

Archivio Storico Fiat, Turin (courtesy): 13 *u*, 258 *ll*

Archivio Storico Olivetti, Ivrea: 12

Archivio Storico Piaggio "Antonella Bechi Piaggio", Ponte-dera: 16-17*, 18 *ul*, 18 *ur*, 18 *c*, 18 *ll*, 20, 21, 22, 23, 24 *ur*, 24 *ll*, 24 *lr*, 25, 26, 27, 30 *ll***, 30 *lr***, 31 *ul*, 31 *ur*, 31 *c*, 32 *ul*, 33 *lr*, 34 *lr*, 36, 37 *ur*, 37 *c*, 37 *l*, 38, 39 *lc*, 39 *lr*, 40-41, 41, 42 *ur*, 50 *ll*, 50 *lr*, 56 *uc*, 56 *ur*, 56 *cr*, 58 *ll*, 59 *u*, 59 *ll*, 60 *ul*, 60ad, 61, 62, 63 *ll*, 63 *lr*, 64, 65, 66, 67, 68, 69, 70, 71 *u*, 71 *lr*, 72 *ul*, 72 *ur*, 73 *u*, 73 *ll*, 75 *ul*, 75 *ur*, 76 *ul*, 76 *ur*, 76 *ll*, 77 *u*, 78 *ul*, 78 *uc*, 78 *ur*, 78 *ll*, 79, 80 *ll*, 80 *lc*, 84 *ll*, 84 *lc*, 84 *lr*, 85, 86***, 87, 88 *ul*, 89 *u*, 89 *ll***, 89 *lr***, 90, 91, 92 *ul*, 92 *l*, 94 *ll*, 94 *lr*, 100 *ll*, 106 *ll*, 106 *lr*, 112as, 112 *cl*, 112 *cr*, 112 *ll*, 112 *lc*, 112 *lr*, 114, 115 *ul*, 115 *l*, 116 *ul*, 116 *uc*, 116 *l*, 118, 119, 120, 121, 122, 123, 124 *ll*, 124 *lr*, 125, 126 *u*, 126 *c*, 127 *ur*, 127 *l*, 128, 129 *ll*, 130, 131 *u*, 132, 133 *ul*, 133 *l*, 134 *ul*, 134 *ur*, 135 *u*, 135 *c*, 138, 140, 141 *u*, 142, 143 *cl*, 146, 147, 148, 150 *ll*, 150 *lr*, 156 *ll*, 156 *lr*, 162 *ll*, 162 *lr*, 168 *ul*, 168 *ll**, 168 *lr**, 171, 172, 173 *l*, 174, 175 *l*, 176, 177 *ul*, 178, 179a, 179 *ll*, 179 *lr**, 180 *l*, 181 *lr*, 183 *ur*, 183 *ll*, 183 *lc*, 184 *ll**, 185 *ll**, 185 *lr**, 186*, 187 *u*, 188 *ul*, 188 *l**, 189 *u*, 189 *l**, 190 *l**, 192 *u*, 192 *c**, 192 *lr**, 193*, 194 *u*, 195 *u*, 196, 197 *u*, 197 *l**, 198 *ur**, 198 *l**, 204 *ll*, 204 *lr**, 205 *ul**, 205 *ur**, 206 *u*, 206 *ll**, 206 *lr**, 208 *ll*, 208 *lr*, 214 *ll*, 214 *lr*, 220 *ll*, 220 *lr*, 226 *ur*, 226 *cl**, 226 *lc*, 228 *s**, 229*, 230 *u*, 232, 233 *u**, 233 *ll**, 233 *lr*, 235 *l*, 238, 239 *c**, 239 *ll*, 239 *lr*, 240 *u*, 240 *l*, 241, 242, 243 *u*, 243 *l**, 244 *u*, 244 *c*, 245, 246, 247 *lr*, 248 *l*, 249 *l*, 251 *u*, 255, 256, 258 *lr*, 264 *ll*, 264 *lr**, 270 *uc*, 270 *ur* (Italo Lupi, foto Leo Torri), 272 *ll* (Ken Cato), 273 *lr* (Alan Fletcher), 277 *u* (Milton Glaser), 277 *l*, 284 *u*, 285 *lr* (Shigeo Fukuda), 287 *u*, 292 (Javier Mariscal), 296 *lc*, 297 *u*, 297 *ll*, 298 *ul*, 300 *ll* (Pierluigi Cerri)

* photo Tam Fagiuoli   *** Astrazioni Fotografia*

AReA Strategic Design, Roma, (photo M. Fadda): 293 *u*

ArteStudio, Stefano Niccolai, Pontedera: 133 *ur*

Bernini Giuseppe – CREC Piaggio, Pontedera (courtesy): 239 *u*

Bettinelli Giorgio (courtesy): 226 *cr*, 236, 237

Corbis / Grazia Neri, Milan: 10, 13 *l*, 28 *ll*, 29 *l*, 44 *ll*, 44 *lr*, 134 *ll*, 137 *ul*, 139 *r*, 143 *lr*, 170, 180 *u*, 183 *ul*, 183 *lr*, 201, 203, 205 *l*, 226 *ur*, 226 *lr*, 240 *c*, 247 *ll*, 248 *l*, 279 *l*, 287 *l*, 300 *lr*

Corbis / De Bellis, Milan: 226 *ll*, 249 *u*, 270 *ll*, 286 *u*

© Disney / photo G. Slocombe / Buena Vista International Italia (courtesy): 144 *lr*

Doveri Carlo (courtesy): 131 *ll*

Electa, Milano, from the volume *Due ruote di libertà, cicli e motocicli, storia tecnica e passione*: 30 *u*

Fedele / Gioffré, Historical Archive in Cavallaro (RC): 56 *ul*

Filippetti Gilberto, Florence (courtesy): 187 *l*, 190 *u*, 273 *u*

Flos, Bovezzo (BS) (courtesy): 14

Fondazione Corriere della Sera (courtesy): 35 *u*

Getty Images / Laura Ronchi, Milan: 280, 281, 282, 283

Granata Press Service, Milan: 286 *l*

Hulton Archive / Laura Ronchi, Milan: 28 *ur*, 29 *ul*, 29 *ur*, 42 *c*, 135 *l*, 136 *l*, 168 *ur*, 168 *c*, 184 *lr*, 199, 228 *r*, 247 *u*

IBM (courtesy): 276

Keystone / Grazia Neri, Milan: 175 *u*

"L'Espresso", Rome (courtesy): 204 *lc*

Magnum / Contrasto, Milan: 226 *ul*, 230 *l*

Marka, Rome: 270 *lr*

Masini Lara-Vinca, Florence: 191 *l*

"Max" – Rcs, Milan (courtesy): 244 *l*

Milagro-Dpp: 234

Mondadori, Milan (courtesy): 177 *l*

"Motociclismo" magazine Archive: 254

Notari Giorgio: 100 *lr*

Olycom, Milan: Publifoto: 32 *ur*, 40 *ul*, 56 *ll*, 56 *lr*, 58 *c*, 59 *lr*, 63 *u*, 71 *ll*, 72 *l*, 74, 75 *l*, 76 *lr*, 77 *l*, 78 *lr*, 84 *c*, 115 *ur*, 117 *u*, 117 *l*, 127 *ul*, 129 *lr*, 134 *lr*, 173 *u*, 194 *l*, 195 *ll*, 195 *lr*

Petronio Giovanni: 11, 46 *cl*, 46 *cr*, 47 *u*, 47 *cl*, 47 *cr*, 52 *cl*, 52 *cr*, 53 *u*, 53 *cl*, 53 *cr*, 96 *cl*, 96 *cr*, 97 *u*, 97 *cl*, 97 *cr*, 102 *u*, 102 *cl*, 102 *cr*, 103 *cl*, 103 *cr*, 108 *cl*, 108 *cr*, 109 *u*, 109 *cl*, 109 *cr*, 152 *cl*, 152 *cr*, 153 *u*, 153 *cl*, 153 *cr*, 158 *cl*, 158 *cr*, 159 *u*, 159 *cl*, 159 *cr*, 164 *cl*, 164 *cr*, 165 *u*, 165 *cl*, 165 *cr*, 210 *cl*, 210 *cr*, 211 *u*, 211 *cl*, 211 *cr*, 216 *u*, 216 *cl*, 216 *cr*, 217 *cl*, 217 *cr*, 222 *cl*, 222 *cr*, 223 *u*, 223 *cl*, 223 *cr*, 260 *cl*, 260 *cr*, 261 *u*, 261 *cl*, 261 *cr*, 266 *cl*, 266 *cr*, 267 *u*, 267 *cl*, 267 *cr*, 300 *u*, 304 *cl*, 304 *cr*, 305 *u*, 305 *cl*, 305 *cr*, 310 *cl*, 310 *cr*, 311 *cl*, 311 *cr*

Photomovie, Milan: 185 *u*, 231

Piaggio & Co.: 270 *c*, 274, 275, 278, 279 *u*, 288, 289, 290, 291, 293 *ll*, 294, 295, 298 *r*, 299, 302 *ll*, 302 *lr*, 308 *ll*, 308 *lr*, 314-315

Pictorial Press, London: 144 *ll*

Reporters Associati, Rome: 112 *ur*, 139 *cl*, 141 *l*, 177 *ur*

Santoro / "Elle" (courtesy): 129 *u*

"Scootering Magazine", Weston-super-Mare, Somerset (UK): 181 *ur*

St. Pauls International, Milan (courtesy): 188 *ur*

Studio Lanza: 2, 5, 6-7, 8, 10-11, 12-13, 15, 19, 31 *l*, 33 *u*, 39 *u*, 43, 44 *u*, 45, 46 *l*, 48, 49, 50 *u*, 51, 52 *ll*, 52 *lr*, 53 *ll*, 53 *lr*, 54, 55, 57, 60 *l*, 73 *lr*, 88 *l*, 93, 94 *u*, 95, 96 *u*, 96 *ll*, 96 *lr*, 97 *l*, 98, 99, 100 *u*, 101, 102 *l*, 103 *u*, 103 *l*, 104, 105, 106 *u*, 107, 109 *l*, 110, 111, 113, 116 *ur*, 131 *lr* (courtesy C. Doveri), 144 *u*, 145 *r*, 149, 150 *u*, 151, 152 *l*, 153 *ll*, 153 *lr*, 154, 155, 156 *u*, 157, 158 *l*, 159 *ll*, 159 *lr*, 160, 161, 162 *u*, 163, 164 *l*, 165 *l*, 166, 167, 169, 207, 208 *u*, 209, 210 *l*, 211 *ll*, 211 *lr*, 212, 213, 214 *u*, 215, 216 *ll*, 216 *lr*, 217 *u*, 218, 219, 220 *u*, 221, 222 *l*, 223 *l*, 224, 225, 227, 235 *u*, 235 *c*, 250, 251 *l*, 252, 253, 257, 258 *u*, 259, 260 *l*, 261 *ll*, 261 *lr*, 262, 263, 264 *u*, 265, 266 *l*, 267 *ll*, 267 *lr*, 268, 269, 270 *ul*, 271, 272 *lr*, 273 *lc*, 293 *lr*, 296 *ll*, 297 *lr*, 301, 302 *u*, 303, 304 *ll*, 304 *lr*, 305 *l*, 306, 307, 308 *u*, 309, 310 *u*, 310 *l*, 311 *u*, 311 *ll*, 311 *lr*, 312, 313, 316, 336

Ministero per i Beni Culturali e Ambientali – Archivio di Stato di Pescara: 18 *lr*, 24 *ul*, 33 *ll*, 33 *lc*, 34 *ll*, 35 *l*, 37 *ul*, 88 *ur* (do not reproduce without authorization)

TBWA / Italia for Absolut Vodka (courtesy): 285 *u*, 285 *ll*

Telepress, Rome: 139 *u*, 143 *u*

Tessera Vittorio, Museo Scooter & Lambretta, via Mazzini 4, Rodano, Milan (courtesy): 80 *lr*, 81 *l*, 82 *ul*, 82-83, 83 *u*

The Audrey Hepburn Foundation: 145 *s*

"Time Out", London: 137 *l*

Piaggio & C.: 274, 275, 278, 279 *u*, 288, 289, 290, 291, 293 *ll*, 294, 295, 298, 299, 302 *ll*, 302 *lr*, 308 *ll*, 308 *lr*, 314-315

Veloce Publishing Ltd. © David Sparrow (courtesy): 182 *c*, 182 *l*

Vespa Club of Japan (courtesy): 284 *l*

Viking Press (courtesy): 92 *ur*

– *u*: up   – *ul*: upper left   – *uc*: upper center   – *ur*: upper right
– *c*: center   – *cl*: center left   – *cr*: center right
– *l*: low   – *ll*: lower left   – *lc*: lower center   – *lr*: lower right

The photographs not listed here are from the Giunti Archives. As regards rights to reproduction, the publisher is willing to pay the amounts due for photographs for which it had been impossible to determine the source.